Dans la même collection

Robert Ardrey : Les enfants de Caïn.
Krishnamurti : La révolution du silence.
Ronald D. Laing : Nœuds.

Se libérer du connu

Du même auteur
aux Editions Stock

Aux étudiants.
L'éveil de l'intelligence.
La première et dernière liberté.
La révolution du silence.

Krishnamurti

Se libérer du connu

Textes choisis par Mary Lutyens
et
traduits par Carlo Suarès

Stock **+** Plus

Titre original

FREEDOM FROM THE KNOWN

Cet ouvrage — en anglais — a été composé et publié sur une première initiative de Krishnamurti et avec son approbation.

Tous les mots sont de lui. Ils proviennent de bandes enregistrées au cours de quelques-unes de ses récentes conférences, dans divers pays, et sont inédits. Leur choix et l'ordre de leur présentation relèvent de ma seule responsabilité.

M.L.

1

La recherche humaine. Les esprits torturés. L'orienta-
tion traditionnelle. Le piège des bien-pensants. L'être
humain et l'individu. Le conflit de l'existence. La
nature fondamentale de l'homme. La responsabilité.
La vérité. Se transformer soi-même. Comment on
dissipe l'énergie. Se libérer de l'autorité.

Au cours des âges, l'homme a toujours cherché un
quelque-chose, au-delà de lui-même, au-delà du bien-
être : un quelque-chose que l'on appelle Dieu, ou la
réalité, ou l'intemporel, que les contingences, la pensée,
la corruption humaine ne peuvent altérer.

L'homme s'est toujours posé, au sujet de l'existence,
la question fondamentale : « De quoi s'agit-il ? La vie
a-t-elle un sens ? » Plongé dans l'énorme confusion
des guerres, des révoltes, des brutalités, des incessants
conflits religieux, idéologiques, nationaux, il se demande,
avec un sens intime de frustration, comment en sortir,
que veut dire vivre, et s'il n'existe rien au-delà.

Et ne trouvant pas cet innommable aux mille noms
qu'il a toujours cherché, il a recours à la foi en un

Sauveur ou en un idéal : à la foi qui invariablement suscite la violence.

En cette perpétuelle bataille que l'on appelle vivre, on cherche à établir un code de comportement adapté à la société, communiste ou prétendument libre, dans laquelle on a été élevé.

Nous obéissons à certaines règles de conduite, en tant qu'elles sont parties intégrantes de notre tradition, hindoue, islamique, chrétienne, ou autre. Nous avons recours à autrui pour distinguer la bonne et la mauvaise façon d'agir, la bonne et la mauvaise façon de penser. En nous y conformant, notre action et notre pensée deviennent mécaniques, nos réactions deviennent automatiques. Nous pouvons facilement le constater en nous-mêmes.

Depuis des siècles, nous nous faisons alimenter par nos maîtres, par nos autorités, par nos livres, par nos saints, leur demandant de nous révéler tout ce qui existe au-delà des collines, au-delà des montagnes, au-delà de la Terre. Si leurs récits nous satisfont, c'est que nous vivons de mots et que notre vie est creuse et vide : une vie, pour ainsi dire de « seconde main ». Nous avons vécu de ce que l'on nous a dit, soit à cause de nos tendances, de nos inclinations, soit parce que les circonstances et le milieu nous y ont contraints. Ainsi, nous sommes la résultante de toutes sortes d'influences et il n'y a rien de neuf en nous, rien que nous ayons découvert par nous-mêmes, rien d'originel, de non corrompu, de clair.

L'histoire des théologies nous montre que les chefs religieux ont toujours affirmé qu'au moyen de rituels, que par des répétitions de prières ou de mantras, que par l'imitation de certains comportements, par le refoulement des désirs, par des disciplines mentales et la sublimation des passions, que par un frein, imposé aux appétits, sexuels et autres, on parvient, après s'être suffisamment torturé l'esprit et le corps, à trouver un quelque-chose qui transcende cette petite vie.

Voilà ce que des millions de personnes soi-disant religieuses ont fait au cours des âges ; soit en s'isolant, en s'en allant dans un désert, sur une montagne ou dans une caverne ; soit en errant de village en village avec un bol de mendiant ; ou bien en se réunissant en groupes, dans des monastères, en vue de contraindre leur esprit à se conformer à des modèles établis.

Mais un esprit torturé, dont les ressorts sont brisés, qui n'aspire plus qu'à échapper aux difficultés de la vie, qui a rejeté le monde extérieur parce que des disciplines et des conformismes l'ont abêti — un tel esprit, chercherait-il longtemps, ne trouverait jamais que l'image de sa propre déformation.

Donc il me semble que la recherche en vue de découvrir s'il existe ou non un quelque-chose au-delà de cette existence angoissée, coupable, apeurée, compétitive, doit s'orienter dans une direction complètement différente.

L'approche traditionnelle consiste à aller de la périphérie vers l'intérieur, avec l'idée que le temps, les dévotions, le renoncement permettront d'atteindre graduellement cette fleur intérieure, cette beauté intérieure, cet amour. En bref, on fait tout ce qu'il faut pour se rendre étroit et mesquin, pour se dégrader : « Epluchez petit à petit ; prenez du temps ; demain ou la prochaine vie feront l'affaire... » et lorsque, enfin, on arrive au centre, on s'aperçoit qu'il n'y a rien, parce qu'on s'est rendu amorphe, incapable, insensible.

Ayant observé ce processus, on est amené à se demander s'il n'existe pas une approche inverse : ne serait-il pas possible d'exploser à partir du centre ?

Le monde entier accepte et pratique l'approche traditionnelle. La cause fondamentale du désordre en nous-mêmes est cette recherche d'une réalité promise par autrui. Nous obéissons mécaniquement à celui qui nous promet une vie spirituelle confortable. Alors que la plupart d'entre nous sont opposés à la tyrannie politique et à la dictature, c'est extraordinaire à quel point nous acceptons l'autorité et la tyrannie de ceux qui déforment nos esprits et qui faussent notre mode de vie. Donc, si nous rejetons complètement — non en pensée, mais en fait — toutes les prétendues autorités spirituelles, toutes les cérémonies religieuses, les rituels et les dogmes, cela veut dire que nous nous retrouvons seuls et que nous sommes déjà en conflit avec la société : en somme, nous cessons d'être ce que l'on appelle des êtres humains « respectables ». Cet être humain « respectable » ne peut en aucune façon parvenir ne serait-ce qu'à proximité de ce quelque-chose, de cette infinie, de cette immesurable réalité.

Supposons maintenant que vous ayez rejeté, comme étant totalement erronée, la voie traditionnelle ; vous ne faites que réagir contre elle, vous engendrez en vous-mêmes un nouveau prototype qui sera un nouveau piège. Si vous vous dites, intellectuellement, que ce rejet est une excellente idée, et n'agissez pas en conséquence, vous n'irez pas plus loin. Si, cependant, vous reniez cette approche parce que vous comprenez qu'elle manque de maturité, et qu'elle est stupide, si vous la rejetez en y appliquant une intelligence profonde parce que vous êtes libres et que vous n'avez pas peur, vous serez la cause d'un grand trouble en vous-mêmes et autour de vous, mais vous aurez échappé au piège de la respectabilité. Alors vous vous apercevrez que vous ne serez plus dans un état de recherche. Et c'est bien cela qu'il faut commencer par apprendre : ne plus chercher. En somme, chercher la vérité c'est passer de la vitrine d'une boutique à une autre.

La question de savoir s'il existe un Dieu, une Vérité, une Réalité (selon le nom qu'on veut lui donner) ne peut jamais trouver de réponse dans des livres, chez des prêtres, des philosophes, ou des Sauveurs. Personne et rien ne peut répondre à cette question si ce n'est vous-mêmes, et c'est pour cela que la connaissance de soi est nécessaire. Manquer de maturité c'est manquer de se connaître. Se connaître est le début de la sagesse.

Et qu'êtes-vous ?... Ce vous individuel, qu'est-il ? Je pense qu'il y a une différence entre l'être humain et l'individu. L'individu est une entité locale, qui vit dans tel pays, qui appartient à telle culture, à telle société, à telle religion. L'être humain n'est pas une entité locale. Il est partout. Si l'individu n'agit que dans un coin du vaste champ de la vie, son action n'aura aucun lien avec la totalité. Veuillez donc tenir présent à l'esprit que ce dont nous parlons est la totalité, non la partie, car dans le plus grand est le plus petit, mais dans le plus petit, le plus grand n'est pas. L'individu est cette petite entité, conditionnée, misérable et frustrée, que satisfont ses petits dieux et ses petites traditions, tandis que l'être humain se sent responsable du bien-être total. de la totale misère et de la totale confusion du monde.

Nous, les êtres humains, sommes ce que nous avons été pendant des millions d'années, colossalement avides, envieux, agressifs, jaloux, angoissés et désespérés, avec d'occasionnels éclairs de joie et d'amour. Nous sommes une étrange mixture de haine, de peur et de gentillesse ; nous sommes à la fois violents et en paix. Il y a eu un progrès extérieur depuis le char à bœufs jusqu'à l'avion à réaction, mais psychologiquement l'individu n'a pas du tout changé et c'est l'individu qui, dans le monde entier, a créé les structures des sociétés. Les structures sociales extérieures sont les résultantes des structures intérieures, psychologiques, qui constituent nos relations humaines, car l'individu est le résultat de l'expérience totale de l'homme, de sa connaissance et de son comportement. Chacun de nous est l'entrepôt de tout le passé. L'individu est l'humain qui est toute l'humanité. L'histoire entière de l'homme est écrite en nous-mêmes.

Veuillez, je vous prie, observer ce qui agit aussi bien en vous-mêmes qu'en dehors de vous, dans la société de compétition où vous vivez : une volonté de puissance, le désir d'acquérir une situation sociale, du prestige, un nom, la recherche du succès... observez les réussites dont vous êtes si fiers, le champ global que vous appelez vivre ; observez les conflits dans tous les domaines des relations, et la haine, la brutalité, les antagonismes, les guerres sans fin qu'ils provoquent. Ce champ, cette vie, est tout ce que nous connaissons ; et comme nous sommes incapables de comprendre l'énorme bataille de l'existence, nous en avons peur et essayons de nous en évader par toutes sortes d'artifices. Et nous avons peur, aussi, de l'inconnu, peur de la mort, peur de ce qui se cache au-delà de demain.

Ainsi, nous avons peur du connu et peur de l'inconnu.

14

Telle est notre vie quotidienne, en laquelle il n'y a pas d'espoir et où toutes les philosophies, toutes les théologies ne sont que des évasions hors de la réalité de ce qui « est » en tout état de fait.

Les structures de tous les changements extérieurs qu'amènent des guerres, des révolutions, des réformes, des lois ou des idéologies, ont été incapables de modifier la nature profonde de l'homme, donc des sociétés. En tant qu'individus humains vivant dans la monstrueuse laideur de ce monde, demandons-nous donc s'il est possible de mettre fin à des sociétés basées sur la compétition, la brutalité et la peur. Posons-nous cette question, non pas comme une spéculation ou un espoir, mais de telle sorte qu'elle puisse rénover nos esprits, les rendre frais et innocents, et faire naître un monde totalement neuf. Cela ne peut se produire, je pense, que si chacun de nous reconnaît le fait central que nous, individus, en tant qu'êtres humains, en quelque partie du monde que nous vivions, ou à quelque culture que nous appartenions, sommes totalement responsables de l'état général du monde.

Nous sommes, chacun de nous, responsables de chaque guerre, à cause de l'agressivité de notre propre vie, à cause de notre nationalisme, de notre égoïsme, de nos dieux, de nos préjugés, de nos idéaux, qui nous divisent. Ce n'est qu'en nous rendant compte — non pas intellectuellement mais d'une façon aussi réelle et actuelle qu'éprouver la faim ou la douleur — que vous et moi sommes responsables de la misère dans le monde entier parce que nous y avons contribué dans nos vies quotidiennes et que nous faisons partie de cette monstrueuse

société, de ses guerres, ses divisions, sa laideur, sa brutalité, et son avidité — ce n'est qu'alors que nous agirons.

Mais que peut faire un être humain ? Que pouvons-
nous faire, vous et moi, pour créer une société complètement différente ? Nous nous posons là une question
très sérieuse : est-il possible de faire quoi que ce soit ?
Que peut-on faire ?... Quelqu'un pourrait-il nous le dire ?
De soi-disant guides spirituels — qui sont censés comprendre ces choses mieux que nous — nous l'ont dit en
essayant de nous déformer, de nous mouler selon certains modèles, et cela ne nous a pas menés loin ; des
savants nous l'ont dit en termes érudits et cela ne nous
a pas conduits plus loin. On nous a affirmé que tous
les sentiers mènent à la vérité : l'un a son sentier en
tant qu'Hindou, l'autre a le sien en tant que Chrétien,
un autre encore est Musulman, et ils se rencontrent tous
à la même porte — ce qui est, si vous y pensez, si
évidemment absurde.
    La Vérité n'a pas de sentier, et c'est cela sa beauté :
elle est vivante. Une chose morte peut avoir un sentier
menant à elle, car elle est statique. Mais lorsque vous
voyez que la vérité est vivante, mouvante, qu'elle n'a
pas de lieu où se reposer, qu'aucun temple, aucune
mosquée ou église, qu'aucune religion, qu'aucun maître
ou philosophe, bref que rien ne peut vous y conduire
— alors vous verrez aussi que cette chose vivante est
ce que vous êtes en toute réalité : elle est votre colère,
votre brutalité, votre violence, votre désespoir. Elle est
l'agonie et la douleur que vous vivez.
    La vérité est en la compréhension de tout cela, vous
ne pouvez le comprendre qu'en sachant le voir dans
votre vie. Il est impossible de le voir à travers une

idéologie, à travers un écran de mots, à travers l'espoir et la peur.

Nous voyons donc que nous ne pouvons dépendre de personne. Il n'existe pas de guide, pas d'instructeur, pas d'autorité. Il n'y a que nous et nos rapports avec les autres et avec le monde. Il n'y a pas autre chose. Lorsque l'on s'en rend compte, on peut tomber dans un désespoir qui engendre du cynisme et de l'amertume, ou, nous trouvant en présence du fait que nous et nul autre sommes responsables de ce monde et de nous-mêmes, responsables de nos pensées, de nos sentiments, et de nos actes, nous cessons de nous prendre en pitié. En général, nous prospérons en blâmant les autres, ce qui est une façon de se prendre en pitié.

Pouvons-nous donc, vous et moi, provoquer en nous-mêmes — sans aucune influence extérieure, sans nous laisser persuader, sans crainte de punition — pouvons-nous provoquer dans l'essence même de notre être une révolution totale, une mutation psychologique, telles que la brutalité, la violence, l'esprit de compétition, l'angoisse, la peur, l'avidité, et toutes les manifestations de notre nature qui ont construit cette société pourrie où nous vivons quotidiennement, cessent d'exister ?

Il est important de comprendre au départ que je ne cherche pas à formuler quelque philosophie, quelque concept, idée ou structure théologique. Il m'apparaît que toutes les idéologies sont totalement idiotes. Ce qui importe, ce n'est pas d'adopter une philosophie de la vie, mais d'observer ce qui a lieu, en toute vérité, dans notre vie quotidienne, intérieurement et extérieurement. Si vous l'observez de très près et si vous l'examinez, vous verrez que tout ce qui se passe est basé sur des conceptions intellectuelles ; et pourtant, l'intellect n'est pas toute la sphère de l'existence : ce n'en est qu'un fragment, et un fragment, quelque habile que soit son assemblage, quelque antique que soit sa tradition, n'est encore qu'une petite partie de l'existence, tandis que ce qui nous importe c'est la totalité de la vie. Lorsque nous voyons ce qui a lieu dans le monde, nous commençons à comprendre que ce n'est pas l'effet de deux processus, l'un extérieur, l'autre intérieur, mais qu'il n'existe qu'un seul processus unitaire, un seul mouvement entier, total : le mouvement intérieur s'exprimant en tant qu'extérieur et l'extérieur réagissant à son tour sur l'intérieur.

Etre capable de regarder tout cela, me semble être la seule chose dont nous ayons besoin, car lorsque nous savons regarder, l'ensemble devient très clair et regarder n'exige ni philosophie ni maître. Il n'est guère utile qu'on vous dise « comment » regarder : regardez, et voilà tout.

Pouvez-vous, alors, voyant le tableau général de ce qui est, le voyant, non pas intellectuellement, mais en fait, pouvez-vous aisément, spontanément, vous transformer ? Là est le point essentiel : est-il possible de provoquer une révolution totale dans la psyché ?

Je me demande comment vous réagissez à une telle question. Peut-être pensez-vous que vous ne voulez pas changer. C'est le cas de beaucoup de personnes, surtout de celles qui se sentent en sécurité socialement et économiquement ; ou de celles qui sont fermement établies dans leurs croyances dogmatiques et qui, volontiers, s'acceptent telles qu'elles sont et acceptent le monde tel qu'il est (ou tel qu'il serait si on le modifiait quelque peu). Ce n'est pas à ces personnes-là que nous nous adressons. Vous pourriez aussi penser, d'une façon plus subtile, que l'entreprise est trop difficile, qu'elle n'est pas pour vous. Dans ce cas vous vous seriez bloqués, vous auriez cessé de vous interroger et il serait inutile de prolonger notre entretien. Vous pourriez encore me dire : « Je vois la nécessité d'un changement fondamental en moi, mais comment dois-je m'y prendre ? Veuillez me montrer la voie, aidez-moi à atteindre ce but. » Dans ce cas, ce ne serait pas le changement qui vous intéresserait, ce ne serait pas une révolution totale : vous ne seriez qu'en quête d'une méthode, d'un système en vue de provoquer ce changement.

Si j'étais assez sot pour vous donner un système et si vous étiez assez sots pour l'adopter, vous ne feriez que copier, imiter, vous conformer, accepter, et en fin de compte ériger en vous-mêmes une autorité, laquelle provoquerait un conflit entre elle et vous. Vous éprouveriez la nécessité de faire ce que l'on vous a dit, tout en vous sentant incapables de le faire. Vos inclinations, vos tendances, vos besoins seraient en conflit avec le système que vous croiriez devoir suivre et vous seriez dans un état de contradiction. Vous mèneriez ainsi une double vie entre l'idéologie du système et la réalité de votre existence quotidienne. En essayant de vous conformer à l'idéologie, vous vous oblitéreriez vous-mêmes tandis que ce qu'il y a de vrai n'est pas l'idéologie : la vérité est ce que vous êtes. Si l'on essaie de s'étudier selon autrui, on demeure indéfiniment une personne « de seconde main ».

L'homme qui dit : « Je veux changer, dites-moi comment m'y prendre » peut paraître très profondément sincère et sérieux, mais il ne l'est pas. Il est à la recherche d'une autorité, dans l'espoir qu'elle mettrait de l'ordre dans sa vie. Mais son ordre intérieur pourrait-il jamais être instauré par une autorité ? Un ordre imposé du dehors provoque presque toujours un désordre.

Tout cela peut être vu intellectuellement. Mais pouvez-vous le vivre en vérité, de telle sorte que votre esprit cesse de projeter toute autorité, celle d'un livre, d'un maître, d'un conjoint, d'un parent, d'un ami, de la société ? Parce que nous avons toujours fonctionné dans le cadre de formules, celles-ci sont devenues notre idéal et notre autorité. Mais aussitôt que nous voyons que la question « comment puis-je changer ? » engendre une nouvelle autorité, nous en avons fini avec l'autorité, une fois pour toutes.

Reprenons clairement la question : je vois la nécessité de changer complètement, depuis les racines de mon être ; je ne peux pas être tributaire d'une tradition parce que les traditions ont engendré cette colossale paresse que sont l'acceptation et l'obéissance ; je ne peux absolument compter sur personne ni sur rien, sur aucun maître, aucun Dieu, aucune croyance, aucun système, aucune pression ou influence extérieures... Que se produit-il alors?

Et d'abord, peut-on rejeter toute autorité ? Si on le peut, c'est que l'on n'a plus peur. Et alors qu'arrive-t-il ? Lorsqu'on rejette une erreur dont on a porté le fardeau pendant des générations, qu'est-ce qui a lieu ?... N'arrive-t-il pas que l'on est animé d'un surcroît d'énergie ? On se sent davantage capable d'agir, on a plus d'élan, plus d'intensité, plus de vitalité. Si ce n'est pas cela que vous ressentez, c'est que vous n'avez pas rejeté le fardeau, c'est que vous ne vous êtes pas débarrassés du poids mort de l'autorité.

Mais lorsqu'on s'en est débarrassé et que l'on possède

cette énergie en laquelle ne subsiste aucune peur, aucune crainte de se tromper, de ne pas savoir choisir entre le bien et le mal, cette énergie n'est-elle pas, alors, la mutation ? Une immense énergie nous est nécessaire, et nous la dissipons dans la peur ; mais lorsque cette vitalité survient du fait que nous avons rejeté la peur sous toutes ses formes, c'est elle-même, cette énergie, qui provoque en nous une révolution radicale : nous n'avons pas à intervenir du tout.

Ainsi l'on reste seul avec soi-même et cet état est effectivement celui de l'homme qui considère ces questions avec beaucoup de sérieux : ne comptant sur l'aide de personne ni de rien, il est libre de s'en aller vers des découvertes. La liberté est inséparable de l'énergie et celle-ci, étant libre, ne peut jamais rien faire qui soit erroné. La liberté diffère totalement de la révolte. La question de « faire bien » ou de « faire mal » ne se pose pas dans la liberté. Etant libre, on agit à partir de ce centre, on est donc sans peur. Un esprit dégagé de toute peur est capable de beaucoup aimer, et l'amour peut agir à son gré.

Ce que nous entreprendrons maintenant, c'est la connaissance de nous-mêmes, non pas cette connaissance selon moi ou selon tel analyste ou tel philosophe, car chercher à se connaître selon quelqu'un c'est recueillir des informations en ce qui le concerne, lui, et pas nous Or ce que nous voulons apprendre, c'est ce que nous sommes nous-mêmes.

Ayant bien compris que nous ne pouvons compter sur aucune autorité pour provoquer une révolution totale dans la structure de notre psyché, nous éprouvons une difficulté infiniment plus grande à rejeter notre propre autorité intérieure : celle qui résulte de nos petites expériences particulières, ainsi que de l'accumulation de nos opinions, de nos connaissances, de nos idées et idéaux. Hier, une expérience vécue nous a appris quelque chose et ce qu'elle nous a appris devient une nouvelle autorité. Cette autorité née de la veille est aussi destructrice que celle que consacrent dix siècles d'existence. Pour nous comprendre, nous n'avons besoin ni d'une autorité millénaire ni de celle d'hier, car nous sommes des êtres vivants, toujours en mouvement selon le flot de l'existence, jamais au repos. Si l'on s'examine du point de vue qu'impose l'autorité d'un passé mort, on manque de comprendre ce mouvement vivant, ainsi que la beauté et la qualité de ce mouvement.

Etre libre de toute autorité, de la nôtre et de celle d'autrui, c'est mourir à tout ce qui est de la veille, de sorte qu'on a l'esprit toujours frais, toujours jeune, innocent, plein de vigueur et de passion. Ce n'est qu'en cet état que l'on apprend et que l'on observe. Et, à cet effet, il faut être conscient avec acuité de ce qui a lieu en nous-mêmes, sans vouloir le rectifier ni lui dire ce qu'il devrait être ou ne pas être, car dès que nous intervenons, nous établissons une autre autorité : un censeur.

Nous allons donc, maintenant, nous explorer nous-mêmes, tous ensemble. Ne considérez pas qu'ici s'exprime une personne qui explique tandis que vous lisez, étant d'accord ou non au fur et à mesure que vous suivez des mots sur la page. Ce que nous allons entreprendre c'est une expédition ensemble, un voyage de découverte dans les recoins les plus secrets de notre conscience. Et pour une telle aventure, on doit partir léger, on ne peut pas s'encombrer d'opinions, de préjugés, de conclusions : de tout ce vieux mobilier que nous avons collectionné pendant deux mille ans et plus. Oubliez tout ce que vous savez à votre propre sujet ; oubliez tout ce que vous avez pensé de vous-mêmes ; nous allons partir comme si nous ne savions rien.

Hier il a plu lourdement et maintenant les cieux commencent à s'éclaircir : nous voici au seuil d'une journée toute neuve. Abordons-la comme si elle était la seule journée. Mettons-nous en route tous ensemble en laissant derrière nous les souvenirs des jours passés et commençons à nous comprendre, pour la première fois.

2

*Apprendre à se connaître. La simplicité et l'humilité.
Le conditionnement.*

Si vous pensez qu'il est important de vous connaître
parce que quelqu'un vous l'a dit (moi ou un autre), je
crains que cela ne mette fin à toute communication entre
nous. Mais si nous sommes d'accord sur le fait qu'il
est vital que nous nous comprenions nous-mêmes
complètement, nous aurons des rapports réciproques
tout autres et nous mènerons notre enquête à notre
propre sujet, diligemment et d'une façon intelligente.
Je ne vous demande pas de croire en moi. Je ne
m'érige pas en autorité. Je n'ai rien à vous enseigner :
pas de nouvelle philosophie, pas de système ou de sentier menant au réel. Il n'y a pas plus de sentier vers la
réalité qu'il n'y en a vers la vérité. Toute autorité de
toute sorte et surtout celle qui s'exerce dans le champ
de la pensée et de l'entendement est destructrice, néfaste.
Les maîtres détruisent les disciples et les disciples
détruisent les maîtres. Il vous faut être votre propre
maître et votre propre disciple. Il vous faut mettre en

25

doute tout ce que l'homme a accepté comme étant valable et nécessaire.

N'étant plus tributaires de personne vous pouvez vous sentir très seuls. Eprouvez donc la solitude. Pourquoi la craignez-vous ? Parce que, face à face avec vous-mêmes tels que vous êtes, vous vous découvrez vides, obtus, stupides, laids, coupables, angoissés ? Si vous êtes cette entité mesquine, de « seconde main », de rebut, affrontez-la, ne la fuyez pas. Dès qu'on fuit, la peur survient.

En menant notre enquête à notre propre sujet, nous sommes loin de nous isoler du reste de l'univers : ce serait malsain. Tous les hommes à travers le monde se débattent dans les mêmes problèmes quotidiens que les nôtres, donc ce n'est pas en névrosés que nous nous examinons, car il n'y a pas de différence entre ce qui est individuel et ce qui est collectif. Le fait réel est que j'ai créé ce monde tel que je suis. Ne nous égarons donc pas dans la bataille au sujet de la partie et du tout.

Je dois prendre conscience du champ total de mon moi-même, et ce champ est l'état de conscience à la fois de l'individu et de la société. Ce n'est qu'alors, lorsque l'on transforme cette conscience individuelle et collective, que l'on devient une lumière à soi-même, qui ne s'éteint jamais.

Or, par où commençons-nous à nous comprendre nous-mêmes? Me voici, ici présent, et comment dois-je m'étudier, m'observer, voir ce qui est réellement en train de se passer en moi ? Je ne peux m'observer qu'en fonction de mes rapports, parce que toute vie est relations. Il est inutile de s'asseoir dans un coin et de méditer sur soi-même. Je ne peux pas exister isolé. Je n'existe que dans mes rapports avec des personnes, des choses, des idées, et en étudiant mes rapports avec le monde exté-rieur, de même que ceux que j'entretiens dans mon monde intérieur, c'est par là que je commence à me comprendre. Toute autre forme de compréhension n'est qu'une abstraction et je ne peux pas m'étudier d'une façon abstraite, n'étant pas une entité abstraite. Je dois donc m'étudier dans l'actualité de ce que je « suis », non en fonction de ce que je souhaiterais être.

Comprendre n'est pas un processus intellectuel. Acqué-rir des connaissances à mon sujet ou me connaître tel que je suis, sont deux choses différentes, car le savoir que je peux accumuler à mon propos appartient tou-jours au passé et un esprit surchargé de passé est tou-jours en peine. M'informer de ce qui est en moi n'est pas « apprendre » dans le sens où l'on acquiert une langue, une technique, une science, ce qui nécessaire-ment exige de la mémoire et une accumulation de données, car il serait absurde de se mettre en état de devoir tout recommencer sans cesse. L'information dans mon propre champ psychologique est toujours une chose du présent ; ce sont les connaissances qui appartiennent au passé mais comme la plupart d'entre nous vivent dans le passé et s'en contentent, les connais-sances ont pris pour nous une importance extraordi-naire : nous vénérons l'érudition, l'habileté, l'astuce. Mais si nous sommes disposés à apprendre en observant et en écoutant, en voyant et en agissant, nous compre-nons alors qu'apprendre est un mouvement perpétuel qui n'a pas de passé.

Si vous pensez pouvoir vous connaître graduellement, en améliorant de plus en plus et petit à petit votre compréhension, c'est que vous ne vous examinez pas tel que vous êtes dans l'instant présent, mais tel que vous vous voyez à travers des connaissances acquises. Apprendre exige une grande sensibilité, et celle-ci est détruite chaque fois qu'une idée, qui appartient nécessairement au passé, domine le présent. L'idée détruit la vivacité de l'esprit, sa souplesse, sa vigilance. Mais la plupart d'entre nous manquent de sensibilité, même physiquement. L'excès de nourriture, le peu de compte en lequel on tient un régime sain, l'abus de tabac et d'alcool rendent le corps épais et insensible ; la qualité d'attention de l'organisme est émoussée. Comment l'esprit peut-il être vif, sensitif, clair, si l'organisme lui-même est alourdi et apathique ? Il peut être sensible à certaines choses qui touchent la personnalité directement, mais pour être complètement sensible à tout ce que la vie implique, il ne faut pas de séparation entre l'organisme et la psyché, car ils constituent un seul mouvement total.

Pour comprendre une chose — quelle qu'elle soit — il faut vivre avec elle, l'observer, connaître tout son contenu, sa nature, sa structure, son mouvement. Avez-vous jamais essayé de vivre avec vous-mêmes ? Dans ce cas, vous avez remarqué que ce vous-même n'est pas un état statique, mais une chose vivante, toujours renouvelée. Et pour vivre avec une chose vivante, l'esprit doit, lui aussi, être vivant. Mais il ne peut pas l'être s'il est pris dans un réseau d'opinions, de jugements, de valeurs.

En vue d'observer le mouvement de votre esprit et de votre cœur, le mouvement de tout votre être, il vous faut avoir un esprit libre, qui ne s'attarde pas à acquiescer, à réfuter, à prendre parti dans une discussion, à argumenter sur des mots, mais qui s'attache à suivre ce qu'il observe, avec l'intention de comprendre. C'est difficile, car la plupart d'entre nous ne savent ni regarder ni écouter leur propre être, pas plus qu'ils ne voient la beauté d'un cours d'eau ou qu'ils n'entendent la brise dans les arbres.

Condamner ou justifier empêche de voir clairement. Il en est de même lorsqu'on bavarde sans arrêt, car alors on n'observe pas « ce qui est » : on ne voit que ce que l'on projette soi-même. Chacun de nous a une image de ce qu'il croit être ou de ce qu'il voudrait être, et cette image nous empêche totalement de voir ce que nous sommes en fait.

Voir quoi que ce soit avec simplicité est une des choses les plus difficiles au monde car nous sommes si complexes que nous avons perdu la qualité de ceux qui sont simples en esprit. Je ne parle pas de cette sorte de simplicité qui s'exprime dans la nourriture et les vêtements, telle que ne posséder qu'un pagne, ou battre des records de jeûne, ou toute autre sottise infantile que cultivent les saints, mais de la simplicité qui permet qu'on regarde directement chaque chose sans peur et soi-même tel que l'on est, sans déformations : si l'on ment, se dire que l'on ment, sans déguisements ni évasions.

Et aussi, pour nous comprendre nous-mêmes, il nous faut une grande humilité. Aussitôt que l'on se dit « je me comprends », on a déjà cessé d'apprendre quoi que ce soit à son propre sujet ; ou si l'on se dit : « après tout, il n'y a rien à apprendre, puisque je ne suis qu'un paquet de souvenirs, d'idées, d'expériences, de traditions », on a également cessé de voir ce que l'on est. Lorsqu'on parvient à une réalisation, on a perdu les qualités propres à l'innocence et à l'humilité. Dès que

29

l'on tient un résultat, ou que l'on cherche à s'informer en se basant sur des connaissances acquises, on est perdu, car on ne fait que traduire tout ce qui vit en termes de ce qui n'est plus. Mais si l'on n'a aucun point d'appui, aucune certitude, on est libre de regarder ; si l'on n'a aucun acquis, on est libre d'acquérir. Ce qu'on voit étant libre est toujours neuf. L'homme plein d'assurance est un être humain mort.

Mais comment pouvons-nous être libres de regarder et d'apprendre, lorsque, depuis notre naissance jusqu'à l'instant de notre mort, nous sommes façonnés par telle ou telle culture, dans le petit moule de notre moi ? Nous avons été conditionnés pendant des siècles par nos nationalités, nos castes, nos classes, nos traditions, nos religions, nos langues ; par l'éducation, la littérature, l'art ; par des coutumes, des conventions, par des propagandes de toutes sortes, des pressions économiques, des modes d'alimentation, des climats différents ; par nos familles et nos amis ; par nos expériences vécues ; bref, par toutes les influences auxquelles on peut penser, et cela, de telle sorte que nos réactions à tous les problèmes qui se présentent sont conditionnées.

« Est-ce que je me rends compte que je suis conditionné ? » C'est la première question à se poser, et non : « Comment puis-je me libérer de mon conditionnement ? » Il se peut que cela ne vous soit pas possible. Donc vous dire : « je dois me libérer » peut vous faire tomber dans un nouveau piège et dans une nouvelle forme de conditionnement. Savez-vous que même lorsque vous regardez un arbre en vous disant que c'est un chêne ou un banyan, ce mot, faisant partie des connaissances en botanique, a déjà si bien conditionné votre esprit qu'il s'interpose entre vous et votre vision de l'arbre ? Pour entrer en contact avec l'arbre nous devons y appuyer la main. Le mot ne nous aidera pas à le toucher.

Comment sait-on que l'on est conditionné ? Qu'est-ce qui nous le fait savoir ?... Comment sait-on que l'on a faim, non en théorie, mais lorsque la faim se fait réellement sentir ? De même, comment, quand, savons-nous que nous sommes conditionnés ? N'est-ce pas lorsque nous réagissons à un problème, à une provocation ? Car nous répondons à l'événement selon notre conditionnement, et celui-ci étant inadéquat réagit toujours d'une façon inadéquate.

Lorsqu'on en devient conscient, est-ce que ce conditionnement d'une race, d'une religion, d'une culture, donne un sens d'emprisonnement ? Considérez une seule forme de conditionnement : votre nationalité. Soyez-en sérieusement, complètement conscients, et sachez si vous en éprouvez un sentiment de plaisir ou de révolte ; sachez si vous vous révoltez ou si vous voulez rompre à travers tout ce qui vous conditionne. Si vous êtes satisfaits de votre conditionnement, vous ne faites évidemment rien à son sujet. Si cependant vous n'êtes pas satisfaits lorsque vous en devenez conscients, vous vous apercevez que vous n'agissez jamais sans lui : jamais ! Et par conséquent vous vivez toujours dans le passé, avec les morts.

On ne peut se rendre compte de la façon dont on est conditionné que lorsque survient un conflit dans une continuité de plaisir ou dans une protection contre la douleur. Si tout est harmonieux autour de nous, notre femme nous aime, nous l'aimons, nous avons une maison agréable, de bons enfants, beaucoup d'argent : dans ce cas nous ne sommes en aucune façon conscients de notre conditionnement. Mais lorsque survient l'accident, la femme infidèle, la perte d'une fortune, une menace de guerre ou toute autre cause de douleur et d'angoisse, alors nous savons que nous sommes conditionnés. Lorsque nous luttons contre une chose, quelle qu'elle soit, qui nous dérange, ou lorsque nous nous défendons contre une quelconque menace, extérieure ou intérieure, alors nous savons que nous sommes conditionnés. Et comme la plupart d'entre nous, la plupart du temps, sont perturbés, soit en surface soit en profondeur, ce trouble, ce désordre indique que nous sommes conditionnés. Tant que l'animal est choyé il réagit agréablement, mais dès qu'il rencontre un antagonisme, la violence de sa nature éclate.

Nous sommes troublés, mal à l'aise, du fait de la vie elle-même, de la situation politique et économique, de l'horreur, de la brutalité, de la douleur dans le monde aussi bien qu'en nous, et tout cela nous révèle combien étroitement nous sommes conditionnés. Et alors, que devons-nous faire ? Accepter d'être ainsi, notre vie durant, comme le font la plupart d'entre nous ? Nous y habituer comme on s'habitue à vivre avec des maux de tête ? Nous en accommoder ?

En chacun de nous est une tendance à s'accommoder des choses, à s'y habituer, à blâmer les circonstances. « Ah ! Si les choses étaient autres, je serais différent », disons-nous. Ou bien : « Donnez-moi une occasion favorable et je me réaliserai. » Ou : « L'injustice de tout cela m'écrase. » Nous ne cessons d'accuser les autres, notre milieu, la situation économique, d'être la cause de tous nos désordres.

Si l'on s'habitue à vivre dans un état troublé et confus, c'est qu'on a l'esprit insensibilisé, tout comme ceux qui s'habituent si bien à la beauté qui les entoure qu'ils ne la remarquent plus : ils deviennent indifférents, durs, leur esprit s'épaississant de plus en plus. Ceux qui ne s'habituent pas à vivre dans cette condition cherchent à s'en évader, soit en se droguant, soit en adhérant à un groupe politique, en s'agitant, en criant, en assistant à des matchs de football, en allant au temple ou a l'église, ou en cherchant d'autres divertissements.

Pourquoi fuyons-nous les faits tels qu'ils sont ? Nous craignons la mort — ceci n'est qu'un exemple — et nous inventons toutes sortes de théories, des raisons d'espérer, des croyances, afin de la déguiser. Mais elle est toujours là. Pour comprendre un fait, il nous faut le regarder, non le fuir. La plupart d'entre nous ont aussi peur de vivre qu'ils ont peur de mourir : peur pour leur famille, peur de l'opinion publique, de perdre un emploi ou une sécurité... peur de mille choses. La vérité toute simple est cette peur, et non notre crainte d'une chose ou l'autre. Cela dit, pouvons-nous affronter ce fait lui-même ? On ne peut l'affronter si ce n'est dans le présent. Si on ne lui permet pas d'être présent, parce qu'on le fuit, on ne peut jamais le rencontrer. Ayant élaborer tout un réseau d'évasions, nous sommes prisonniers de notre habitude de fuir.

Si l'on est tant soit peu sensitif et sérieux, on ne se rend pas seulement compte du fait que l'on est conditionné mais aussi du danger qui en résulte, de la brutalité et de la haine qu'il engendre. Voyant ce danger, pourquoi n'agissons-nous pas ? Est-ce parce que nous sommes paresseux, la paresse étant un manque d'énergie ? Et pourtant, nous ne manquerions pas d'énergie si nous nous trouvions devant un danger immédiat, tel qu'un serpent sur le chemin, un précipice ou un incendie. Pourquoi donc ne faisons-nous rien lorsque nous voyons le danger de notre conditionnement ? Si vous perceviez le danger que le nationalisme fait courir à votre sécurité n'agiriez-vous pas ?

La réponse est que vous ne voyez pas. Peut-être, par un processus intellectuel d'analyse, voyez-vous que le nationalisme est un phénomène d'auto-destruction. Mais il n'y a, en cela, aucun contenu émotionnel, lequel, seul, confère de la vitalité. Si votre vision du danger que représente votre conditionnement n'est qu'un concept intellectuel, vous ne ferez jamais rien pour y parer.

Tant que la perception du danger demeure dans le champ des idées, il se produit un conflit entre l'idée et l'action, et ce conflit absorbe votre énergie. On n'agit que lorsqu'on voit, dans l'immédiat, à la fois le conditionnement et le danger, à la façon dont on se verrait au bord d'un précipice. Ainsi, « voir » c'est « agir ».

En général, nous traversons l'existence d'une façon inattentive, réagissant sans réflexion au milieu qui nous a formés. De telles réactions ne font que créer de nouvelles sujétions et nous conditionner davantage, mais sitôt que nous accordons à cette emprise une attention totale, nous sommes complètement affranchis du passé : il se détache de nous tout naturellement.

3

Le champ de la conscience. La totalité de la vie. Etre
pleinement conscient.

Ceux qui deviennent conscients de leur conditionnement saisissent tout le champ de leur conscience,
lequel est celui où fonctionne la pensée et où existe
l'ensemble des rapports et des relations. Mobiles, inten-
tions, désirs, plaisirs, craintes, inspirations, espérances,
espoirs, douleurs, joies : tout est dans ce champ. Mais
nous en sommes venus à diviser la conscience en deux,
une partie active, et l'autre en sommeil, se situant à
deux niveaux différents : nos pensées, nos activités, ce
qui nous est sensible étant à la surface, et au-dessous,
le prétendu subconscient, lequel se compose de tout ce
qui ne nous est pas familier et qui s'exprime, à l'occasion, par des émissions, des intuitions, des rêves.

Un seul petit coin de notre conscience occupe presque
toute notre vie, cependant que nous ne savons même
pas pénétrer dans le reste, que nous appelons le
subconscient, avec ses impératifs, ses peurs, ses qualités raciales, héritées ou acquises.

Or, je vous le demande : existe-t-il vraiment quoi que
ce soit que l'on puisse appeler subconscient ? nous
employons ce mot très librement. Nous avons accepté
qu'existe la chose qu'il désigne. Les locutions, le jargon
des analystes, des psychologues en général, ont pénétré
dans notre langage courant, mais existe-t-elle ? Pourquoi lui accordons-nous une telle importance ? Le
subconscient m'apparaît, quant à moi, aussi insignifiant
et stupide que le conscient : aussi étroit, crédule, conditionné, angoissé, vulgaire.

Est-il donc possible d'être conscient dans le champ
total de la conscience et non simplement dans une de
ses parties, dans un de ses fragments ? Si on l'est, on
vit constamment dans un état de totale attention, au
lieu de n'être que partiellement attentif. Il est important de comprendre ce fait, car lorsqu'on est réellement
conscient du champ total de la conscience, on n'est
pas dans un état de conflit. C'est lorsqu'on divise en
couches superposées la conscience, laquelle est « tout »
le penser, le sentir, et l'agir, que se produisent les frottements et les conflits intérieurs.

Nous vivons fragmentés. Nous sommes un personnage au bureau, un autre dans notre foyer ; nous parlons de démocratie et sommes autocrates en nos cœurs ;
nous parlons d'aimer le voisin que nous tuons par notre
esprit compétitif ; une partie de nous-mêmes travaille,
regarde, agit indépendamment de l'autre.

Etes-vous conscients de la fragmentation de vos
existences ? Est-il possible à un cerveau qui a mis en
pièces la structure de sa pensée de percevoir le champ
total de la conscience ? Nous est-il possible d'appré-
hender tout notre état de conscience, complètement,

absolument, c'est-à-dire de devenir des êtres humains achevés ?

Si, dans le dessein de comprendre la structure totale du moi, du soi-même, avec son extraordinaire complexité, nous cherchons à avancer pas à pas, en mettant à nu une couche de conscience après l'autre, en examinant chaque pensée, chaque émotion, chaque mobile, nous nous empêtrons dans un processus analytique qui pourrait durer des semaines, des mois, des années ; et lorsqu'on introduit le temps dans l'entreprise de se connaître, on doit prévoir l'intervention de toutes sortes de déformations, car le soi est une entité complexe, qui bouge, vit, lutte, désire, renie, et subit les nombreuses contraintes et influences qui ne cessent d'agir sur elle.

Nous nous rendons compte, ainsi, que cette voie n'est pas la bonne, et nous comprenons que la seule façon de se voir doit être totale, immédiate, sans l'intervention de la durée, ce qui ne peut se faire que lorsque l'esprit n'est pas fragmenté. La Vérité est ce que l'on voit en totalité. Y parvenez-vous ? La plupart d'entre nous en sont incapables, n'ayant jamais abordé ce problème assez sérieusement : ils ne se sont jamais vus eux-mêmes, jamais, blâmant les autres, noyant la question sous des explications, ou ayant peur de se regarder. Mais si vous vous percevez totalement, avec toute votre attention, tout votre être, ou ce qui est vous, vos yeux, vos oreilles, vos nerfs ; si vous vous abandonnez à votre propre présence, il n'y a pas de place pour la peur, pas de place pour des contradictions, donc pas de conflit.

L'attention et la concentration sont deux choses différentes. La concentration procède par exclusions. tandis que l'attention, qui est un état de pleine conscience, n'exclut rien. Il me semble qu'en général nous ne sommes pas plus conscients de ce dont nous parlons que de ce qui nous entoure, des couleurs, des gens, de la forme des arbres, des nuages, du mouvement de l'eau. Peut-être sommes-nous trop préoccupés de nous-mêmes, de nos petits problèmes, de nos idées, de nos plaisirs, de nos aspirations, pour être objectivement lucides. Et pourtant, nous parlons beaucoup de vision objective. Une fois, en Inde, je voyageais en voiture, assis près du chauffeur, et trois messieurs, assis à l'arrière, discutaient avec animation, m'interrogeant au sujet de la vision claire et objective des choses. Il se trouva que le chauffeur, distrait, écrasa malencontreusement une chèvre, cependant que les trois continuaient à discuter, sans s'être aperçus de rien. Lorsque ce manque d'attention leur fut signalé, ils en demeurèrent fort surpris.

Il en va de même pour la plupart d'entre nous. Nous ne sommes pleinement conscients ni du monde extérieur ni de notre monde intérieur. Si nous voulons comprendre la beauté d'un oiseau, d'une mouche, d'une feuille ou d'une personne avec toutes ses complexités, il nous faut y appliquer toute notre attention avec lucidité. Mais nous ne le faisons que s'il nous importe de comprendre, c'est-à-dire si nous aimons comprendre. Alors nous nous y mettons de tout cœur, avec toute notre intelligence.

L'état d'une conscience si totalement présente est semblable à celui où l'on se trouverait en vivant avec un serpent dans la chambre : on observerait tous ses mouvements, on serait très, très sensible au moindre bruit qu'il ferait. Un tel état d'attention est une plénitude d'énergie où la totalité de nous-mêmes se révèle en un instant.

Lorsqu'on s'est examiné aussi profondément, on peut aller plus profondément encore. Ces mots ne doivent pas être pris dans un sens comparatif. Nous pensons en termes de comparaisons, tels que superficiel et profond, heureux et malheureux. Nous ne cessons de mesurer, de comparer. Mais existe-t-il en nous un état profond par opposition à un état creux ? Lorsque je me dis que mon esprit est creux, mesquin, étroit, limité, comment l'ai-je appris ? Est-ce en comparant mon intelligence à la vôtre, plus brillante, plus large, plus vive ? Puis-je, au contraire, me savoir médiocre sans me comparer à qui que ce soit ? Si j'ai faim, je ne compare pas ma faim à celle d'hier. Celle d'hier est une idée, un souvenir.

Si je me mesure tout le temps par rapport à vous, faisant des efforts pour être à votre image, je me nie moi-même, donc, je crée une illusion. Lorsque je comprends que toute comparaison, quelle qu'elle soit, ne peut que conduire vers de nouvelles illusions et de nouveaux maux, j'élimine complètement cette façon de penser, tout comme j'élimine l'analyse psychologique, l'étude de moi-même morceau par morceau, ou mon identification avec quelque chose d'extérieur à moi, une idéologie, un Sauveur, l'Etat. Lorsque je vois que tous ces processus ne mènent qu'à intensifier des conformismes, c'est-à-dire des conflits, je les écarte résolument. Alors je ne suis plus dans un esprit de recherche et c'est cela qu'il est important de comprendre : je ne tâtonne plus, je ne cherche plus, je ne consulte plus personne. Ce n'est pas que je sois satisfait des choses telles qu'elles sont, mais je ne suis plus encombré d'illusions, et lorsque l'esprit s'est ainsi affranchi, il peut se mouvoir dans une tout autre dimension. La dimension dans laquelle nous vivons habituellement, cette vie quotidienne faite de douleur, de plaisir et de crainte, nous a conditionné l'esprit, a limité sa nature, et lorsque cette douleur, ce plaisir et cette crainte ont disparu (ce qui ne veut pas dire que l'on soit sans joie : la joie est tout autre chose que le plaisir), l'esprit peut alors fonctionner dans une dimension où n'existe aucun conflit, aucun sens de séparation entre le moi et « l'autre ».

Sur le plan verbal nous ne pouvons aller que jusque-là. Ce qui est au-delà ne peut pas être mis en mots car le mot n'est pas la chose. Jusque-là, nous pouvons décrire, expliquer, mais aucun mot, aucune explication ne peuvent ouvrir la porte. Ce qui ouvrira la porte, c'est notre lucidité quotidienne, notre attention ; c'est la perception aiguë de ce que nous disons, de comment nous parlons, marchons, pensons. Cela peut se comparer au fait de nettoyer une chambre et de la tenir en ordre. Mettre de l'ordre dans la chambre est important dans un certain sens, mais, en un autre sens, n'a aucune espèce d'importance, car l'ordre, pour nécessaire qu'il soit, n'ouvrira ni la porte ni la fenêtre. Ce n'est pas non plus votre volition, votre désir qui l'ouvriront. Et vous ne pouvez inviter personne à le faire pour vous. Tout ce que vous pouvez faire, c'est maintenir l'ordre, c'est-à-dire être vertueux pour l'ordre lui-même, non pour ce qu'il pourrait susciter : être sain, rationnel, ordonné. Alors peut-être, avec de la chance, la fenêtre s'ouvrira et la brise pénétrera. Elle pourrait aussi ne pas pénétrer : cela dépendrait de votre état d'esprit. Et cet état d'esprit ne peut être compris que par vous-mêmes si vous l'observez sans essayer jamais de le façonner, ni de prendre parti, ni de lui résister, et sans jamais acquiescer, justifier, condamner, juger, c'est-à-dire si vous l'observez sans option. Par cette observation impartiale la porte pourra, peut-être, s'ouvrir pour vous, et vous saurez ce qu'est cette dimension en laquelle il n'y a pas de conflits et pas de temps.

4

La poursuite du plaisir. Le désir. La perversion de la pensée. La mémoire. La joie.

Nous avons dit dans le chapitre précédent que la joie est tout autre chose que le plaisir. Voyons donc ce qu'implique le plaisir et s'il serait possible de vivre dans un monde qui n'en offrirait pas, mais où existerait une joie immense, une félicité.

Nous sommes tous engagés à la poursuite du plaisir, sous une forme ou l'autre, intellectuelle, sensuelle, culturelle ; nous avons le plaisir de réformer, de donner des conseils, de corriger, de faire du bien ; celui de l'érudition, des jouissances physiques ; celui d'acquérir de l'expérience, une plus grande compréhension de la vie, et celui de toutes les ruses, des artifices de l'esprit, le plaisir ultime étant, bien sûr, celui de connaître Dieu.

Le plaisir est la structure même de la société. Depuis l'enfance jusqu'à la mort, en secret avec ruse, ou ouvertement, nous sommes à sa poursuite. Donc, quelle que soit notre forme de plaisir, je pense qu'il nous faut être très clairs à son sujet, car elle guidera et façonnera toute notre existence. Il est important que chacun explore de très près, avec hésitation et délicatement, cette question, car trouver son plaisir et ensuite l'alimenter est une exigence fondamentale de la vie, sans laquelle l'existence deviendrait morne, stupide, solitaire et n'aurait pas de sens.

Vous pouvez alors demander pourquoi la vie ne devrait pas être guidée par le plaisir. Pour la simple raison que le plaisir engendre nécessairement de la douleur, des frustrations, la peur, et celle-ci la violence. Si c'est ainsi que vous voulez vivre, vivez ainsi, puisque d'ailleurs presque tout le monde le fait, mais si vous voulez vous affranchir de la douleur, il vous faut comprendre toute la structure du plaisir.

Comprendre le plaisir, ce n'est pas y renoncer. Nous ne le condamnons pas, nous ne disons pas que c'est bien ou mal de le poursuivre ; mais faites-le, du moins, les yeux ouverts, en sachant que sa recherche constante trouve toujours son ombre : la douleur. Plaisir et douleur ne peuvent être séparés, bien que nous courions après l'un et essayions d'éviter l'autre.

Demandons-nous pourquoi le plaisir est un besoin. Pourquoi accomplissons-nous des actes nobles et ignobles, poussés par ce besoin ? Pourquoi ces sacrifices et ces souffrances sur le fil ténu du plaisir ? Qu'est-il et comment naît-il ? Je me demande combien parmi vous se sont posé ces questions en allant jusqu'au bout des réponses.

Le plaisir prend forme en quatre étapes : perception, sensation, contact, désir. Je vois, par exemple, une belle voiture ; j'en ai la sensation, puis, en la regardant, se produit en moi une réaction ; je touche ou je m'imagine toucher la voiture ; ensuite vient le désir de la posséder et de me montrer en train de la conduire. Ou encore, je vois un beau nuage, une montagne claire se détachant sur le ciel, une feuille que le printemps vient de faire surgir, une vallée resplendissante, un superbe coucher de soleil, ou le visage, intelligent, vivant, d'une personne qui cessant d'être présente à elle-même, perdrait de sa beauté. Je vois ces choses avec une joie intense et pendant que j'observe, il n'y a pas d'observateur, mais une beauté telle que l'amour. Pendant un instant, je suis absent, moi et mes problèmes, mes angoisses, mes tracas : il n'y a que cette merveille. Je peux la voir avec joie et l'instant suivant l'oublier ; mais si la pensée et l'émotion interviennent, le problème commence ; je me remémore ce que j'ai vu, je pense à cette beauté, je me dis que je voudrais la revoir de nombreuses fois. La pensée se met à comparer, à juger, à vouloir un lendemain : la continuité d'une expérience qui a donné une seconde de plaisir est alimentée par la pensée.

Il en va de même du désir sexuel et de toute autre forme de désir. Il n'y a rien de mal à désirer. Toute réaction est parfaitement normale. Si vous me piquez avec une épingle, je réagis, sauf si je suis insensible. Mais dans certains cas, la pensée intervient pour ruminer une réaction. Elle la transforme ainsi en plaisir. Elle veut répéter l'expérience, et plus on la répète, plus elle devient mécanique. Plus on y pense, plus on confère de l'énergie au plaisir. La pensée crée et alimente le plaisir au moyen du désir : elle lui donne une continuité, de sorte que la réaction naturelle qui consiste à désirer un bel objet est pervertie par la pensée. La pensée transforme le désir en mémoire et la mémoire est alimentée parce qu'on y revient maintes fois par la pensée.

La mémoire a, bien sûr, sa place à un certain niveau. Dans notre vie quotidienne, nous ne pourrions pas exister sans elle. Il la faut efficace dans son propre champ, mais il existe un état d'esprit où la mémoire occupe fort peu de place. L'esprit que ne mutile pas la mémoire est véritablement libre.

Avez-vous jamais remarqué que lorsqu'on réagit, lorsqu'on répond à quelque chose totalement, de tout son cœur, très peu de mémoire s'y attache ? Ce n'est que lorsqu'on ne répond pas de tout son être à une provocation que se produit un conflit, une lutte, qui créent de la confusion, du plaisir, ou de la douleur. Cette lutte engendre une mémoire, tout le temps, à laquelle s'ajoutent d'autres, et ce sont elles qui répondent aux événements. Tout ce qui résulte de la mémoire est vieux, et par conséquent n'est jamais libre. La liberté de pensée n'existe pas. C'est une sottise que de le croire.

La pensée n'est jamais neuve, car elle est une réaction de la mémoire, de l'expérience, du savoir. Parce qu'elle est vieille, elle vieillit l'objet que vous avez regardé avec délectation et que vous avez, dans l'instant, senti profondément. Et c'est ce qui est vieux qui donne du plaisir, jamais ce qui est neuf, car, dans le neuf, le temps n'existe pas.

Donc si vous pouvez considérer chaque chose sans permettre au plaisir d'intervenir : un visage, un oiseau, la couleur d'un sari, la beauté d'une nappe d'eau brillante de soleil, ou tout autre objet délectable ; si vous pouvez la regarder sans vouloir que l'expérience se répète, aucune douleur, aucune crainte n'interviendront, et il se produira une joie immense.

C'est la lutte en vue de répéter et de perpétuer le plaisir qui devient de la souffrance. Observez cela en vous. Vouloir cette répétition c'est inviter la douleur, car l'expérience d'hier, répétée, n'est plus la même. On fait de grands efforts pour retrouver non seulement le même plaisir et le même sens esthétique, mais aussi la même qualité interne de l'esprit, et on est blessé et déçu car elle vous est refusée.

Avez-vous observé ce qui vous arrive lorsqu'un petit plaisir vous est refusé ? Lorsqu'on n'obtient pas ce que l'on veut, on devient anxieux, envieux, on se prend à haïr. Avez-vous remarqué que lorsque vous sont refusés vos plaisirs — boisson, tabac, sexe ou autre chose —, avez-vous observé les batailles qui se livrent en vous ? Et tous ces conflits sont des aspects de la peur, n'est-ce pas ? Vous avez peur de ne pas trouver ce que vous cherchez ou de perdre ce que vous avez. Lorsque telle ou telle foi ou idéologie, dont vous avez été tributaires pendant des années, chancelle ou vous est arrachée par une logique ou par les circonstances, n'avez-vous pas peur de vous retrouver seuls, sans secours ? Cette croyance, pendant des années, vous a procuré de la satisfaction et du plaisir. Lorsqu'elle vous est retirée, vous demeurez égarés et vides, et la peur s'installe en vous jusqu'à ce que vous trouviez une autre forme de plaisir, une autre croyance.

Tout cela me semble très simple et parce que c'est si simple nous refusons de voir sa simplicité. Nous aimons tout compliquer. Si votre femme vous délaisse, n'êtes-vous pas jaloux ? N'êtes-vous pas en colère ? Ne haïssez-

47

vous pas l'homme qui l'a attirée ? Et qu'est tout cela si ce n'est la peur de perdre ce qui vous a procuré beaucoup de plaisir, une vie en commun, une sorte de sécurité dans la possession ?

Donc si vous comprenez que la recherche du plaisir est toujours accompagnée de souffrance, et si vous voulez vivre ainsi, du moins faites-le en connaissance de cause. Mais si, par contre, vous voulez mettre fin au plaisir, ce qui veut dire mettre fin aussi à la douleur, il vous faut être attentifs à toute la structure du plaisir. Il ne s'agit pas de l'expulser à la façon de ces moines et sannyasis qui s'interdisent de regarder les femmes, pensant que ce serait un péché, et qui, de ce fait, détruisent la vitalité de leur entendement, mais de comprendre tout son sens et sa signification. Alors vivre sera pour vous une joie immense. On ne peut penser à la joie : c'est une chose immédiate. En y pensant, on la transforme en plaisir. La vie dans le présent est la perception immédiate de la beauté et la délectation qu'elle comporte, sans la recherche du plaisir qu'elle pourrait procurer.

5

Se préoccuper de soi-même. Aspirer à une situation.
Les craintes et la peur totale. La fragmentation de la
pensée. Mettre fin à la peur.

Avant que nous n'allions plus loin, je voudrais vous
demander quel est votre intérêt fondamental et permanent, dans la vie. Laissant de côté toutes les réponses
obliques et abordant cette question directement et
honnêtement, que répondriez-vous ? Le savez-vous ? Que
le centre de votre intérêt n'est autre que vous-mêmes ?
C'est ce que la plupart d'entre nous répondraient s'ils
étaient sincères : je m'intéresse à mon évolution, à mon
travail, à ma famille, au petit coin dans lequel je vis,
à obtenir une meilleure situation, plus de prestige et de
pouvoir, à mieux dominer les autres, etc. Je crois
qu'il serait logique, n'est-ce pas, d'admettre que ce qui
nous intéresse au premier chef c'est « moi d'abord » ?
   Certains pourraient dire qu'il ne faudrait pas s'intéresser principalement à soi-même. Mais quel mal y
a-t-il à cela, si ce n'est que nous l'admettons rarement
en toute honnêteté ? Il arrive que nous en éprouvions

comme un sentiment de honte. Mais voilà qui est dit : notre intérêt fondamental est nous-mêmes, quoique pour différentes raisons, idéologiques ou traditionnelles, nous pensons que c'est un mal. Toutefois ce que l'on pense ne change rien : pourquoi introduire ici cette notion de mal ? Ce n'est qu'une idée, un concept. Le « fait » est que ce qui nous intéresse d'une façon fondamentale et durable, c'est nous-mêmes.

Vous pourriez me dire que l'on éprouve plus de satisfaction à aider les autres qu'à penser à soi. Où est la différence ? Si aider les autres est ce qui vous donne le plus de satisfaction, c'est que vous êtes intéressés par ce qui peut le plus vous satisfaire, vous. Pourquoi y introduire un concept idéologique ? Pourquoi ne pas vous dire que ce que vous désirez réellement, c'est vous satisfaire, soit par l'érotisme, soit par la charité, ou en devenant un grand saint, un homme de science, un homme politique ? C'est toujours le même processus, n'est-ce pas ? Notre satisfaction par les moyens les plus divers, subtils ou grossiers : c'est cela que nous voulons. Lorsque nous disons que nous voulons la « libération », c'est que nous pensons qu'il s'agit de trouver un état qui satisfasse merveilleusement, et l'ultime satisfaction serait, bien sûr, l'idée saugrenue de la « réalisation » personnelle. En vérité, nous aspirons à une satisfaction qui ne comporterait rien qui puisse nous déplaire.

La plupart d'entre nous ont un désir dévorant d'occuper une position sociale, craignant de n'être que des rien du tout. La société est faite de telle façon que l'homme qui occupe une belle situation est traité avec beaucoup de courtoisie, tandis que celui qui n'est rien socialement est malmené. Tout homme au monde veut avoir sa place, dans la société, dans sa famille, où à la droite de

Dieu, et cette situation doit être reconnue, sans quoi ce ne serait pas une situation du tout. Il nous faut toujours être sur une estrade. Intérieurement, nous sommes des remous douloureux et désordonnés. Etre considérés par le monde, passer pour des personnages importants, nous procure une grande compensation.

Ce désir d'avoir du prestige, d'être puissant et d'être reconnu tel par la société, est en somme un désir de dominer, ce qui est une forme d'agression. Le saint qui aspire à être dans un certain état de sainteté est aussi agressif que, dans sa basse-cour, la poule qui picore. Et quelle est la cause de cette agressivité ? La peur, n'est-ce pas ?

La peur est un des plus grands problèmes inhérents à la vie. Etre sa victime c'est avoir l'esprit confus, déformé, violent, agressif, en perpétuel conflit. C'est ne pas oser s'éloigner d'un mode conventionnel de pensée, qui engendre l'hypocrisie. Tant qu'on n'est pas délivré de la peur, on peut escalader les plus hautes montagnes, inventer toutes sortes de dieux, mais on demeure dans les ténèbres.

Vivant dans une société stupide et corrompue comme la nôtre, dont l'éducation compétitive engendre la peur, nous sommes tous surchargés du fardeau de la peur. Il pèse horriblement sur nous, de toutes les façons. Il ternit, déforme et corrompt nos existences.

Une peur physique existe, mais ce n'est qu'une réaction qui provient de notre hérédité animale. Seules les peurs psychologiques nous intéressent ici, car lorsqu'on les comprend telles qu'elles sont, profondément ancrées en nous, on peut affronter les peurs animales, tandis que nous attaquer à celles-ci d'abord ne nous aidera jamais à comprendre celles de la psyché.

La peur a toujours un objet ; elle n'est jamais abstraite ; elle est toujours reliée à quelque chose. Savez-vous quelles sont vos peurs ? Perdre son emploi, manquer de nourriture ou d'argent, être victime de médisances ou de calomnies, ne pas réussir, perdre une position sociale, être méprisé ou ridiculisé ; ou la peur de la souffrance et de la maladie; celles d'être assujetti, de ne pas connaître l'amour, de n'être pas aimé, de perdre sa femme ou ses enfants; ou encore : la peur de la mort ; celle de vivre dans un monde semblable à la mort, celle de périr d'ennui, celle de ne pas être à la hauteur de l'image que l'on se fait de vous, celle de perdre la foi... de toutes ces peurs, et d'autres innombrables, savez-vous quelles sont les vôtres ? Et d'habitude, que faites-vous à leur sujet ? Vous les fuyez, n'est-ce pas ? Ou vous inventez des idées et des images pour les camoufler. Mais fuir la peur ne fait que l'accroître.

Une des causes majeures de la peur est notre refus de nous voir tels que nous sommes. Nous devons, donc, non seulement connaître nos peurs, mais aussi examiner le réseau d'artifices que nous avons élaboré en vue de nous débarrasser d'elles. Si nous mettons à l'œuvre nos facultés — qui comprennent celles du cerveau — pour dominer la peur, la réprimer, la discipliner, la maîtriser, ou lui donner une autre apparence, le conflit qui en résulte est une perte d'énergie.

La première question à nous poser est de savoir ce qu'est, au juste, la peur et comment elle naît. Qu'entendons-nous par ce mot peur ? Je me pose la question : « Qu'est-ce que la peur ? » et non « de quoi ai-je peur ? »

Je mène une certaine vie ; je pense d'une certaine

façon ; j'ai mes croyances, j'accepte certains dogmes ; et je ne veux pas perdre ces armatures de mon existence car j'ai mes racines en elles. Je ne veux pas qu'on les conteste, je ne veux pas que l'on vienne me troubler, car je me trouverais dans l'incertitude détestable de celui qui ne sait pas. Si l'on m'arrachait à tout ce que je sais et crois, je voudrais avoir une certitude raisonnée quant à ma nouvelle condition. Ainsi il se trouve que les cellules de mon cerveau se tracent certains circuits et qu'elles refusent d'en tracer d'autres, qui comporteraient une part d'incertitude. Le passage de la certitude à l'incertitude est ce que j'appelle la peur.

En ce moment, étant assis ici, je n'ai aucune crainte. Je n'éprouve pas de peur en cet instant présent, rien ne m'arrive, on ne menace ni ma personne ni mon bien. Mais au-delà du moment actuel, en mon esprit, une couche profonde pense consciemment ou inconsciemment à ce qui pourrait arriver dans l'avenir, ou se tracasse au sujet de quelque événement passé dont les suites pourraient me rattraper. Ainsi, j'ai peur du passé et du futur. J'ai divisé le temps en passé et futur, et la pensée intervient et dit : « Prenez garde que ceci ne recommence ; ou préparez-vous à cela, qui peut arriver ; l'avenir peut être dangereux pour vous ; ce que vous possédez aujourd'hui, il se pourrait que demain vous ne l'ayez plus ; demain vous pouvez mourir, votre femme pourrait vous quitter, vous pouvez perdre votre emploi ; la solitude vous guette ; assurez votre avenir. »

Considérez maintenant votre forme particulière de peur. Regardez-la et observez vos réactions. Pouvez-vous la regarder sans un seul mouvement de fuite, sans la justifier, la condamner ou la réprimer ? Pouvez-vous la regarder sans l'intervention du mot qui la provoque? Pouvez-vous, par exemple, penser à la mort sans le mot qui engendre la peur de la mort ? Ce mot suscite une vibration nerveuse particulière, de même que le mot amour qu'accompagnent ses propres images. Est-ce l'image que vous avez de la mort, est-ce le souvenir de tant de morts dont vous avez été témoins, est-ce votre association avec ces événements, qui engendrent en vous la peur ? Ou, en fait, est-ce votre disparition qui vous fait peur, et non l'image de cette fin ? Est-ce le mot mort qui vous terrorise ou est-ce votre fin ? Si c'est le mot, si ce sont vos souvenirs, ce que vous ressentez n'est pas du tout la peur.

Supposons que l'un de vous ait été malade il y a deux ans et que la mémoire ait enregistré cette souffrance ; elle vous dit maintenant d'être prudent, de crainte d'une rechute. La mémoire et ses associations provoquent ainsi en vous une peur apparente mais qui n'est pas du tout réelle, puisqu'en ce moment vous êtes en bonne santé. La pensée — qui est toujours vieille car elle est une réaction de la mémoire, laquelle est toujours vieille — a créé, dans le champ de la durée, un sentiment de peur, qui n'est pas un fait réel. La vérité est que vous vous portez bien. Mais l'expérience qui est enregistrée en vous en tant que mémoire vous dit d'être prudent, de crainte de retomber malade.

Nous voyons donc que la pensée engendre une peur d'une sorte. Mais en dehors de cela, la peur existe-t-elle ? Est-elle toujours le résultat de la pensée, et si elle l'est, assume-t-elle d'autres aspects ? Nous avons peur de la mort, c'est-à-dire d'un événement qui aura lieu demain ou après, dans la sphère du temps. Il y a une distance entre l'actuel et ce qui sera. La pensée a constaté cet état, elle a observé la mort et dit : « Je mourrai. » Ainsi elle crée la peur de la mort ; mais dans le cas où elle ne la crée pas, la peur existe-t-elle en aucune façon ?

La peur est-elle le produit de la pensée ? Si elle l'est, la pensée étant toujours vieille, la peur l'est aussi. Ainsi que nous l'avons dit, il n'existe pas de pensée neuve : si nous la reconnaissons, c'est qu'elle est vieille. Ce que nous redoutons, c'est une répétition du passé : la pensée de ce qui « a été » se projetant dans le futur. C'est donc elle, la pensée, qui est responsable de la peur. Vous pouvez d'ailleurs vous en assurer vous-mêmes. Lorsqu'on est face à face avec l'immédiat, on n'a aucune peur : elle ne survient que lorsque intervient la pensée.

Notre question est donc : nous est-il possible de vivre complètement, totalement, dans le présent ? Ce n'est qu'ainsi que l'on s'affranchit de la peur. Mais pour le comprendre, vous devez comprendre toute la structure de la pensée, de la mémoire, du temps, et cela, non pas intellectuellement, non pas verbalement, mais en toute vérité, avec votre cœur, avec votre esprit, avec vos entrailles. Alors serez-vous libérés de la peur ; alors pourrez-vous, sans l'engendrer, vous servir de la pensée.

La pensée, tout comme la mémoire, nous est évidemment nécessaire pour vivre quotidiennement. C'est le seul instrument que nous ayons pour communiquer, agir, travailler, etc. La pensée est une réaction de la mémoire, laquelle s'accumule par l'expérience, les connaissances, les traditions, le temps. C'est en fonction de cet arrière-plan que nous réagissons et cette réaction est la pensée. Celle-ci est essentielle à certains niveaux, mais lorsqu'elle se projette psychologiquement en tant que futur et passé, engendrant la peur ainsi que le plaisir, elle rend l'esprit obtus, donc forcément inactif. Alors je me demande pourquoi, pourquoi, pourquoi je pense au futur et au passé en termes de plaisir et de douleur, sachant qu'une telle pensée engendre la peur. N'est-il pas possible à la pensée psychologique de s'arrêter, faute de quoi la peur ne finira jamais ?

Une des fonctions de la pensée est d'être occupée tout le temps. Ce que nous désirons, en général, c'est penser toujours à une chose ou l'autre, afin de ne pas nous voir tels que nous sommes. Nous redoutons notre vacuité. Nous avons peur de voir nos peurs. A fleur de conscience nous les connaissons, mais les couches plus profondes de notre conscience les perçoivent-elles ? Et comment vous y prendrez-vous pour découvrir celles qui s'y cachent, secrètes ? Pouvez-vous réellement considérer deux sortes de peurs, les conscientes et les inconscientes ? Cette question est très importante. Les spécialistes, les psychologues, les analystes les classent ainsi, en couches de profondeurs différentes, mais si vous vous basez sur ce qu'ils disent — ou sur ce que je dis — ce sont nos théories, nos dogmes, nos connaissances que vous comprenez, ce n'est pas vous-mêmes.

Il est impossible de se connaître selon Freud, selon Jung ou selon ce que je dis. Les théories des autres n'ont absolument aucune importance. C'est à « vous-mêmes » que vous devez poser la question de savoir si la peur peut être divisée en consciente et inconsciente, ou si elle est un fait indivisible que l'on envisage sous différents aspects.

Chacun de nous n'a jamais qu'un seul désir. Il y a nous-mêmes et, en chacun, du désir. Les objets changent, le désir est toujours lui-même. Et, peut-être, en est-il ainsi de la peur. Nous avons peur de toutes sortes de choses, mais elle est une. Lorsqu'on s'en rend compte, on s'aperçoit que l'on a, de ce fait, écarté totalement le problème du subconscient et ainsi frustré les psychologues et les analystes. Lorsque l'on comprend que la peur est un seul et unique mouvement qui s'exprime de diverses façons et lorsqu'on voit ce mouvement lui-même plutôt que l'objet vers lequel il se dirige, on se trouve en face d'une question immense : comment le regarder sans qu'intervienne la fragmentation de notre conscience que nous avons si bien cultivée ?

Il n'existe en nous qu'une seule peur totale, mais comment, habitués comme nous le sommes à une pensée compartimentée, pouvons-nous en avoir une vue d'ensemble ? Cela nous est-il possible ? Ayant vécu une existence émiettée, nous ne voyons pas la peur totale, car le processus de cette machinerie qu'est la pensée consiste à tout émietter. Je vous aime, je vous hais, vous êtes mon ennemi, vous êtes mon ami ; j'ai mes particularités et mes tendances, mon emploi, ma situation, mon talent, ma femme, mon enfant ; il y a mon pays et votre pays, mon Dieu et votre Dieu... tout cela est de la pensée fragmentée. Et c'est cette pensée qui, cherchant à voir l'état total de la peur, le met en morceaux. Nous comprenons donc que l'on ne peut regarder cette peur totale que lorsque tout mouvement de la pensée s'arrête.

Pouvez-vous observer la peur sans rien en conclure, sans qu'interviennent les connaissances que vous avez accumulées à son sujet ? Si vous ne le pouvez pas, c'est que vous observez le passé, non la peur ; si vous le pouvez, c'est que vous observez la peur pour la première fois, sans qu'intervienne le passé. Cela ne peut se produire que lorsque la pensée est très silencieuse, de même que l'on ne peut écouter un interlocuteur que lorsqu'on ne bavarde pas intérieurement, poursuivant un dialogue avec soi-même au sujet d'inquiétudes et de problèmes personnels.

De la même façon, pouvez-vous regarder votre peur sans vouloir la résoudre au moyen de son opposé, le courage ? La regarder vraiment sans essayer de vous en libérer ? Lorsqu'on dit : « Je dois la dominer, je dois m'en débarrasser, je dois la comprendre », c'est qu'on cherche à la fuir.

Nous pouvons observer d'un esprit assez tranquille un nuage, un arbre, ou le courant d'une rivière, qui n'ont, pour nous, que peu d'importance, mais nous observer nous-mêmes est bien plus difficile, car nos exigences sont d'un ordre pratique, et nos réactions sont si immédiates ! Lorsque nous nous trouvons directement en contact avec la peur, ou le désespoir, ou la solitude, ou la jalousie, ou avec tout autre état d'esprit haïssable, pouvons-nous le regarder assez complètement pour que nos esprits se calment et nous permettent de voir ?

Pouvons-nous percevoir la peur elle-même dans sa totalité, et non ses différents aspects, non les sujets de notre peur ? Si nous considérons ceux-ci en détail, en les abordant un à un, nous ne parviendrons jamais au cœur de la question, qui consiste à apprendre à vivre avec la peur.

Pour vivre avec une chose vivante telle que la peur, il faut avoir l'esprit et le cœur extraordinairement subtils, n'ayant rien conclu à son sujet, et qui peuvent, par conséquent, suivre tous les mouvements de la peur. Si, alors, vous l'observez et vivez avec elle — ce qui ne prendrait pas toute une journée, car en une minute, en une seconde on peut percevoir toute sa nature — si vous vivez avec elle, vous vous demandez inévitablement quelle est l'entité qui vit avec la peur. Qui est celui qui l'observe, qui épie les mouvements de ses différentes formes, tout en étant conscient de ce qu'elle est en essence ? L'observateur est-il une entité morte, un être statique, ayant acquis de nombreuses informations et connaissances à son propre sujet ? Est-ce bien cette chose inanimée qui observe la peur et qui vit en son mouvement ? L'observateur n'est-il rien que du passé ou est-il une chose vivante ? Que répondez-vous à cela ? Ce n'est pas à moi que vous devez répondre, mais à vous-mêmes. Etes-vous, vous l'observateur, une entité morte essayant d'observer une chose vivante, ou un être vivant, qui observe une vie en mouvement ? Remarquez que dans l'observateur ces deux états existent. Il est le censeur qui refuse la peur. L'observateur est la somme de toutes ses expériences de la peur ; il est donc séparé de cette chose qu'il appelle peur, de sorte que se produit un espace entre lui et elle. Soit qu'il cherche à l'affronter pour la subjuguer, soit qu'il la fuie, il en résulte toujours une bataille, qui est une telle perte d'énergie !

En l'observant vous apprendrez que l'observateur n'est qu'un paquet d'idées et de mémoires sans validité ni substance, cependant que la peur étant un fait actuel vous ne pourrez jamais la comprendre au moyen d'une abstraction. Et, en vérité, l'observateur qui dit « j'ai peur » est-il autre chose que cette peur qu'il observe ? La peur, c'est lui. Lorsque cela est compris, on ne

59

dissipe plus tant d'énergie pour s'en débarrasser et la distance entre elle et l'observateur disparaît. Lorsque vous voyez que vous êtes une partie intégrante de la peur, que vous êtes elle en vérité, vous ne pouvez plus ien faire à ce sujet, et la peur parvient à sa fin ultime.

6

*La violence. La colère. Justifier et condamner. L'idéal
et l'actuel.*

La peur, le plaisir, la douleur, la pensée et la violence
sont intimement reliés. La plupart d'entre nous prennent
du plaisir à être violents, à détester des individus, à
haïr des groupes ou des races, à éprouver un sentiment
quelconque d'inimitié. Mais lorsque naît en nous un
état d'esprit où toute violence a pris fin, une joie l'accom-
pagne, très différente du plaisir que donnent la violence
et ses manifestations telles que les conflits, les haines,
les terreurs.

Pouvons-nous parvenir aux racines mêmes de la
violence et nous en libérer ? A défaut de cela, nous
vivrons indéfiniment en état de guerre les uns contre
les autres. Si c'est ainsi que vous voulez vivre — et c'est
ce qu'apparemment veulent la plupart des personnes
— continuez à dire que, encore que vous le déploriez,
la violence ne pourra jamais cesser. Mais dans ce cas,
nous n'aurons, entre nous, aucun moyen de communication, car vous vous serez bloqués. Si, au contraire,

vous pensez qu'il serait possible de vivre autrement, alors nous pourrons communiquer les uns avec les autres.

Examinons donc, entre ceux qui s'entendent, la question de savoir si l'on peut mettre fin, en soi-même, à toute forme de violence tout en vivant dans ce monde monstrueusement brutal. Je crois que c'est possible. Je ne veux avoir en moi aucun élément de haine, de jalousie, d'angoisse ou de peur. Je veux vivre totalement en paix... ce qui ne revient pas à dire que je souhaite mourir : je veux vivre sur cette merveilleuse terre, si belle, si pleine, si riche ; je veux voir les arbres, les fleurs, les cours d'eau, les vallées, les femmes, les garçons et les filles, et en même temps vivre tout à fait en paix avec moi-même et avec le monde. Que puis-je faire pour cela ?

Si nous pouvons observer la violence, non seulement dans la société — avec ses guerres, ses émeutes, ses conflits nationaux, ses antagonismes de classes — mais aussi en nous, alors, peut-être, pourrons-nous aller au-delà.

Ce problème est très complexe. Pendant des siècles et des siècles l'homme a été violent ; des religions, dans le monde entier, ont essayé de le rendre plus amène, et n'y sont pas parvenues. Si donc nous avons l'intention de pénétrer dans cette question, nous devons — il me semble — être pour le moins très sérieux, car elle nous conduira dans un tout autre domaine, tandis que si nous ne l'abordons qu'en tant que divertissement intellectuel, nous n'irons pas très loin.

Peut-être croyez-vous être très sérieux, lorsque vous vous dites que tant que le reste du monde ne s'orientera pas résolument vers la solution du problème de la violence, vous n'y pourrez rien. En ce qui me concerne, peu m'importe l'attitude des autres. J'envisage cette question avec le plus profond intérêt. Je ne suis pas le gardien de mon frère. En tant qu'être humain je ressens très profondément la nécessité de mettre fin à la violence et je veillerai à y mettre fin en moi-même. Mais je ne peux vous dire, ni à vous ni à quiconque, de ne pas être violents. Cela n'aurait aucun sens, sauf si vous en aviez le désir. Si donc vous avez réellement la volonté de découvrir ce qu'est la violence, poursuivons ensemble un voyage d'exploration dans ce domaine.

Ce problème est-il ailleurs ou ici ? Cherchez-vous à le résoudre dans le monde extérieur ou à examiner la violence elle-même, telle qu'elle existe en vous ? Si vous êtes libres de toute violence en vous-mêmes la question qui se pose est : « Comment puis-je vivre dans un monde rempli de violence, d'ambition, d'avidité, d'envie, de brutalité ? Ne serais-je pas détruit ? » Telle est la question inévitable que l'on se pose intérieurement.

Il me semble que lorsqu'on soulève cette question, c'est qu'on ne vit pas en paix, car dans le cas contraire on ne se poserait aucun problème. On peut se faire emprisonner parce qu'on refuse d'être mobilisé, ou fusiller parce qu'on refuse de se battre. Eh bien, on est fusillé : cela n'est pas un problème. Il est extrêmement important de le comprendre. J'essaie ici de voir la violence en tant que fait, non en tant qu'idée : en tant qu'elle existe dans l'être humain, et en tant que cet être est moi-même. A cet effet, il me faut être « complètement » vulnérable : je dois m'ouvrir à cette exploration, m'exposer à ma propre présence (pas nécessairement à la vôtre, car cela pourrait ne pas vous intéresser); je dois être dans un état d'esprit qui me pousserait jusqu'à l'extrême limite de ma recherche, sans m'arrêter à aucune étape en la jugeant suffisante.

Il doit m'apparaître avec évidence, maintenant, que je suis un être humain violent. J'ai reconnu la violence dans mes colères, dans mes exigences sexuelles, dans mes haines, dans les inimitiés que j'ai suscitées, dans ma jalousie ; j'en ai fait l'expérience vécue ; je l'ai connue ; et je me dis que je veux la comprendre tout entière, ne pas m'arrêter à une quelconque de ses manifestations (telle que la guerre) mais dégager le sens de l'agressivité dans l'homme, qui existe aussi chez les animaux, et dont je suis partie intégrante.

La violence ne consiste pas uniquement à nous entre-tuer. Nous sommes violents dans nos altercations, nous le sommes lorsque nous écartons quelqu'un de notre chemin, nous le sommes lorsque la crainte nous incite à obéir. La violence n'est pas seulement ces boucheries humaines organisées au nom de Dieu, d'une société, d'un pays. Elle existe aussi dans des sphères plus subtiles, plus secrètes et c'est là, dans ses grandes profondeurs, qu'il nous faut la chercher.

Lorsque vous vous dites Indien, Musulman, Chrétien, Européen, ou autre chose, vous êtes violents. Savez-vous pourquoi ? C'est parce que vous vous séparez du reste de l'humanité, et cette séparation due à vos croyances, à votre nationalité, à vos traditions, engendre la violence. Celui qui cherche à comprendre la violence n'appartient à aucun pays, à aucune religion, à aucun parti politique, à aucun système particulier. Ce qui lui importe c'est la compréhension totale de l'humanité.

Deux façons de penser existent au sujet de la violence.

Selon une école, elle est innée dans l'homme ; selon l'autre elle est le résultat de son héritage social et culturel. Aucune de ces deux façons de voir ne nous intéresse : elles n'ont aucune importance ; l'important est le fait que nous sommes violents, non de raisonner à ce sujet.

Une des manifestations les plus habituelles de la violence est la colère. Si ma femme ou ma sœur sont attaquées, je me dis que ma colère est juste. J'éprouve également cette juste colère lorsque mon pays, mes idées, mes principes, mon mode de vie sont attaqués. Je l'éprouve encore lorsque mes habitudes, mes petites opinions sont menacées. S'il arrive qu'on me marche sur les pieds ou qu'on m'insulte, je me mets en colère, ou encore si quelqu'un m'enlève ma femme et que je suis jaloux : cette jalousie passera pour être bienséante et juste, parce que cette femme est ma propriété. Tous ces aspects de la colère sont justifiés moralement, ainsi que tuer pour mon pays. Donc lorsque nous parlons de la colère, qui est une forme de violence, distinguons-nous, selon notre inclination et les influences du milieu, celle qui est juste de celle qui ne l'est pas, ou considérons-nous la colère en tant que telle ?

Une colère juste ? Cela peut-il exister ? Ou la colère a-t-elle une qualité intrinsèque, tout comme l'influence qu'exerce la société, que je qualifie de bonne ou mauvaise, selon qu'elle me convient ou non ? Dès que vous protégez votre famille, votre pays, un bout de chiffon coloré que vous appelez un drapeau, ou une croyance, une idée, un dogme, ou l'objet de vos désirs, ou ce que vous possédez, cette protection même est un indice de colère. Pouvez-vous examiner cette colère sans l'expliquer ou la justifier, sans vous dire qu'il vous faut protéger votre bien, ou que vous avez le droit d'être en colère, ou qu'il est absurde de l'être ? Pouvez-vous la regarder comme une chose en soi ? La regarder complètement, objectivement, c'est-à-dire sans l'absoudre ni la condamner ? Le pouvez-vous ?

Puis-je vous voir objectivement si je suis votre adversaire ou si je pense que vous êtes un être merveilleux ? Je ne peux vous voir tel que vous êtes que si je vous regarde avec une attention que n'altèrent pas de tels rapports. Mais puis-je regarder la colère de la même façon ? Etre vulnérable à ce phénomène extraordinaire ? Ne pas lui résister ? L'observer sans la moindre réaction ? C'est très difficile de l'observer sans passion, parce que la colère fait partie de mon être. Et pourtant c'est ce que j'essaie de faire.

Me voici, être humain violent, blanc, noir, brun ou rouge, et il ne m'intéresse pas de savoir si j'ai hérité cette violence ou si la société l'a engendrée en moi : ce qu'il m'importe de savoir, c'est si je peux m'en libérer. Cette question pour moi prime tout le reste, nourriture, besoin sexuel, situation sociale, car elle me corrompt, me détruit et détruit notre monde. Je veux la comprendre, la transcender. Je me sens responsable de toute la colère et de toute la violence du monde. Je m'en sens réellement responsable ; ce ne sont pas que des mots : je me dis : « Je ne peux agir dans ce sens que si je suis au-delà de la colère, au-delà de la violence, au-delà des particularismes nationaux. »

Ce sentiment de devoir comprendre la violence en moi engendre une immense vitalité, une passion de savoir. Mais pour aller au-delà de la violence, je ne dois ni la refouler, ni la nier, ni me dire : « Elle fait partie

de moi, je n'y peux rien. » ou : « Je veux la rejeter. »
Je dois la regarder, l'étudier, entrer dans son inti-
mité et à cet effet je ne dois ni la condamner ni la
justifier. C'est, pourtant, ce que nous faisons. Je vous
demande donc de suspendre, pour l'instant, vos jugements à son sujet.

Si vous voulez mettre fin à la violence et aux guerres,
demandez-vous combien de vous-mêmes, combien de
votre vitalité vous y mettez. N'êtes-vous pas profondément affectés de voir que vos enfants sont tués, que
vos fils sont enrégimentés, assujettis, assassinés ? Cela
vous est-il indifférent ? Grand Dieu, si cela ne vous
émeut pas, qu'est-ce qui vous intéresse ? Conserver votre
argent ? Vous divertir ? Vous droguer ? Ne voyez-vous
pas que votre propre violence est en train de détruire
vos enfants ? Ou n'est-ce là qu'une abstraction pour
vous ?

Fort bien. Si la question vous intéresse, adonnez-
vous à elle de tout votre cœur et de tout votre esprit.
Ne demeurez pas assis en me demandant de vous en
parler. J'attire votre attention sur le fait qu'il est
impossible de réellement voir la colère et la violence
si on les condamne ou les justifie, et que si elles ne
représentent pas un problème brûlant, on ne peut pas
s'en libérer. Commencez donc par apprendre. Apprenez à regarder la colère, à voir votre mari, votre
femme, vos enfants ; à écouter les hommes politiques.
Apprenez à voir pourquoi vous n'êtes pas objectifs,
pourquoi vous condamnez ou justifiez : si vous condamnez ou justifiez c'est parce que cela fait partie de la
structure de la société où vous vivez.

Vous êtes conditionnés en tant qu'Allemands, Indiens,

Nègres, Américains, au hasard de votre naissance, et votre condition a alourdi vos esprits. Pour découvrir une vérité fondamentale on doit pouvoir explorer ses profondeurs. On n'y parvient pas si l'outil dont on dispose est émoussé. Ce que nous faisons en ce moment c'est aiguiser cet outil, qui est cet esprit devenu obtus à force de condamner et de justifier. On ne peut explorer des profondeurs qu'avec un esprit pénétrant comme une aiguille, dur comme le diamant.

Il est inutile de s'asseoir dans un fauteuil et de se demander : « Comment puis-je avoir un esprit fait de la sorte ? » Il faut le sentir comme on a faim, et il faut se rendre compte que ce qui abêtit l'esprit est son sentiment d'invulnérabilité, qui l'a enfermé dans des murs. Ce sentiment est présent chaque fois que l'on condamne ou que l'on justifie. Si l'on peut s'en débarrasser, on peut regarder, étudier, pénétrer un problème et peut-être parvenir à un état où l'on en est totalement conscient.

Revenons au cœur de la question : pouvons-nous déraciner la violence en nous-mêmes ? Si je vous disais : « Pourquoi n'avez-vous pas changé ? » ce serait une forme de violence. Ce n'est pas du tout cela que je vous dis. Je n'ai en aucune façon le désir de vous convaincre de quoi que ce soit. C'est votre vie, non la mienne, et chacun la vit comme il l'entend. Je demande simplement s'il est possible à un être humain, psychologiquement intégré à une société quelle qu'elle soit, de se débarrasser de sa propre violence. Si un tel processus est possible, il ne peut manquer de susciter une nouvelle façon de vivre.

La plupart d'entre nous ont accepté que la violence

soit à la base de leur mode de vie. Deux guerres horribles ne nous ont appris qu'à dresser des barrières de plus en plus nombreuses entre les hommes — c'est-à-dire entre vous et moi. Mais ceux qui veulent s'affranchir de la violence, comment doivent-ils s'y prendre ? Je ne pense pas qu'ils puissent y parvenir en s'analysant ou en se faisant analyser par un spécialiste. Ils pourraient, par ce moyen, se modifier quelque peu, vivre un peu plus paisiblement, dans un meilleur climat affectif, mais ils ne pourraient acquérir la perception totale qu'ils recherchent.

Toutefois, il nous faut savoir nous analyser, car ce processus aiguise considérablement l'esprit et lui confère une qualité d'attention, de pénétration, de sérieux, qui lui permettra de parvenir à une perception totale. Nous n'avons pas la faculté innée de percevoir un ensemble d'un seul coup d'œil. Cette clarté de vision n'est possible que lorsqu'on a appris à bien voir les détails, après quoi on peut « sauter ».

Il arrive que pour essayer de n'être plus violents nous nous appuyions sur un concept, un idéal appelé la « non-violence », pensant qu'en faisant appel à l'opposé de la violence nous pourrions abolir le fait lui-même. Mais nous n'y parviendrons pas. Nous avons des idéaux en grand nombre ; tous les livres sacrés en sont pleins ; et pourtant nous sommes encore violents. Pourquoi donc ne pas affronter la violence elle-même et oublier le mot qui la désigne ?

Si l'on veut comprendre l'actuel, on doit y consacrer toute son attention, toute son énergie, lesquelles font défaut lorsqu'on pense à un monde idéal fictif. Mais pouvons-nous bannir tout idéal de notre pensée ? Une personne sérieuse. qui a un intense désir de découvrir la vérité, de savoir ce qu'est l'amour dans le vrai sens de ce mot, ne doit avoir dans l'esprit aucun concept d'aucune sorte. Elle doit vivre dans ce qui « est » : dans l'actuel.

Pour voir en fait ce qu'est la colère, on ne doit passer aucun jugement à son sujet, car aussitôt que l'on pense à son opposé on la condamne, ce qui empêche de la voir. Lorsque vous déclarez détester ou haïr quelqu'un, cela peut paraître brutal, mais le fait est là, et si vous l'examinez à fond, complètement, il disparaît, tandis que si vous vous dites : « Je ne dois pas haïr ; je dois avoir de l'amour en mon cœur », vous vivez dans un monde hypothétique, avec une double série de valeurs.

Vivre dans le présent, complètement, totalement, c'est vivre avec ce qui « est », avec l'actuel, sans le condamner ni le justifier. Tout problème vu dans cette clarté est résolu.

Pouvez-vous voir ainsi le visage de la violence, non seulement dans le monde extérieur, mais aussi le visage réel qu'elle assume en vous, ce qui veut dire vous en libérer parce que vous n'avez admis aucune des idéologies qui la combattent ? Cela nécessite une méditation profonde, non un acquiescement verbal ou une dénégation.

Vous avez maintenant lu toute une série d'assertions, mais les avez-vous comprises ? Vos esprits conditionnés, vos façons de vivre, toute la structure de la société vous empêchent de voir un fait tel qu'il est et de vous en affranchir séance tenante. Vous dites : « J'y penserai ; je verrai s'il m'est possible ou non de m'affranchir de la violence ; j'essaierai. » Cette déclaration « j'essaierai » est une des pires que l'on puisse faire.

Essayer, faire de son mieux, cela n'existe pas. On fait la chose ou on ne la fait pas. Vous voulez du temps pour prendre une résolution lorsque la maison brûle. Elle brûle à cause de la violence dans le monde, et vous dites : « Donnez-moi le temps de trouver l'idéologie la plus propre à éteindre l'incendie. » Lorsque la maison brûle, discutez-vous sur la couleur des cheveux de celui qui apporte de l'eau ?

7

Les rapports humains. Les conflits. Le social. La pauvreté. Les drogues. La dépendance. Les comparaisons. Les désirs. Les idéaux. L'hypocrisie.

La cessation de la violence — que nous venons de considérer — n'implique pas nécessairement un état d'esprit paisible en lui-même, donc en paix dans ses rapports humains. Ces rapports s'établissent toujours sur des images, sur des mécanismes de défense : chacun se fait le portrait de ce que sont les autres personnes et les rapports sont ceux de ces images entre elles, non ceux des personnes elles-mêmes. Le mari a une image de sa femme — peut-être pas consciemment, mais elle est là —, la femme en a une de son mari, nous avons celle de notre pays, celle que nous formons à notre sujet, et nous les renforçons toutes, en y ajoutant sans cesse quelque chose. Ce sont elles qui déterminent nos prétendus rapports réciproques. Tant que subsiste cette formation d'images, les rapports entre deux personnes ou entre de nombreux êtres humains, n'existent pas, et ceux qui s'établissent ne peuvent évidemment jamais instaurer une paix, car ces images sont fictives ; or la vie dans l'abstrait est impossible.

Malgré cela, c'est ainsi que nous existons : dans un monde d'idées, de théories, de symboles, d'images, que nous avons créé à notre sujet et au sujet d'autrui, et qui n'a aucune réalité. Tous les rapports que nous avons, soit avec des idées, soit avec les biens matériels ou les êtres humains, sont basés essentiellement sur cette formation d'images, et donnent lieu, par conséquent, à des conflits.

Comment vivre en paix avec nous-mêmes et avec les autres ? Après tout, la vie est un mouvement en relations, sans quoi elle n'existerait pas, et si nous basons cette vie sur une abstraction, une idée, ou des opinions spéculatives, une telle existence abstraite engendre des relations qui deviennent des champs de bataille.

Est-il en aucune façon possible à l'homme de vivre une vie intérieure tout à fait ordonnée, sans aucune forme de contrainte, d'imitation, de refoulement ou de sublimation ? Peut-il engendrer en lui-même un ordre qui serait une qualité vivante, non enfermée dans un cadre d'idées — une tranquillité intérieure qui ne connaîtrait aucun trouble à aucun moment —, non dans quelque monde fantastique, abstrait, mythique, mais dans sa vie quotidienne, à son travail et dans son foyer ?

Je pense qu'il nous faut examiner cette question très soigneusement, car aucun recoin de notre conscience n'est à l'abri des conflits. Ils sont là, dans nos rapports avec nos intimes, avec nos voisins ou avec la société ; ils se manifestent dans nos contradictions, nos divisions, ils nous séparent les uns des autres dans un état de dualité. Observez vos rapports avec la société : vous y verrez, à tous les niveaux, des conflits mineurs ou majeurs, qui provoquent des réactions superficielles ou des résultats dévastateurs.

L'homme a accepté que l'état de conflit soit une partie intégrante de l'existence quotidienne, car il a admis que la compétition, la jalousie, l'avidité, le désir de posséder, l'agressivité soient un mode de vie naturel. Il accepte, en somme, la structure de la société et sa propre existence dans le cadre de la respectabilité. C'est le piège où tombent la plupart d'entre nous, car nous voulons être si respectables ! Mais si nous examinons nos esprits, nos cœurs, notre façon de penser, de sentir, d'agir, dans nos existences quotidiennes, nous voyons que tant que nous nous conformerons ainsi aux valeurs de la société, nous vivrons dans un champ de bataille. Mais si nous ne les acceptons pas — et aucune personne religieuse ne peut les accepter — nous serons tout à fait affranchis de la structure psychologique de la société.

Nous sommes, pour la plupart, riches de tout ce que produit la société, de tout ce qu'elle a créé en nous et de ce que nous avons créé en nous-mêmes : riches en avidité, envie, colère, haine, jalousie, angoisse. En cela nous sommes très riches. Des religions, à travers le monde, ont prêché la pauvreté. Le moine revêt sa robe, change de nom, se rase la tête, entre dans une cellule et fait vœu de pauvreté et de chasteté. En Orient il ne dispose que d'un pagne, d'une robe, d'un repas par jour, et nous respectons cette pauvreté. Mais ceux qui l'ont assumée sont encore, intérieurement, riches de tous les produits de la société, car ils recherchent une situation, un prestige. Appartenant à tel ou tel ordre, à telle ou telle religion, ils vivent toujours dans ce qui divise et sépare les cultures et les traditions. Ce n'est pas cela la pauvreté, car elle consiste à être totalement libre par rapport à la société, encore que l'on puisse avoir quelques vêtements de plus et consommer

quelques repas de plus. Grand Dieu, qui en fait cas ?
Mais, malheureusement, beaucoup de personnes sont
avides de ce genre d'exhibitionnisme.

La pauvreté devient une chose merveilleuse quand
on s'est libéré psychologiquement de la société. On
devient pauvre intérieurement car on n'a plus rien du
tout dans l'esprit, ni recherches, ni exigences, ni désirs :
rien. Ce n'est que cette pauvreté intérieure qui peut
percevoir la vérité d'une vie en laquelle n'existe aucun
conflit. Une telle vie est une bénédiction qu'aucune
église, qu'aucun temple ne peuvent donner.

Comment peut-on se libérer de la structure psychologique de la société, c'est-à-dire de ce qui constitue
l'essence même des conflits ? Il n'est pas difficile de
tailler, d'émonder certaines branches d'un conflit, mais
nous nous demandons comment parvenir à une paix intérieure totale, donc à une parfaite tranquillité extérieure
où, loin de végéter, loin d'être dans un état d'inertie,
on serait dynamique, plein de vitalité et d'énergie.

Pour comprendre un problème et s'en libérer, il faut
une énergie passionnée et soutenue. Il ne suffit pas
qu'elle soit physique et intellectuelle ; encore faut-il
qu'elle ne dépende d'aucun motif et d'aucun stimulant
psychologique ou sous forme de drogues. Le stimulant
dont on est tributaire est cela même qui engourdit
l'esprit et le rend insensible. En prenant certaines drogues on peut temporairement avoir assez d'énergie
pour voir les choses très clairement, mais on retombe
dans l'état où l'on se trouvait, et l'on devient de plus
en plus assujetti à ces stupéfiants.

Tout stimulant, que ce soit l'église, l'alcool, les
drogues, la parole écrite ou prononcée, nous met inévi-

tablement dans un état de dépendance qui fait obstacle à notre vision directe. Or c'est cette vision qui déclenche la vitalité de notre énergie.

Nous dépendons tous, psychologiquement, de quelque chose. Et pourquoi ? Pourquoi avons-nous cet intense désir d'être assujettis ?...

... C'est tous ensemble que nous entreprenons ce voyage d'exploration. N'attendez pas que je vous apprenne les causes de l'état de dépendance où vous vous trouvez. Si nous explorons ensemble, les découvertes que nous ferons seront les vôtres, et étant vôtres elles vous donneront de la vitalité.

Je découvre en moi-même que je suis tributaire de quelque chose. Disons, par exemple, qu'un auditoire me stimule. Parler à un grand nombre de personnes me donne une sorte d'énergie ; je dépends donc de ces personnes, qu'elles soient ou non d'accord avec ce que je dis. Leur désaccord suscite même plus d'énergie en moi que leur acquiescement, car une acceptation passive n'établit que des rapports creux, sans contenu. Je découvre donc que j'ai besoin d'un auditoire et qu'il est très stimulant de m'adresser à lui. Pourquoi ? Pourquoi ce besoin ? Parce qu'au plus profond de moi-même je suis vide ; parce que je ne trouve pas en moi la source de vie, toujours pleine, riche, mouvante. Je m'appuie donc à quelque chose, et voilà que j'ai découvert la cause de ma dépendance.

Mais cette découverte m'affranchit-elle ? Evidemment pas, car elle n'est qu'intellectuelle. L'acceptation intellectuelle d'une idée ou l'acquiescement émotionnel à une idéologie ne peuvent pas libérer l'esprit de son état de dépendance : son besoin d'être stimulé demeure. Ce qui le libère c'est la vision de la structure de la stimulation, la vision de la nature de cette dépendance qui abêtit l'esprit, le rend stupide et inactif. Seule le libère cette vision totale.

Il me faut maintenant comprendre en quoi consiste cette vision totale. Tant que je considère la vie d'un point de vue particulier ; ou en fonction d'une expérience vécue que je chéris ; ou à partir de certaines connaissances que j'ai amassées (toutes ces données étant mon arrière-plan, c'est-à-dire mon moi), je ne peux percevoir aucune structure dans sa totalité. J'ai découvert intellectuellement, verbalement, par une analyse, la cause de ma dépendance, mais tout ce qu'explore la pensée est inévitablement fragmentaire. Ainsi donc je ne peux voir en sa totalité le processus de ma dépendance que lorsque la pensée n'intervient pas.

Je vois alors le fait lui-même ; je vois en toute réalité ce qui « est » ; je le vois sans plaisir ni déplaisir ; je ne veux ni me débarrasser de cette dépendance ni me libérer de sa cause ; je l'observe et lorsque se produit une telle observation, c'est l'image tout entière qui m'apparaît, non un simple fragment. Cette vision est un état de liberté.

J'ai maintenant découvert que la fragmentation est une perte d'énergie : j'ai découvert l'origine de cette dissipation.

On peut croire qu'il n'y a aucune perte d'énergie lorsqu'on imite, lorsqu'on accepte une autorité, lorsqu'on est subordonné à une autorité religieuse ou sous l'emprise d'un rituel, d'un dogme, d'un parti, d'une idéologie. Mais cette soumission, cette acceptation d'un mode de pensée — qu'il soit bon ou mauvais, sublime ou terre à terre — n'est qu'une activité fragmentaire qui crée une séparation entre ce qui « est » et ce qui « devrait être ». Cette séparation provoque toujours un conflit, qui est une perte d'énergie.

Si l'on se pose la question : « Comment me libérer de cet état de conflit ? » on se crée un nouveau problème et on intensifie la lutte ; mais si on peut regarder cette question comme un objet concret, d'une façon claire et directe, on comprend en son essence la vérité d'une vie qui ne comporte aucun conflit.

Abordons cette question d'un autre point de vue. Nous ne cessons de mettre en regard ce que nous sommes et ce que nous devrions être. Ce qui, selon nous, « devrait » être est notre idée, projetée, de ce qui « doit » être. Toute comparaison entraîne une contradiction, non seulement entre deux personnes ou entre une personne et un objet, mais entre ce qu'on était hier et ce qu'on est aujourd'hui, donc il y a conflit entre ce qui a été et ce qui est.

Ce qui « est » n'a de réalité pour nous que lorsque nous vivons en sa présence, sans nous livrer à aucune comparaison. C'est alors que nous pouvons paisiblement accorder toute notre attention à ce qui se trouve en nous : désespoir, laideur, brutalité, peur, anxiété ou solitude, et vivre avec, complètement. Ayant enfin aboli les contradictions, nous échappons aux conflits.

Mais nous ne cessons de nous comparer à ceux qui sont plus riches, plus brillants, plus intelligents, plus célèbres, plus ceci ou cela que nous.

Ce « plus » joue un rôle extrêmement important dans nos vies. Cette habitude de nous mesurer toujours à quelque chose ou à quelqu'un est une des principales causes de nos conflits. Pourquoi nous comparons-nous toujours à d'autres ? Pourquoi ce sens de comparaison est-il ancré en nous ? On nous l'a inculqué depuis notre enfance. Dans chaque école, « A » apprend à se comparer à « B », et se détruit en s'efforçant d'être l'égal de « B ».

Lorsque ce processus de comparaison est absent, lorsque l'on n'a ni idéal ni opposant, c'est-à-dire aucun facteur de dualité, et que l'on cesse de lutter pour devenir autre que ce que l'on est, que se produit-il en nous ? Ayant cessé de créer notre opposant, notre intelligence et notre sensibilité s'aiguisent ; ayant cessé de lutter, nous ne dissipons plus l'énergie vitale qui est passion ; nous sommes devenus capables de cette passion immense, sans laquelle rien ne se fait.

Si l'on ne se compare à personne, on devient ce que l'on est. A l'imitation de quelqu'un, on espère évoluer, s'élever en intelligence et en beauté. Y parvient-on ? La « réalité » est ce que vous êtes ; vous fragmentez ce fait par des comparaisons ; mais le regarder sans se référer à autrui confère l'immense énergie qu'il faut pour le voir. On se trouve alors au-delà du champ des comparaisons, non que l'esprit soit devenu stagnant de contentement ; il a compris en essence comment il dissipe l'énergie vitale si nécessaire pour pénétrer la vie dans sa totalité.

Je ne veux pas savoir avec qui je suis en conflit. Je ne veux pas connaître les conflits périphériques de mon être. Je veux savoir pourquoi les conflits existent. Lorsque je me pose cette question, je découvre en moi une cause fondamentale qui est toute différente des éléments périphériques des conflits et de leurs solutions. C'est cette essence centrale qui m'intéresse, et je vois — peut-être le voyez-vous aussi ? — que la nature même du désir, si elle n'est pas bien comprise, conduit inévitablement à des conflits.

Tout désir est contradictoire. On désire toujours deux choses opposées. Je ne dis pas qu'il faut détruire le désir, le refouler, le dominer ou le sublimer, mais qu'il faut le voir en tant que contradiction. Ce ne sont pas ses objets qui s'opposent : c'est en sa nature propre qu'existent toujours deux opposés, et c'est cela que je dois comprendre avant de chercher à comprendre mes conflits ; c'est en nous-mêmes qu'existe un état contradictoire, lequel est engendré par notre désir fondamental de poursuivre le plaisir et d'éviter la douleur... Mais nous avons examiné cette question plus haut.

Nous voyons que le désir est à l'origine d'un état contradictoire qui consiste à vouloir une chose tout en ne la voulant pas. C'est, en somme, une activité à deux sens. On n'effectue aucun effort, n'est-ce pas ? à faire ce qui est agréable, mais ce plaisir engendre une souffrance. On entreprend alors une lutte pour l'éviter, ce qui est une perte d'énergie.

Pourquoi entretenons-nous cette dualité ? Elle existe, évidemment, dans la nature ; dans la lumière et l'ombre, la nuit et le jour, l'homme et la femme... mais psychologiquement, intérieurement, pourquoi existe-t-elle ? Veuillez y penser avec moi ; n'attendez pas que je vous le dise. Il vous faut exercer vos facultés pour le savoir, car mes mots ne sont qu'un miroir qui vous permet de vous observer vous-mêmes. Pourquoi donc cette dualité psychologique ? Est-ce parce que nous avons été entraînés à toujours mettre en regard ce qui « est » et ce qui « devrait être » ?

On nous a conditionnés par des notions de bien et de

mal, de ce qui est bon ou mauvais, moral ou immoral. Cette dualité est-elle là parce que nous croyons qu'en pensant aux opposés de la violence, de l'envie, de la jalousie, de la mesquinerie, nous nous en débarrasserons ? Utilisons-nous ces opposés comme des leviers à cet effet, ou en tant que voies d'évasions, pour échapper à l'actuel, ne sachant pas comment l'aborder ? Est-ce parce que l'on nous a dit, au cours de milliers d'années de propagande, qu'il nous faut avoir pour idéal le contraire de ce qui « est », afin de bien vivre dans le présent ?

On pense qu'un idéal nous délivrera de ce qui « est », mais il n'y parvient jamais. Vous pouvez prêcher la non-violence toute votre vie, et pendant ce temps semer les graines de la violence. Lorsqu'on a une conception de ce qu'on devrait être et de comment on devrait agir, et qu'on s'aperçoit que l'on ne cesse d'agir d'une façon opposée, on se rend compte que les principes, les croyances, les idéaux doivent inévitablement faire tomber dans l'hypocrisie et la malhonnêteté. C'est l'idéal qui engendre le contraire de ce qui « est » ; si l'on sait suivre avec la réalité de ce qui « est », l'idéal est inutile.

Essayer de se façonner à l'imitation de quelqu'un, ou selon un idéal, est une des principales causes de nos contradictions, de notre état de confusion et de conflit. Un esprit confus, à quelque niveau qu'il agisse, demeure confus ; toute action émanant de cette confusion ne fait que l'accentuer. Je vois cela très clairement ; je le vois comme si je me trouvais devant un danger physique immédiat. Qu'arrive-t-il alors ? Je cesse d'agir en termes d'une confusion, quelle qu'elle soit. Cette inaction est une action totale.

8

*La liberté. La révolte. La solitude. L'innocence. Vivre
avec soi-même tel que l'on est.*

Aucun tourment des refoulements, aucune brutale
discipline des conformismes n'ont conduit à la vérité.
Pour la rencontrer on doit avoir l'esprit complètement
libre, sans l'ombre d'une déviation.

Mais demandons-nous d'abord si nous voulons réellement être libres. Lorsque nous en parlons, pensons-
nous à une liberté totale ou à nous débarrasser d'une
gêne ou d'un ennui ? Nous aimerions ne plus avoir de
pénibles souvenirs de nos malheurs et ne conserver
que ceux de nos jours heureux, des idéologies, des formules, des contacts qui nous ont le plus agréablement
satisfaits. Mais rejeter les uns et retenir les autres est
impossible, car, ainsi que nous l'avons vu, la douleur
est inséparable du plaisir.

Il appartient donc à chacun de nous de savoir s'il
veut être absolument libre. Si nous le voulons, nous
devons commencer par comprendre la nature et la
structure de la liberté.

Est-ce de « quelque chose » que nous voulons nous libérer ? De la douleur ? De l'angoisse ? Cela ne serait pas vouloir la liberté, qui est un état d'esprit tout différent. Supposons que vous vous libériez de la jalousie. Avez-vous atteint la liberté ou n'avez-vous fait que réagir, ce qui n'a en rien modifié votre état ?

On peut très aisément s'affranchir d'un dogme en l'analysant, en le rejetant, mais le mobile de cette délivrance provient toujours d'une réaction particulière due, par exemple, au fait que ce dogme n'est plus à la mode ou qu'il ne convient plus. On peut se libérer du nationalisme parce que l'on croit à l'internationalisme ou parce que l'on pense que ce dogme stupide, avec ses drapeaux et ses valeurs de rebut, ne correspond pas aux nécessités économiques. S'en débarrasser devient facile. On peut aussi réagir contre tel chef spirituel ou politique qui aurait promis la liberté moyennant une discipline ou une révolte. Mais de telles conclusions logiques, de tels raisonnements ont-ils un rapport quelconque avec la liberté ?

Si l'on se déclare libéré de « quelque chose », cela n'est qu'une réaction qui engendrera une nouvelle réaction, laquelle donnera lieu à un autre conformisme, à une nouvelle forme de domination. De cette façon, on déclenche des réactions en chaîne et l'on imagine que chacune d'elles est une libération. Mais il ne s'agit là que d'une continuité modifiée du passé, à laquelle l'esprit s'accroche.

La jeunesse, aujourd'hui, comme toutes les jeunesses, est en révolte contre la société, et c'est une bonne chose en soi. Mais la révolte n'est pas la liberté parce qu'elle n'est qu'une réaction qui engendre ses propres valeurs, lesquelles, à leur tour, enchaînent. On les imagine neuves, mais elles ne le sont pas : ce monde nouveau n'est autre que l'ancien, dans un moule différent. Toute révolte sociale ou politique fera inévitablement retour à la bonne vieille mentalité bourgeoise.

La liberté ne survient que lorsque l'action est celle d'une vision claire ; elle n'est jamais déclenchée par une révolte. Voir clairement c'est agir, et cette action est aussi instantanée que lorsqu'on fait face à un danger. Il n'y a, alors, aucune élaboration cérébrale, aucune controverse, aucune hésitation ; c'est le danger lui-même qui provoque l'acte. Ainsi, voir c'est à la fois agir et être libre.

La liberté est un état d'esprit, non le fait d'être affranchi de « quelque chose » ; c'est un sens de liberté ; c'est la liberté de douter, de remettre tout en question ; c'est une liberté si intense, active, vigoureuse, qu'elle rejette toute forme de sujétion, d'esclavage, de conformisme, d'acceptation. C'est un état où l'on est absolument seul, mais peut-il se produire lorsqu'on a été formé par une culture de façon à être toujours tributaire, aussi bien d'un milieu que de ses propres tendances ? Peut-on, étant ainsi constitué, trouver cette liberté qui est solitude totale, en laquelle n'ont de place ni chefs spirituels, ni traditions, ni autorités ?

Cette solitude est un état d'esprit qui ne dépend d'aucun stimulant, d'aucune connaissance. Elle n'est pas, non plus, le résultat de l'expérience et des conclusions que l'on en peut tirer. La plupart d'entre nous ne sont jamais seuls, intérieurement. Il y a une différence entre l'isolement, la réclusion, et l'état de celui qui se sait seul. Nous savons tous en quoi consiste l'isolement : on construit des murs autour de soi afin de n'être atteint par rien, de n'être pas vulnérable ; ou on cultive le détachement, qui est une autre forme d'agonie ; ou on vit dans la tour d'ivoire onirique de quelque idéologie. Se savoir seul, c'est tout autre chose.

On n'est jamais seul tant qu'on est rempli des souvenirs, des conditionnements, des soliloques du passé : les déchets accumulés du passé encombrent les esprits. Pour être seul on doit mourir au passé. Lorsqu'on est seul, totalement seul, on n'appartient ni à une famille, ni à une nation, ni à une culture, ni à tel continent : on se sent un étranger. L'homme qui, de la sorte, est complètement seul, est innocent et c'est cette innocence qui le délivre de la douleur.

Nous traînons avec nous le fardeau de ce que des milliers de personnes ont dit, et la mémoire de toutes nos infortunes. Abandonner définitivement tout cela, c'est être seul et non seulement innocent, mais jeune aussi — non en nombre d'années, mais innocent, jeune, vivant à tout âge — et l'on peut alors pénétrer la vérité ; pénétrer ce qui n'est pas mesurable en paroles.

En cette solitude, on commence à comprendre la nécessité de vivre avec soi-même tel que l'on est, et non tel qu'on devrait être ou tel que l'on a été. Voyez si vous pouvez vous voir sans émotion, ni fausse modestie, ni crainte, ni justifications ou condamnations, si vous pouvez vivre avec vous-mêmes tels que vraiment, vous êtes.

On ne comprend une chose qu'en vivant intimement avec elle. Mais dès qu'on s'y habitue — dès qu'on s'habitue, par exemple, à l'angoisse ou à la jalousie — on ne vit plus avec elle. Si l'on vit près d'un torrent, au bout de quelques jours on ne l'entend plus ; un tableau dans votre chambre, après quelque temps, disparaît à votre regard. Il en est de même des montagnes, des vallées, des arbres ; il en est de même de votre famille, de votre mari, de votre femme. Mais pour vivre avec la jalousie, l'envie, l'inquiétude, il ne faut jamais s'y habituer, jamais les accepter. Il faut en prendre soin tout comme on soigne un arbre nouvellement planté, l'abritant du soleil et des orages ; en prendre soin sans condamnation ni justification. Alors on commence à l'aimer. En prendre soin, c'est l'aimer. Ce n'est pas que l'on aime être envieux ou anxieux, ainsi que cela arrive à tant de personnes, mais plutôt que l'on éprouve un penchant naturel à observer.

Pouvez-vous donc — pouvons-nous, vous et moi — vivre avec ce que nous sommes réellement, nous sachant ternes, envieux, craintifs, incapables d'affection alors que nous nous croyons pleins d'amour, vite blessés dans notre amour-propre, facilement flattés, blasés... pouvons-nous vivre avec tout cela, sans l'accepter ni le nier, mais en un état d'observation qui ne serait ni morbide, ni déprimé, ni exalté ?

Posons-nous une autre question : pourrions-nous atteindre cette liberté, cette solitude, ce contact avec la structure entière de ce que nous sommes, en y mettant du temps ? En d'autres termes : la liberté peut-elle être conquise par un processus graduel ? Evidemment pas, car la durée, aussitôt qu'on l'introduit, nous rend de plus en plus esclaves. On ne peut pas devenir libre graduellement. Cela n'est pas une affaire de temps.

Et maintenant posons-nous la question qui résulte des précédentes : peut-on devenir conscient de cette liberté ? Si vous dites : « je suis libre », c'est que vous ne l'êtes pas, de même que l'homme qui se dit heureux ne l'est pas, car s'il le dit, c'est qu'il revit la mémoire d'un certain passé. La liberté ne peut se produire que d'une façon naturelle, non en la souhaitant, en la voulant, en aspirant à elle. Elle ne se laisse pas atteindre, non plus, à travers l'image que l'on s'en fait. Pour la rencontrer, on doit apprendre à considérer la vie — qui est un vaste mouvement — sans la servitude du temps, car la liberté demeure au-delà du champ de la conscience.

9

Le temps. La douleur. La mort.

Je suis tenté de vous répéter l'histoire d'un grand disciple qui alla chez Dieu pour lui demander de lui enseigner la vérité. Ce pauvre Dieu lui dit : « Mon ami, cette journée est si chaude, apporte-moi, je te prie, un verre d'eau. » Le disciple s'en va, et frappe à la première porte qu'il rencontre. Une belle jeune femme ouvre, il en tombe amoureux, ils se marient et ont plusieurs enfants. Or, un jour, la pluie survient, il pleut, il pleut, il pleut tellement que les torrents enflent, que les rues sont inondées et les maisons emportées. Le disciple, soutenant sa femme et portant ses enfants, crie, en détresse : « Seigneur, viens à notre secours ! » Et le Seigneur répond : « Où est le verre d'eau que je t'avais demandé ? »

C'est une assez bonne histoire, car nous pensons en termes de durée. L'homme vit dans la sphère du temps. Inventer un futur a été le jeu favori de ses évasions.

Nous pensons que des changements peuvent se produire en nous au cours du temps, que l'ordre peut se construire petit à petit, en y ajoutant chaque jour quelque chose. Mais le temps n'amenant ni l'ordre ni la paix, nous devons cesser de penser en termes d'évolutions graduelles. Cela veut dire que n'existe pour nous aucun lendemain paisible : c'est dans l'instant immédiat qu'il nous faut mettre de l'ordre en nous-mêmes.

Lorsqu'un danger immédiat nous menace, le temps disparaît, n'est-ce pas ? L'action est immédiate. Mais nous ne voyons pas le danger que constituent un grand nombre de nos problèmes, et, par conséquent, nous inventons le temps comme moyen pour les surmonter. Toutefois, le temps est trompeur, car il ne nous aide en rien à provoquer un changement en nous. Le temps est un mouvement que l'homme a divisé en passé, présent et futur. Tant qu'il le divisera ainsi, il vivra dans un état de conflit.

Est-ce qu'apprendre est une affaire de temps ? Nous n'avons pas appris, après tant de milliers d'années, qu'il y a une meilleure façon de vivre que de nous haïr et de nous entre-tuer. Le problème du temps est très important à comprendre si nous voulons trouver une issue à cette vie que nous avons contribué à rendre monstrueuse au point qu'elle n'a plus aucun sens. Mais ce que l'on doit d'abord comprendre c'est que l'on ne peut pénétrer la nature du temps que si l'on a cette fraîcheur, cette innocence d'esprit dont nous parlions.

Nos nombreux problèmes nous plongent dans une confusion qui nous égare. Or, si l'on est égaré dans une forêt, que fait-on ? On commence par s'arrêter et regarder, n'est-ce pas ? Mais dans la confusion de la vie, plus nous nous égarons, plus nous courons d'un côté à l'autre, cherchant, interrogeant, quémandant, sollicitant. La première chose à faire, si je peux me permettre de vous le proposer, est de mettre fin complètement à cette quête intérieure. Cet arrêt psychologique permet d'avoir un esprit paisible et très clair. Alors on peut examiner le processus du temps.

Les problèmes psychologiques n'existent que dans le temps, c'est-à-dire lorsque notre contact avec l'événement est incomplet. C'est cette rencontre partielle qui crée le problème. Lorsque nous répondons partiellement, d'une façon fragmentaire, à une provocation, ou lorsque nous essayons de l'éviter — c'est-à-dire lorsque nous ne lui accordons pas toute notre attention — nous nous créons une difficulté d'ordre psychologique qui durera tant que notre attention sera incomplète : tant que nous espérons la résoudre « un de ces jours ».

Savez-vous ce qu'est le temps ? Non pas le temps des montres, le temps chronologique, mais le temps psychologique ? C'est l'intervalle entre l'idée et l'action. Le mobile de l'idée est l'auto-protection : on a l'idée d'une sécurité. L'action est toujours dans l'immédiat ; elle n'a lieu ni dans le passé ni dans le futur ; mais agir est si dangereux et si incertain que l'on se conforme à l'idée dont on espère qu'elle apportera une sorte de sécurité.

Voyez donc cela en vous-mêmes. Vous avez une idée du bien et du mal, ou une conception idéologique en ce qui vous concerne, vous et la société, et vous vous préparez à agir. Votre action sera autant que possible conforme à votre idée ; elle cherchera à s'en rapprocher et il en résultera un conflit. Ainsi se produisent l'idée, l'intervalle et l'action. Dans cet intervalle, constitué essentiellement par de la pensée, se trouve tout le champ du temps psychologique. Lorsque vous pensez à un bonheur futur, vous vous imaginez tel que vous serez, après avoir obtenu, avec du temps, un certain résultat. La pensée, au moyen de l'observation, du désir et de la continuité de ce désir appuyée par un appoint de pensée, dit : « Demain je serai heureux ; demain j'aurai du succès ; demain le monde sera beau. » C'est ainsi qu'elle crée l'intervalle qui est le temps.

Demandons-nous dès lors s'il est possible de mettre un point final à ce temps. Est-il possible de vivre si complètement qu'il n'y ait pas de lendemains pour absorber la pensée ? Car le temps est douleur. Je veux dire qu'hier, ou il y a mille hiers, vous avez aimé, ou vous avez eu un compagnon qui est mort, et cette mémoire demeure. Vous pensez à ce plaisir et à cette douleur. Vous regardez en arrière, désirant, espérant, regrettant. Votre pensée ressasse indéfiniment les mêmes thèmes et, ce faisant, elle engendre la chose que l'on appelle douleur, et elle donne continuité au temps.

Tant qu'existe un intervalle de temps cultivé par la pensée, la douleur est présente, ainsi qu'une continuité de peur. Alors on en vient à se demander si cet intervalle peut disparaître. Si vous vous demandez : « peut-il jamais disparaître ? », cette question émane déjà d'une idée, car vous pensez en termes de réussite, vous créez un intervalle et vous revoici dans le piège du temps.

Considérez maintenant la question de la mort. Elle pose un problème immense à la plupart des personnes. Vous connaissez la mort ; elle est là, marchant à vos côtés jour après jour. Est-il possible de l'aborder si totalement qu'elle ne soit plus un problème ? Pour un tel contact, toute croyance, toute espérance, toute peur à son sujet doivent parvenir à leur fin, sans quoi on approche cette chose extraordinaire à travers une conclusion, une image, une anticipation inquiète, ce qui revient à faire intervenir une notion de temps.

Ce temps est un intervalle entre l'observateur et la chose observée ; cela veut dire que vous, l'observateur, avez peur de rencontrer cette chose qui s'appelle la mort. Vous ne savez pas ce qu'elle signifie ; vous avez toutes sortes d'espoirs et de théories à son sujet : vous croyez à la réincarnation ou à la résurrection, ou à ce qu'on appelle l'âme, l'atman, à une entité spirituelle intemporelle à laquelle on donne des noms différents.

Est-ce vous qui avez découvert par vous-mêmes que l'âme existe ? Ou est-ce une idée qu'on vous a transmise ? Existe-t-il vraiment une chose qui soit permanente, continue, au-delà de la pensée ? Si on peut la concevoir, c'est qu'elle est dans le champ de la pensée, et ne peut donc pas être permanente, car dans ce champ il n'y a rien de permanent. Découvrir qu'il n'y a rien de permanent a une immense importance car alors seulement a-t-on l'esprit libre, alors seulement peut-on voir clair, et en cela est une grande joie.

On ne peut pas avoir peur de l'inconnu, pour la simple raison qu'on ne le connaît pas. La mort n'est qu'un mot. Ce qui crée la peur c'est le mot, l'image. Pouvez-vous penser à la mort sans son image, étant donné que toujours l'image donne lieu à une pensée ? Cette pensée provoque une peur que l'on rationalise en créant une résistance contre l'inévitable, ou dont on se protège en inventant d'innombrables croyances. Il en résulte un espace entre la personne et ce dont elle a peur, l'espace d'une durée, un intervalle qui comporte nécessairement un conflit, où l'on se prend en pitié à cause de la peur et de l'inquiétude que l'on éprouve.

La pensée, qui engendre la peur de la mort, dit : « Remettons-la à plus tard, évitons-la, qu'elle s'éloigne le plus possible de nous, n'y pensons pas »... et pendant tout ce temps, on ne fait qu'y penser. Lorsque l'on s'interdit d'y penser, on a déjà élaboré les moyens de l'éviter. On en a peur parce qu'on l'éloigne.

L'homme a séparé la vie de la mort. L'intervalle entre vivre et mourir est une peur : c'est elle, la peur, qui crée le temps de l'intervalle. Vivre, c'est notre torture quotidienne, ce sont les insultes de tous les jours, les souffrances et un état de confusion avec des ouvertures occasionnelles sur des mers enchantées. C'est ce que nous appelons vivre, et nous avons peur de la mort qui met fin à ces misères. Nous préférons nous accrocher au connu plutôt que d'affronter l'inconnu, le connu étant notre maison, nos meubles, notre famille, notre travail, ainsi que notre caractère, notre savoir, notre célébrité, notre solitude, nos dieux. En somme, le connu est cette petite entité qui tourne incessamment autour d'elle-même, dans les limites de son existence amère.

Nous pensons que vivre a toujours lieu dans le présent et que mourir est un événement qui nous attend dans un avenir lointain. Mais nous ne nous sommes jamais demandé si la bataille quotidienne de nos existences peut vraiment s'appeler vivre. Nous voulons des preuves de la survivance de l'âme, nous écoutons les déclarations des voyants, et les résultats des recherches métapsychiques, mais jamais, au grand jamais, nous ne nous demandons comment vivre, comment vivre dans la délectation et l'enchantement d'une beauté quotidienne.

Nous avons accepté que la vie soit cette agonie et cette désespérance : nous nous y sommes habitués, et nous pensons que la mort doit être soigneusement évitée. Mais cependant, la mort est extraordinairement semblable à la vie lorsque nous savons vivre. On ne peut vivre sans, en même temps, mourir. On ne peut pas vivre sans mourir psychologiquement toutes les minutes. Cela n'est pas un paradoxe intellectuel, je dis bien que pour vivre complètement, totalement, chaque journée, en tant qu'elle présente une beauté toute neuve, on doit mourir à tout ce qu'était la journée d'hier, sans quoi on vit mécaniquement et l'on ne peut savoir ce qu'est l'amour, ce qu'est la liberté.

En général, nous avons peur de mourir parce que nous ne savons pas ce que veut dire vivre. Nous ne savons pas vivre, et, par conséquent, nous ne savons pas mourir. Tant que nous aurons peur de la vie, nous aurons peur de la mort. L'homme que la vie n'effraie pas ne craint pas de se trouver dans une insécurité totale, car il sait qu'intérieurement, psychologiquement, il n'y a pas de sécurité.

Ne pas rechercher une sécurité, c'est participer à un incessant mouvement où la vie et la mort sont une seule et même chose. L'homme qui vit sans conflits, qui vit en présence de la beauté et de l'amour, ne craint pas la mort, car aimer c'est mourir.

Si vous mourez à tout ce que vous connaissez, y compris votre famille, votre mémoire, et à tout ce que vous avez vécu, la mort devient une purification, un processus de rajeunissement ; elle confère une innocence et seuls les innocents sont passionnés, non les croyants, ni ceux qui cherchent à savoir ce qu'il advient après la mort.

Pour savoir réellement ce qui se produit lorsqu'on meurt, on doit mourir... cela n'est pas une plaisanterie : on doit mourir, non pas physiquement, mais intérieurement, mourir à ce que l'on a chéri et à ce qui a provoqué de l'amertume. Si l'on a su mourir à l'un des plaisirs que l'on a eus, le plus insignifiant ou le plus intense, peu importe, mais d'une façon naturelle, sans contrainte ni argumentation, on sait ce que veut dire mourir.

Mourir c'est se vider totalement l'esprit de ce que l'on est, c'est se vider de ses aspirations, des chagrins et des plaisirs quotidiens. La mort est un renouvellement, une mutation, où n'intervient pas la pensée qui est toujours vieille. Lorsque se présente la mort, elle apporte toujours du nouveau. Se libérer du connu c'est mourir, et alors on vit.

10

L'amour.

Aspirer à une sécurité dans nos relations c'est, inévitablement, vivre dans la souffrance et la crainte. Cette
recherche d'une sécurité invite l'insécurité. Avez-vous
jamais trouvé une certitude dans vos rapports humains ?
L'avez-vous trouvée ? Nous désirons cet apaisement
lorsque nous aimons et que nous voulons qu'on nous
aime en retour ; mais deux personnes peuvent-elles
s'aimer lorsque chacune d'elles est à la recherche de
sa propre sécurité, selon sa voie particulière ? On ne
nous aime pas, parce que nous ne savons pas aimer.

Qu'est-ce que l'amour ? Ce mot est si galvaudé et
corrompu, que j'ose à peine le prononcer. Tout le monde
parle de l'amour : tous les périodiques, tous les jour-
naux ; et les missionnaires parlent d'un amour éternel.
« J'aime mon pays, j'aime mon roi, j'aime tel livre,
j'aime cette montagne, j'aime le plaisir, j'aime ma
femme, j'aime Dieu »... l'amour est-il une idée ? Dans
ce cas on peut le cultiver, le nourrir, le chérir, le
promouvoir, le déformer de toutes les façons.

Lorsque vous déclarez que vous aimez Dieu, qu'est-ce que cela veut dire ? Que vous aimez une projection issue de votre imagination, une projection de vous-même, revêtue d'une sorte de respectabilité, conforme à ce que vous croyez être noble et saint. Dire « J'aime Dieu » est une absurdité. Adorer Dieu c'est s'adorer soi-même, ce n'est pas de l'amour.

Parce que nous ne trouvons pas de solution à l'amour entre humains, nous avons recours à des abstractions. L'amour pourrait bien être l'ultime solution à toutes les difficultés des hommes entre eux, à leurs problèmes, à leur peine, mais comment nous y prendre pour savoir ce que c'est ? En le définissant ? L'Eglise le définit d'une façon, la société d'une autre, et il y a, en outre, toutes sortes de déviations et de perversions : adorer quelqu'un, coucher avec quelqu'un, échanger des émotions, vivre en compagnie, est-ce cela que nous appelons l'amour ? Mais oui, c'est bien cela, et ces notions sont, malheureusement, si personnelles, si sensuelles, si limitées, que les religions se croient tenues de proclamer l'existence d'un amour transcendantal. En ce qu'elles appellent l'amour humain, elles constatent du plaisir, de la jalousie, un désir de s'affirmer, de posséder, de capter, de dominer, d'intervenir dans la pensée d'autrui, et voyant toute cette complexité, elles affirment qu'existe un autre amour, divin, sublime, infrangible, impollué.

Des hommes saints, partout dans le monde, soutiennent que regarder une femme est mal ; qu'il est impossible de se rapprocher de Dieu si l'on prend plaisir à des rapports sexuels ; et, ce faisant, ils refoulent leurs désirs qui les dévorent. En niant la sexualité, ils se bouchent les yeux et s'arrachent la langue, car ils nient toute la beauté de la terre. Ils ont affamé leur cœur et leur esprit. Ce sont des êtres déshydratés, ils ont banni la beauté, parce que la beauté est associée à la femme.

Peut-on diviser l'amour en amour sacré et profane, divin et humain, ou est-il indivisible? Se rapporte-t-il à une personne et pas au nombre ? Lorsqu'on dit : « Je t'aime », est-ce que cela exclut l'amour pour d'autres ? L'amour est-il personnel ou impersonnel ? Moral ou immoral ? Est-il réservé à la famille ? Et si l'on aime l'humanité, peut-on aimer une personne ? Est-ce un sentiment ? Une émotion ? Un plaisir ? Un désir ?

Toutes ces questions indiquent, n'est-ce pas, que nous avons des idées au sujet de l'amour, des idées sur ce qu'il devrait être ou ne pas être, en somme un critérium ou un code élaboré par la culture à laquelle nous appartenons.

Pour voir clair en cette question, il nous faut donc, au préalable, nous libérer des incrustations des siècles, mettre à l'écart tous les idéaux et idéologies au sujet de ce qu'il faut ou de ce qu'il ne faut pas que soit l'amour. Créer une séparation entre ce qui « est » et ce qui « devrait être » est la façon la plus illusoire de considérer la vie.

Comment saurai-je ce qu'est cette flamme qu'on appelle l'amour ? Je ne cherche pas à savoir comment exprimer l'amour, mais je veux comprendre en quoi il consiste. Je commence donc par rejeter tout ce que m'ont dit à ce sujet les églises, la société, mes parents, mes amis, et toutes les personnes que j'ai rencontrées et

99

les livres que j'ai lus, car c'est par moi-même que je veux savoir.

Voici donc un énorme problème, qui englobe l'humanité entière. Il y a eu des milliers de façons de le définir et je suis moi-même pris dans le réseau des choses qui me plaisent et dont je jouis dans l'instant. Ne devrais-je pas, pour comprendre ce problème, commencer par me libérer de mes inclinations et de mes préjugés ? Me voici dans un état de confusion, déchiré par mes désirs, et je me dis : « Commence par te vider de cette confusion ; alors, peut-être, découvriras-tu ce qu'est l'amour, par le truchement de ce qu'il n'est pas. »

L'Etat nous dit d'aller tuer par amour de la patrie. Est-ce cela, l'amour ? La religion nous dit de renoncer à notre sexualité par amour pour Dieu. Est-ce cela, l'amour ? L'amour est-il désir ?... Ne dites pas non ! Il l'est, pour la plupart d'entre nous : c'est un désir et son plaisir, le plaisir des sens, de l'attachement sexuel, d'une plénitude.

Je ne suis pas contre les pratiques sexuelles, mais voyez ce qu'elles impliquent : elles vous mettent momentanément dans un état de total abandon de vous-mêmes, et lorsque vous vous retrouvez plongés dans vos désordres habituels, vous désirez que se répète encore cet état en lequel vous n'aviez pas de soucis, pas de problèmes, pas de moi.

Vous prétendez aimer votre femme. Cet amour comprend un plaisir sexuel, le plaisir d'avoir quelqu'un à la maison pour s'occuper de vos enfants, pour faire la cuisine. Vous avez besoin de cette femme qui vous a donné son corps, ses émotions, ses encouragements, un certain sens de sécurité et de bien-être. Puis, elle

100

se détourne de vous, par ennui, ou pour partir avec quelqu'un, et tout votre équilibre est détruit. Ce désagrément, vous l'appelez jalousie ; il comporte une souffrance, une inquiétude, de la haine, de la violence. Ce qu'en réalité vous dites à votre femme c'est : « Quand vous m'appartenez je vous aime, dès l'instant que vous ne m'appartenez pas je vous hais. Tant que je peux compter sur vous pour satisfaire mes exigences, sexuelles et autres, je vous aime ; dès que vous cessez de me fournir ce que je demande vous me déplaisez. » Voici créés entre vous deux un antagonisme et un sens de séparation qui excluent l'amour. Si, cependant, vous pouvez vivre avec votre femme sans que la pensée crée ces états contradictoires, sans entretenir en vous-même ces perpétuelles querelles, alors peut-être... peut-être... saurez-vous ce qu'est l'amour, et vous serez libre, et elle le sera aussi, car nous sommes esclaves de la personne dont dépendent nos plaisirs. Ainsi lorsqu'on aime il faut être libre, non seulement de l'autre personne, mais par rapport à soi.

Le fait d'appartenir à quelqu'un, d'être nourri psychologiquement par cette personne, cet état de dépendance, comporte toujours de l'inquiétude, des craintes, de la jalousie, un sens de culpabilité. La peur exclut l'amour. Un état douloureux, sentimental ou émotionnel, le plaisir et le désir n'ont rien de commun avec lui.

L'amour n'est pas un produit de la pensée. La pensée, étant le passé, ne peut pas le cultiver. L'amour ne peut pas être enclos dans le champ de la jalousie. La jalousie est le passé et l'amour le présent actif. Les mots « j'aimerai », « j'ai aimé » n'ont pas de sens. Si l'on sait ce qu'est aimer, on n'est tributaire de personne

L'amour n'obéit pas. Il est en dehors des notions de respect ou de familiarité.

Ne savez-vous pas ce que veut dire aimer réellement une personne, sans haine, ni jalousie, ni colère, sans vouloir vous mêler de ce qu'elle fait ou pense, sans condamnation ni comparaison ? Ne le savez-vous pas ? Lorsqu'on aime, compare-t-on ? Lorsqu'on aime de tout son cœur, de tout son corps, de son être entier, compare-t-on ? Lorsqu'on s'abandonne totalement à cet amour, « l'autre » n'est pas.

L'amour a-t-il des responsabilités et des devoirs, et se sert-il de ces mots ? Lorsqu'on agit par devoir, y a-t-il de l'amour ? La notion de devoir ne l'exclut-elle pas ? La structure du devoir emprisonne l'homme et le détruit. Tant qu'on s'oblige à agir par devoir, on n'aime pas ce que l'on fait. L'amour ne comporte ni devoir ni responsabilité.

La plupart des parents se sentent, malheureusement, responsables de leurs enfants, et ce sens de responsabilité les pousse à leur dire ce qu'ils doivent faire, ce qu'ils ne doivent pas faire, ce qu'ils doivent devenir. Les parents veulent que leurs enfants aient une situation sûre dans la société. Ce qu'ils appellent responsabilité fait partie de cette respectabilité pour laquelle ils ont un culte, et il me semble que là où est cette respectabilité il n'y a pas d'amour. Ils n'aspirent, en fait, qu'à devenir de parfaits bourgeois. Lorsqu'ils éduquent leurs enfants en vue de les adapter à la société, ils perpétuent les conflits, les guerres, la brutalité. Est-ce cela que vous appelez protection et amour ? Protéger l'enfance avec amour, c'est se comporter à la façon du jardinier qui soigne ses plantes, les arrose, étudie avec douceur et tendresse leurs besoins, le sol qui leur convient le mieux. Mais lorsque vous préparez vos enfants à être adaptés à la société, vous les préparez à se faire tuer. Si vous aimiez vos enfants, vous n'auriez pas de guerres.

Lorsqu'on perd un être aimé, on verse des larmes. Sont-elles pour vous, ou pour la personne qui vient de mourir ? Pleurez-vous pour vous-même ou pour quelqu'un ? Avez-vous jamais pleuré pour qui que ce soit ? Avez-vous jamais pleuré pour votre fils, tué sur le champ de bataille ?... Vous avez pleuré, bien sûr, mais était-ce parce que vous vous preniez en pitié ou parce qu'un être humain avait été tué ?

Si l'on pleure parce qu'on se prend en pitié, ces larmes, versées sur soi, n'ont aucun sens. Si l'on pleure parce qu'on est privé d'une personne en qui l'on a placé beaucoup d'affection, c'est que ce n'était pas de l'affection. Lorsque vous pleurez votre frère mort, que ce soit donc pour lui. Il vous est facile de pleurer pour vous en pensant qu'il est parti. En apparence, vous pleurez parce que votre cœur est blessé, mais ce n'est pas pour votre frère que vous souffrez, c'est pour vous, car vous vous prenez en pitié, et cette pitié vous endurcit, vous replie sur vous-même, vous rend terne et stupide.

Pleurer sur soi, est-ce de l'amour ? Pleurer par solitude, parce qu'on a été abandonné, ou parce qu'on a perdu son prestige, ou parce qu'on se plaint du sort, ou parce qu'on accuse le milieu, c'est toujours ce « vous-même » en pleurs. Comprenez-le, entrez aussi directement en contact avec cette réalité que si vous touchiez un arbre, un pilier, une main, et vous verrez que cette douleur est auto-engendrée, qu'elle est créée par la pensée. La douleur est le produit du temps. « J'avais

103

un frère il y a trois ans, maintenant il est mort, et me voici seul, affligé, sans personne qui vienne me consoler et me tenir compagnie ; et c'est cela qui me fait venir les larmes aux yeux » : c'est tout cela que vous pouvez voir se produire en vous, dès que vous l'observez ; vous pouvez le voir complètement, totalement, d'un seul coup d'œil, sans prendre du temps pour l'analyser.

On peut voir en un instant toute la structure et la nature de cette pauvre petite chose appelée le moi, avec ses larmes, sa famille, sa nation, ses croyances, sa religion, avec toute cette laideur : tout cela est en nous, et lorsqu'on le voit du plus profond du cœur et non par le seul intellect, on tient la clé qui met fin à la douleur.

La douleur et l'amour ne peuvent aller de pair, mais dans le monde chrétien on a idéalisé la douleur, on l'a mise sur une croix et on l'adore, entendant par là qu'il est impossible d'y échapper, sauf par cette porte particulière. Telle est toute la structure d'une société qui exploite religieusement.

Lorsqu'on demande ce qu'est l'amour, il arrive que l'on soit trop effrayé par la réponse pour l'accepter, car elle peut provoquer un bouleversement complet, rompre des liens familiaux. On peut découvrir que l'on n'aime pas sa femme, son mari, ses enfants... (Les aimez-vous ?)... on peut aller jusqu'à démolir l'édifice que l'on a construit autour de soi ; ne jamais aller au temple.

Si, malgré cela, vous voulez le savoir, vous verrez que la peur n'est pas l'amour, que la jalousie n'est pas l'amour, que la possession et la domination ne sont pas l'amour, que la responsabilité et le devoir ne sont pas l'amour, que se prendre en pitié n'est pas l'amour, que la grande souffrance de n'être pas aimé n'est pas l'amour. L'amour n'est pas plus l'opposé de la haine que l'humilité n'est l'opposé de la vanité. Si donc vous pouvez éliminer toutes ces choses, non par la force mais en les faisant disparaître à la façon dont la pluie lave la feuille chargée de la poussière de nombreuses journées, peut-être rencontrerez-vous cette étrange fleur à laquelle, toujours, les hommes aspirent.

Tant que vous n'aurez pas d'amour, non en petite dose mais en grande abondance, tant que vous n'en serez pas remplis, le monde ira vers des désastres. Vous savez, cérébralement, que l'unité de l'homme est essentielle et que l'amour est la seule voie. Mais qui vous apprendra à aimer ? Est-ce qu'aucune autorité, aucune méthode, aucun système vous diront comment aimer ? Si qui que ce soit vous le dit, ce n'est pas l'amour. Pouvez-vous dire : « Je m'exercerai à aimer ; j'y penserai jour après jour, je m'entraînerai à être doux et charitable, je m'efforcerai de me pencher sur les autres » ? Pouvez-vous vraiment me dire que vous vous disciplinerez, que vous appliquerez votre volonté à aimer ? Si vous le faisiez, l'amour s'enfuirait par la fenêtre.

Par la pratique de quelque méthode ou de quelque système en vue d'acquérir de l'amour, vous pourriez devenir extraordinairement habiles ou un peu plus bienveillants, ou parvenir à un état de non-violence, mais tout cela n'aurait aucun rapport avec l'amour.

Dans le déchirant désert de ce monde, l'amour est absent, parce que le plaisir et le désir y jouent les rôles principaux. Pourtant, sans amour la vie quotidienne n'a aucun sens. Et il ne peut exister d'amour sans beauté. La beauté n'est pas dans ce que l'on voit : elle n'est pas celle dont on dit : « C'est un bel arbre, un beau tableau, un bel édifice, une belle femme. » Il n'y a de beauté que lorsque le cœur et l'esprit savent ce qu'est l'amour. Sans l'amour et sans cette beauté, il n'y a pas de vertu, et vous savez fort bien que, quoi que vous fassiez : que vous amélioriez la société, ou nourrissiez les pauvres, vous ne feriez qu'ajouter au chaos, car sans amour il n'y a que laideur et pauvreté dans votre cœur et votre esprit. Mais avec la présence de l'amour et de la beauté, tout ce que l'on fait est bien fait, ordonné, correct. Si l'on sait aimer, on peut faire ce que l'on veut, parce que cela résoudra tous les autres problèmes.

Nous arrivons au point suivant : peut-on entrer en contact avec l'amour sans disciplines, ni impositions, ni livres sacrés, ni le secours de guides spirituels, et même sans l'intervention de la pensée ? Le rencontrer, en somme, à la façon dont on aperçoit soudain un beau coucher de soleil ?

Une chose, me semble-t-il, est nécessaire à cet effet : une passion sans motif, une passion non engagée, et qui ne soit pas d'ordre sensuel. Ne pas connaître cette qualité de passion c'est ne pas savoir ce qu'est l'amour, car l'amour ne peut prendre naissance que dans un total abandon de soi.

Chercher l'amour — ou la vérité — n'est pas le fait d'un esprit réellement passionné. Rencontrer l'amour sans l'avoir cherché est la seule façon de le trouver : le rencontrer sans s'y attendre, non en tant que résultat d'efforts, ni parce que l'on a acquis de l'expérience. Un tel amour n'est pas tributaire du temps, il est à la fois personnel et impersonnel, il s'adresse à la fois à l'individu et au nombre. Semblable à la fleur qui a son parfum, on peut s'en délecter ou passer outre. Cette fleur-là est pour tous, tout autant que pour celui qui prend la peine de la respirer profondément et de la regarder avec joie. Que l'on soit tout près d'elle dans son jardin, ou qu'on en soit éloigné, cela importe peu à la fleur, car elle est remplie de son parfum et le partage avec tout le monde.

L'amour est toujours neuf, frais, vivant. Il n'a pas d'hier et pas de demain. Il est au-delà des mêlées qu'engendre la pensée. Seul l'esprit innocent sait ce qu'est l'amour et un esprit innocent peut vivre dans ce monde qui n'est pas innocent. Cette chose extra-ordinaire que l'homme a toujours cherchée, par le sacrifice, l'adoration, les rapports sexuels, par des plaisirs et des peines de toutes sortes, ne peut être trouvée que lorsque la pensée, se comprenant elle-même, arrive à sa fin naturelle. Alors l'amour n'a pas d'opposé, alors l'amour n'a pas de conflit.

Vous vous demandez peut-être : « Si je trouve un pareil amour, qu'adviendra-t-il de ma femme, de mes enfants, de ma famille ? Il leur faut une certaine sécurité. » Si vous vous interrogez de la sorte, c'est que vous ne vous êtes jamais trouvés au-delà du champ de la pensée, au-delà du champ de la conscience. Si vous vous y trouviez une seule fois, vous ne poseriez pas de telles questions, car vous sauriez ce qu'est l'amour, en lequel il n'y a pas de pensée, donc pas de temps.

Il se peut que la lecture de tout cela vous enchante et, en quelque sorte, vous hypnotise, mais aller au-delà de la pensée et du temps — ce qui veut dire au-delà de la douleur — c'est se rendre compte qu'il existe une autre dimension qui s'appelle l'amour. Ne sachant pas comment atteindre cette source extraordinaire, que faites-vous ? Rien, n'est-ce pas ? Absolument rien. Dans ce cas vous voilà, intérieurement, complètement silencieux. Comprenez-vous ce que cela veut dire ? Cela veut dire que vous ne cherchez plus, que vous ne désirez plus, que vous ne poursuivez plus rien, bref qu'il n'y a plus de centre du tout. Alors l'amour est là.

11

Voir et écouter. L'art. La beauté. L'austérité. Les images.
Les problèmes. L'espace.

Nous nous sommes interrogés sur la nature de l'amour
et nous sommes parvenus à un point qui, me semble-t-il,
nécessite une plus grande pénétration, car il nous faut
prendre davantage conscience de ses prolongements.

Nous avons découvert que, pour la plupart des personnes, l'amour est le réconfort que procure une existence assurée, la garantie d'une satisfaction émotion-
nelle capable de durer toute une vie. Je me suis avancé
alors et j'ai posé la question : « Est-ce cela, l'amour ? »
Je vous ai incités à regarder en vous-mêmes et peut-
être cherchez-vous à ne pas voir la réponse à cette
question car elle est de nature à vous troubler. Peut-
être préféreriez-vous que nous nous entretenions de ce
qu'est l'âme ou de la situation économique ? Mais en
supposant que je vous aie mis le dos au mur, vous avez
pu vous rendre compte que ce que vous avez jusqu'ici
appelé amour n'est que satisfaction mutuelle et exploi-
tation réciproque

Lorsque je dis : « L'amour n'a pas d'hier et pas de demain », ou bien : « Où il n'y a pas de centre est l'amour », cela a une réalité pour moi, mais pas pour vous. Vous pouvez citer ces phrases et en faire des formules, mais cela n'aurait aucune validité. Il vous faut voir clair en vous-mêmes, mais pour cela, vous devez avoir la liberté de regarder sans juger : sans condamner ou absoudre, rejeter ou acquiescer.

Voir est une des choses les plus difficiles au monde : voir ou entendre, ces deux perceptions sont semblables. Si vos yeux sont aveuglés par vos soucis, vous ne pouvez pas voir la beauté d'un coucher de soleil. Nous avons, pour la plupart, perdu le contact avec la nature. La civilisation nous concentre de plus en plus autour de grandes villes ; nous devenons de plus en plus des citadins, vivant dans des appartements encombrés, disposant de moins en moins de place, ne serait-ce que pour voir le ciel un matin ou un soir. Nous perdons ainsi beaucoup de beauté. Je ne sais pas si vous avez remarqué combien peu nombreuses sont les personnes qui regardent le soleil se lever ou se coucher, ou des clairs de lune, ou des reflets dans l'eau.

N'ayant plus ces contacts, nous avons une tendance naturelle à développer nos capacités cérébrales. Nous lisons beaucoup, nous assistons à de nombreux concerts, nous allons dans des musées, nous regardons la télévision, nous avons toutes sortes de distractions. Nous citons sans fin les idées d'autrui, nous pensons beaucoup à l'art et en parlons souvent. A quoi correspond cet attachement à l'art ? Est-ce une évasion ? Un stimulant. Lorsqu'on est directement en contact avec la nature lorsqu'on observe le mouvement de l'oiseau sur son aile ; lorsqu'on voit la beauté de chaque mouvement du ciel ; lorsqu'on regarde le jeu des ombres sur les collines ou la beauté d'un visage, pensez-vous que l'on éprouve le besoin d'aller voir des peintures dans un musée ? Peut-être est-ce parce que vous ne savez pas voir tout ce qui est autour de vous que vous avez recours à quelque drogue pour stimuler votre vision.

Il y a l'histoire d'un maître religieux qui parlait tous les jours à ses disciples. Un matin où il se trouvait sur son estrade, s'apprêtant à parler, un petit oiseau se posa sur le rebord de la fenêtre et se mit à chanter de tout cœur. Lorsqu'il se tut et qu'il s'envola, le maître dit : « Le sermon de ce matin est terminé. »

Une de nos plus grandes difficultés est, à mon sens, celle qui consiste à voir par nous-mêmes, d'une façon réellement claire, non seulement le monde extérieur, mais notre vie intérieure. Lorsque nous pensons voir un arbre, une fleur, ou une personne, les voyons-nous réellement, ou voyons-nous l'image que le mot a créée ? Lorsque vous regardez un arbre, un nuage, par une soirée lumineuse et délicieuse, ne les voyez-vous qu'avec vos yeux et votre intellect, ou les voyez-vous totalement, complètement ?

Avez-vous jamais essayé de regarder un élément quelconque du monde objectif — un arbre, par exemple — sans les associations et les connaissances que vous avez acquises à son sujet, sans préjugés, sans jugements, sans aucun des mots qui font écran entre vous et l'arbre et qui vous empêchent de le voir tel qu'il est dans sa réalité ? Essayez donc, et voyez ce qui se produit lorsqu'on observe de tout son être, avec la totalité de son énergie. Vous verrez que dans cette intensité il n'y a

111

pas du tout d'observateur : il n'y a que de l'attention. Ce n'est que l'inattention qui sépare l'observateur de la chose observée. Dans l'attention totale il n'y a pas de place pour des concepts, des formules ou des souvenirs. Il est important de comprendre ce point, car nous allons entrer dans un domaine qui exigera une très soigneuse investigation.

Seuls ceux qui savent regarder un arbre, les étoiles, les eaux scintillantes d'un torrent, dans un état de complet abandon, savent ce qu'est la beauté. Cet état de vision « réelle » est l'amour. En général c'est par des comparaisons, ou à travers ce que l'homme a assemblé que nous apprécions la beauté, ce qui veut dire que nous l'attribuons à quelque objet. Je vois ce que je considère être un bel édifice, et j'apprécie sa beauté à cause de mes connaissances en architecture qui me permettent de le comparer à d'autres édifices que j'ai vus. Mais je me demande maintenant : « Existe-t-il une beauté sans objet ? » Lorsque l'observateur, qui est le penseur, le censeur, celui qui vit l'expérience vécue, est présent, la beauté est un attribut extérieur que l'observateur voit et juge. Mais lorsque cet observateur n'est pas là — ce qui demande des recherches et de longues méditations — alors apparaît une beauté sans objet.

La beauté réside dans le total abandon de l'observateur et de l'observé, et cet abandon de soi n'est possible qu'en un état d'austérité absolue. Ce n'est pas l'austérité du prêtre avec sa dureté, ses sanctions, ses règles, son obéissance ; ce n'est pas l'austérité des vêtements, des idées, du régime alimentaire, du comportement ; c'est celle de la simplicité totale, qui est une complète humilité. Il n'y a, alors, rien à accomplir, aucune échelle à grimper, mais un premier pas à faire, et le premier pas est celui de toujours.

Supposez que vous vous promeniez seul, ou en compagnie, que vous ayez cessé de parler, et que vous soyez plongé dans la nature. Aucun aboiement ne se fait entendre, pas un bruit de voiture, pas un battement d'ailes. Vous êtes complètement silencieux et la nature autour de vous est totalement silencieuse aussi. Cet état de silence, à la fois de l'observateur et de l'observé, lorsque le témoin ne traduit pas en pensées ce qu'il observe, ce silence dégage une beauté d'une qualité particulière où ni la nature ni l'observateur ne sont là, mais un état d'esprit entièrement, complètement seul : seul, non isolé, seul en une immobilité qui est beauté.

Lorsque vous aimez, l'observateur est-il là ? Il n'est là que lorsque l'amour est désir et plaisir. Mais lorsque le plaisir et le désir ne lui sont pas associés, l'amour est intense ; il est, telle la beauté, quelque chose de totalement neuf tous les jours. Ainsi que je l'ai dit, il n'a pas d'hier et pas de demain.

Lorsqu'on est capable de voir sans préjugés une image, quelle qu'elle soit, alors seulement peut-on entrer en contact direct avec ce que présente la vie. Tous nos rapports sont imaginaires, en ce sens qu'ils s'établissent sur des images que forme la pensée. Si j'ai une image de ce que vous êtes et si vous en avez une de ce que je suis, il est évident que nous ne nous voyons pas tels que nous sommes. Ces images réciproques nous empêchent d'être en contact, et c'est pour cela que nos rapports s'altèrent.

Lorsque je dis que je vous connais, c'est de la per-

sonne telle qu'elle était hier dont je parle. En fait, en
« ce moment même », je ne vous connais pas. Tout ce
que je connais, c'est mon image de vous. Elle s'est
constituée selon les mots élogieux ou insultants que
vous avez dits à mon sujet, et selon votre comportement à mon égard ; elle a été assemblée par les souvenirs que j'ai de vous ; et l'image que vous avez de moi
est formée de la même façon. Les rapports que ces
images ont entre elles rendent toute communion entre
nous impossible.

Deux personnes qui ont vécu longtemps ensemble ont,
l'une de l'autre, des images qui les empêchent d'avoir
des rapports réels. Si nous savions en quoi consistent
ces rapports authentiques entre personnes, nous pourrions, vous et moi, entreprendre ensemble quelque
action ; mais il ne peut pas y avoir de coopération par
l'entremise d'images, de symboles, de conceptions idéologiques, il ne peut pas y avoir d'amour tant que l'on
ne comprend pas ce que sont ces rapports directs. Les
images éliminent l'amour.

Il est donc important de comprendre, non pas intellectuellement, mais en toute « réalité » dans votre vie
quotidienne, comment vous construisez ces images de
votre femme, de votre mari, de votre voisin, de votre
enfant, de votre pays, de vos chefs, de vos politiciens,
de vos dieux. Il n'y a, en vous, que des images, et elles
créent un espace entre vous et ce que vous observez,
un espace source de conflits.

Nous allons, maintenant, vous et moi ensemble, voir
s'il est possible d'être libéré de l'espace que l'on crée
non seulement en dehors de soi, mais en soi-même :
l'espace qui divise les personnes dans tous leurs
rapports.

L'attention même que l'on accorde à un problème est l'énergie qui le résout. Lorsqu'on lui donne une attention complète — je veux dire avec tout ce qu'on a en soi — il n'y a pas d'observateur du tout ; il n'y a qu'un état d'attention qui est totale énergie, et celle-ci est la plus haute forme d'intelligence. Naturellement, cet état d'esprit doit être complètement silencieux et ce silence, cette immobilité se produisent dans l'attention totale, non dans une immobilité disciplinée.

Ce silence total, en lequel il n'y a ni observateur ni observé est la forme la plus élevée de l'esprit religieux. Mais ce qui se produit en cet état ne peut pas être mis en mots, parce que ce qui est dit avec des mots n'est pas le fait. Pour découvrir cet état il faut passer par lui.

Chaque problème est relié à tous les autres problèmes, de sorte que si vous pouvez en résoudre un complètement — quel qu'il soit — vous verrez que vous serez capable d'aborder tous les autres aisément et de les résoudre. Nous parlons, évidemment, des problèmes psychologiques. Nous avons vu qu'ils n'existent que dans le temps, c'est-à-dire lorsque nous les abordons d'une façon incomplète. Donc, non seulement devons-nous prendre conscience de la nature et de la structure d'un problème, et le voir complètement, mais nous devons l'affronter dès qu'il apparaît et le résoudre immédiatement afin qu'il ne s'enracine pas dans notre esprit. Si l'on permet à un problème de durer un mois, un jour, ou même quelques minutes, il déforme l'esprit. Est-il possible de l'affronter immédiatement, sans déformations, et d'en être tout de suite complètement délivré, sans permettre à une mémoire, à une éraflure, de demeurer ? Ces mémoires sont les images que nous portons en nous et ce sont ces images qui prennent contact avec cette chose extraordinaire qu'on appelle la vie, d'où résultent nos contradictions et nos conflits. La vie est très réelle, ce n'est pas une abstraction ; nos problèmes psychologiques proviennent de ce que nous la rencontrons à travers des images.

Est-il possible d'aborder les événements sans cet intervalle d'espace-temps, sans cette séparation entre nous-mêmes et ce dont nous avons peur ? Ce n'est possible que lorsque l'observateur n'a aucune continuité, l'observateur, ce constructeur d'images, cette collection de mémoires et d'idées, ce paquet d'abstractions.

Lorsque vous regardez les étoiles, il y a vous qui les regardez dans le ciel. Il est inondé d'étoiles brillantes, l'air est frais, et il y a vous, l'observateur, celui qui vit l'événement, le penseur : vous et votre cœur douloureux, vous ce centre qui crée de l'espace. Vous ne comprendrez jamais l'espace qu'il y a entre vous et les étoiles, entre vous et votre femme, ou votre mari, ou votre ami, parce que vous n'avez jamais regardé sans images, et c'est pour cela que vous ne savez pas ce qu'est la beauté ni ce qu'est l'amour. Vous en parlez, vous écrivez à leur sujet, mais vous ne les avez jamais connus, sauf, peut-être, à de rares moments d'abandon du moi. Tant qu'existe un centre qui crée de l'espace autour de lui, il n'y a ni amour ni beauté. Lorsqu'il n'y a ni centre ni circonférence, l'amour est là. Et lorsqu'on aime, on « est » cette beauté.

Lorsqu'on regarde un visage en face de soi, c'est d'un centre qu'on regarde, lequel crée l'espace entre une personne et l'autre, et c'est pour cela que nos vies sont si vides et si insensibles.

On ne peut cultiver ni l'amour et la beauté, ni

inventer la vérité. Mais si l'on est tout le temps conscient de ce que l'on fait, on peut cultiver cette lucidité et grâce à elle commencer à voir la nature du plaisir, du désir, de la douleur, de la solitude et de la lassitude morale de l'homme. Alors peut-on se trouver en présence de cette chose qu'on appelle l'espace.

Lorsque vous percevez une distance entre vous et l'objet de votre observation, constatez en cette distance l'absence de l'amour, et sachez que sans amour quelque ardeur que vous mettiez à réformer le monde, à instaurer un nouvel ordre social, à parler de progrès, vous ne créerez que des tourments.

Tout cela est entre vos mains. Il n'existe pas de maître, il n'existe pas d'instructeur, il n'existe personne pour vous dire ce que vous devez faire. Chacun de nous est seul dans ce monde fou et brutal.

12

L'observateur et l'observé.

Je vous en prie, accompagnez-moi encore un bout de chemin. Cela sera peut-être quelque peu complexe et subtil, mais veuillez poursuivre.

Lorsque je construis une image de vous — ou de n'importe quoi — j'ai la faculté de l'observer. Il y a donc l'image et son observateur. Je vois, par exemple, quelqu'un avec une chemise rouge et ma réaction immédiate est qu'elle me plaît ou qu'elle me déplaît. Ce plaire et déplaire est le résultat de ma culture, de mon éducation, de mes associations, de mes inclinations, de mes caractéristiques acquises ou héritées. C'est de ce centre que j'observe et que j'émets mes jugements, et c'est ainsi que l'observateur se sépare de ce qu'il observe.

Mais l'observateur est conscient de plus que d'une seule image : il en crée des milliers. Toutefois, en diffère-t-il ? N'est-il pas, lui, qu'une autre image ? Il ne cesse d'ajouter ou de soustraire à ce qu'il est ; il est une chose vivante qui, tout le temps, soupèse, compare,

119

juge, se modifie, et change en tant qu'il est une résultante de pressions extérieures et intérieures. Il vit dans le champ de conscience que constituent ses connaissances, les influences qu'il reçoit et d'innombrables calculs.

En même temps, si vous regardez l'observateur — qui est vous-même — vous voyez qu'il est fait de mémoires, d'expériences, d'accidents, d'influences, de traditions, et d'une variété infinie de souffrances : tout cela étant le passé. Ainsi l'observateur est à la fois le passé et le présent ; et le lendemain qui est en attente est aussi une partie de lui. Il est mi-vivant, mi-mort et au moyen de cette mort-vie il regarde, en compagnie des feuilles des arbres, mortes et vivantes.

C'est en cet état d'esprit, qui est dans le champ du temps, que vous (observateur), regardez la peur, la jalousie, la guerre, et cette entité vilainement enclose qui s'appelle la famille. C'est ainsi que vous essayez de résoudre les problèmes que vous pose ce que vous observez, problèmes qui sont la provocation, le neuf. Vous ne faites jamais que traduire le neuf en termes du vieux et, par conséquent, vous vous trouvez dans de sempiternels conflits.

Une image, en tant qu'observateur, observe des douzaines d'autres images autour d'elle et en elle, et dit : « Celle-ci me plaît, je la garde », ou « celle-là me déplaît, je vais m'en débarrasser ». Mais cet observateur lui-même a été fabriqué par les différentes images qui ont été créées par des réactions à diverses autres images. Nous arrivons alors au point où nous pouvons dire que l'observateur est aussi une image, mais qui s'est séparée des autres, et qui observe. Ayant été engendré par des images variées, cet observateur se croit pourtant permanent et il se produit entre lui et celles qu'il crée une division, un intervalle de temps. Cela provoque un conflit entre lui et les images qu'il accuse d'être la cause de ses tracas. Il dit alors : « Je dois me délivrer de ce conflit », et ce désir même qu'il a de s'en dégager crée, encore, une nouvelle image.

S'être rendu compte de tout cela — et c'est la vraie méditation — a révélé qu'il y a une image centrale assemblée par toutes les autres, qui est l'observateur, le censeur, celui qui perçoit l'expérience, celui qui évalue. C'est le juge qui veut conquérir ou subjuguer les images qui l'ont créé, ou même les détruire, incité par celles qui résultent de ses jugements, de ses opinions, de ses conclusions. Mais ces images qui l'ont créé le voient, à leur tour, et c'est alors que l'observateur « est » l'observé.

Ainsi la lucidité a révélé les différents états qui composent notre état de conscience ; elle a révélé les images contrastantes qui s'y trouvent et la nature de leurs contradictions ; elle a révélé les conflits qui engendrent ces contradictions, le désespoir de n'y rien pouvoir faire, et les divers moyens que l'on met en pratique pour s'en évader ; tout cela par une quête prudente et hésitante à la suite de quoi il est apparu que l'observateur « est » l'observé. Il n'est pas une entité supérieure, devenue consciente. Il n'est pas un surmoi. Ces « Soi » exaltés ne sont que des inventions, des images qui s'ajoutent à toutes les autres : c'est la lucidité elle-même qui a révélé que l'observateur est l'observé.

Lorsque vous vous posez une question, quelle est l'entité qui recevra la réponse ? Et quelle est l'entité qui cherche à s'informer ? Si elle est une partie de votre conscience, une partie de votre pensée, elle sera incapable de trouver ce qu'elle cherche. Tout ce qu'elle peut trouver, c'est un état lucide. Mais si dans cet état il y a encore une entité qui dit : « Je dois être lucide, je dois m'exercer à l'être », ce n'est encore qu'une nouvelle image.

La perception du fait que l'observateur est l'observé n'est pas un processus d'identification avec l'observé. S'identifier à quelque chose est assez facile. C'est ce que font la plupart d'entre nous : ils s'identifient à leur famille, à leur mari ou à leur femme, à leur nation, ce qui conduit à de grandes souffrances et à des guerres.

Ce dont nous parlons est totalement différent, et nous devons le comprendre non pas verbalement, mais avec notre être le plus profond, alerté jusqu'à ses racines. Dans la Chine ancienne, un peintre, avant de commencer à peindre quoi que ce soit — un arbre, par exemple — s'asseyait devant son sujet pendant des jours, des mois, des années — peu importait le temps — jusqu'à « devenir » l'arbre. Il ne s'identifiait pas à lui, il était cet arbre. Cela veut dire qu'il n'y avait pas d'espace entre l'arbre et lui, pas d'espace entre l'observateur et l'observé, pas d'entité vivant sa perception de la beauté, du mouvement, de l'ombre, de la profondeur d'une feuille, de la qualité de sa couleur. Il était l'arbre totalement et en cet état seulement pouvait-il peindre.

Tout mouvement de l'observateur, s'il ne s'est pas rendu compte qu'il est l'observé, ne peut créer que de nouvelles séries d'images, où il se retrouve captif. Mais que se passe-t-il lorsque l'observateur est conscient d'être l'observé ? Examinez cette question lentement, très lentement, car nous entrons maintenant dans

quelque chose de très complexe. Que se passe-t-il ?
L'observateur, ainsi conscient, n'agit plus du tout. Il
s'était toujours dit : « Je dois faire quelque chose en
ce qui concerne ces images, les abolir ou leur donner
de nouvelles formes » ; il avait toujours été actif au
sujet de ce qu'il observait, agissant et réagissant, soit
avec passion, soit avec indolence. Ce mode d'agir, basé
sur le plaire et le déplaire, a toujours été qualifié de
positif : « Ceci me plaît, je le retiens, cela me déplaît,
je m'en débarrasse. »

Lorsque l'observateur se rend compte que ce sur quoi
il agissait n'était autre que « lui-même » en sa qualité
d'observateur, tout conflit cesse entre lui et ses images.
Il est « cela », il n'en est pas séparé. Lorsqu'il s'en
séparait, il agissait, ou essayait d'agir sur ce qu'il voyait,
mais maintenant, sachant que ces tentatives s'exer-
çaient sur lui-même, le plaire et le déplaire ne sont plus
en jeu, et le conflit cesse.

Que peut-il faire ? Que peut-on faire au sujet d'une
chose qui est soi-même ? On ne peut ni se révolter
contre elle, ni la fuir, ni même l'accepter. Elle est
« là » ! Alors toute action qui provient des réactions
du plaire et du déplaire parvient à sa fin, et on découvre
une lucidité qui est devenue extrêmement vivante. Elle
n'est tributaire ni de l'activité d'un centre, ni d'images.
De son intensité se dégage une attention d'une qualité
telle, que l'esprit — qui est cette lucidité — devient
extraordinairement sensitif et hautement intelligent.

13

Qu'est-ce que penser ? Les idées et l'action. Les provocations. La matière. L'origine de la pensée.

Examinons maintenant en quoi consiste la pensée, et commençons par distinguer celle que l'on doit exercer sainement, logiquement, avec grand soin, dans la vie quotidienne, de celle qui ne correspond à rien. Tant que nous ne serons pas très avertis de leurs natures, nous ne pourrons pas pénétrer certaines profondeurs que la pensée ne peut atteindre.

Essayons donc de comprendre l'ensemble de cette structure complexe qu'est la pensée. Voyons ce qu'est la mémoire, comment la pensée prend naissance, comment elle conditionne tous nos actes ; et, en comprenant tout cela, peut-être rencontrerons-nous quelque chose que la pensée n'a jamais pu découvrir, une chose à laquelle la pensée n'a jamais pu ouvrir la porte.

Pourquoi la pensée est-elle devenue si importante dans nos vies ? Je parle de celle qui manipule des idées, de celle qui n'est pas la réaction de mémoires accumulées dans les cellules de nos cerveaux. Il se peut que certains d'entre vous ne se soient même jamais posé cette question, ou se l'étant posée qu'ils l'aient écartée comme étant de peu d'importance, pensant que seule compte l'émotion. Mais je ne vois pas comment on pourrait séparer les deux. Si la pensée ne donne pas continuité au sentiment, celui-ci meurt vite. Pourquoi dans nos vies quotidiennes, dans nos vies assujetties aux labeurs et aux adversités, la pensée a-t-elle pris une importance hors de toute proportion ? Demandez-le-vous, comme je me le demande. Pourquoi sommes-nous tributaires de cette pensée, si rusée, si habile, si capable d'organiser, de mettre en route, d'inventer des choses, d'engendrer des guerres, de semer la terreur, de susciter les inquiétudes, de multiplier des images à l'infini, de poursuivre des chimères ; de cette pensée qui, ayant joui des plaisirs d'hier, leur donne continuité dans le présent, et aussi dans le futur ; de cette pensée toujours active, bavarde, remuante, qui ne cesse de construire, de démolir, d'additionner, de supposer ?

Les idées sont devenues pour nous beaucoup plus importantes que l'action : les idées qu'exposent les intellectuels avec tant de talent, sur toutes les questions. Plus elles sont habiles et subtiles, plus nous leur rendons un culte, à elles et aux livres qui les contiennent. Nous « sommes » ces idées, nous « sommes » ces livres, étant si lourdement conditionnés par eux. Nous discutons inlassablement d'idées et d'idéaux, et, dialectiquement, nous offrons nos opinions. Chaque religion a ses dogmes, ses formules, ses échafaudages pour atteindre les dieux, et maintenant, alors que nous nous interrogeons sur l'origine de la pensée, nous contestons l'importance de tout cet édifice.

Nous avons séparé les idées de l'action, parce qu'elles sont toujours du passé tandis que l'action est toujours du présent : vivre est toujours du présent. Nous avons peur de vivre, et c'est pour cela que le passé, en tant qu'idées, est si important pour nous.

En vérité, il est extraordinairement intéressant d'observer la façon dont opère notre pensée, de simplement voir comment nous pensons et d'où surgit cette réaction que nous appelons penser. Il est évident qu'elle a sa source dans la mémoire. Mais la pensée a-t-elle un commencement ? Si elle en a un, pouvons-nous le découvrir, c'est-à-dire découvrir comment naît la mémoire, puisque, sans elle, il n'y aurait pas de pensée ?

Nous avons vu comment la pensée nourrit le plaisir et lui donne une continuité, et aussi comment elle alimente le contraire du plaisir, c'est-à-dire la crainte et la douleur, et nous avons vu que celui qui est le lieu de cette expérience vécue, le penseur, « est » à la fois le plaisir, la douleur et l'entité qui les nourrit. Il distingue le plaisir de la douleur, et ne voit pas qu'en recherchant le plaisir il invite la souffrance et la peur. Dans les relations humaines, la pensée est toujours à la recherche de son plaisir qu'elle déguise de mots tels que loyauté, aider, donner, soutenir, servir.

Je me demande pourquoi nous voulons servir. Les postes d'essence offrent un bon service : que veulent dire ces mots, aider, donner, servir ? De quoi s'agit-il ? Est-ce qu'une fleur, pleine de lumière, de beauté, dit : « Je donne, j'aide, je sers » ? Elle « est » ! Et parce qu'elle n'essaie pas de faire quelque chose, elle recouvre la terre.

La pensée est si rusée, si habile, qu'elle déforme tout,

selon ce qui lui convient. Mais dans sa demande de plaisir, elle se met elle-même en esclavage. Elle est la génératrice de la dualité dans toutes nos relations, faisant naître en nous une violence qui nous donne du plaisir, mais aussi un désir de paix, un désir d'être doux et bienveillants. Cette dualité se produit tout le temps dans nos vies, mais en plus de ces contradictions, la pensée accumule les mémoires innombrables, enregistrées en nous, de nos plaisirs et de nos douleurs. De ces mémoires elle renaît. Ainsi que je l'ai dit, la pensée est le passé, elle est toujours vieille.

Comme nous affrontons toutes les provocations en termes du passé, et qu'elles sont toujours neuves, nos prises de contact sont toujours inadéquates, d'où nos contradictions, nos conflits, les misères, les souffrances qui sont notre héritage. Nos petits cerveaux sont dans un état de conflit « quoi qu'ils fassent ». Leurs aspirations, leurs imitations, leurs conformismes, leurs répressions ou leurs sublimations, ou les drogues que nous prenons pour élargir notre conscience, « rien » de tout cela ne nous sort de l'état de conflit. Au contraire, tout nous y maintient.

Ceux qui pensent beaucoup sont très matérialistes parce que la pensée est matière. Elle l'est tout comme le sont un plancher, des murs, un appareil téléphonique. L'énergie fonctionnant dans le cadre d'une forme est matière. Il y a de l'énergie, et il y a de la matière. En cela est toute la vie. Nous pouvons croire que la pensée n'est pas de la matière, pourtant elle l'est. Elle l'est en tant qu'idéologie. L'énergie, là où elle se trouve, devient matière. Matière et énergie sont reliées entre elles. L'une ne peut pas exister sans l'autre, et plus il y a d'harmonie entre elles, plus nos cellules cérébrales sont équilibrées et actives. La pensée a créé une structure de plaisir, de douleur, de peur, et a fonctionné à l'intérieur de cette structure, qu'elle ne peut pas briser, l'ayant construite pendant des milliers d'années.

Aucun fait nouveau ne peut être vu par la pensée. Il peut être compris par elle, verbalement, à une date ultérieure, mais la perception d'un fait nouveau n'est pas une réalité pour elle. Elle ne peut résoudre aucun problème psychologique. Malgré son habileté, ses artifices, son érudition, les structures qu'elle crée par la science, par des cerveaux électroniques, sous le coup de contraintes ou de nécessités, la pensée n'est jamais neuve et ne peut, par conséquent, jamais répondre à l'urgence d'une question essentielle. Le vieux cerveau est incapable de résoudre l'énorme problème de vivre.

La pensée est difforme, contrefaite, car elle peut inventer n'importe quoi et voir des choses qui ne sont pas. Elle peut jouer les tours les plus extraordinaires. On ne peut donc pas compter sur elle. Mais si vous comprenez toute la structure de votre mode de pensée : comment, pourquoi vous pensez ; les mots que vous employez ; votre façon de vous comporter dans votre vie quotidienne ; la manière dont vous parlez aux gens, et dont vous les traitez ; votre façon de marcher, de manger ; si vous êtes conscient de tout cela, vous ne serez pas trompé par votre pensée : elle ne disposera d'aucun élément pour vous induire en erreur. L'esprit, alors, n'est pas quelque chose qui exige, qui subjugue, il devient extraordinairement calme, souple, sensible, seul, et, dans cet état, il n'y a plus d'erreurs ni d'illusions.

Avez-vous jamais observé que lorsqu'on est dans un

état de complète attention, l'observateur, le penseur, le centre, le « moi » arrive à une fin ? En cet état d'attention, la pensée commence à s'étioler, à disparaître.

Lorsqu'on veut voir une chose très clairement, on doit avoir l'esprit très tranquille, sans tous ces préjugés, ces bavardages, ces dialogues, ces images, ces tableaux : tout cela doit être mis de côté, afin de regarder. Et ce n'est que dans le silence que l'on peut observer le début de la pensée, non lorsqu'on cherche, posant des questions, attendant des réponses. Ce n'est que lorsqu'on est complètement silencieux, jusqu'au fond de son être, que, s'étant posé la question : « Quel est le commencement de la pensée ? », on peut voir, provenant de ce silence, comment la pensée prend forme.

Si on se rend compte de la façon dont naît la pensée, on n'a plus besoin de la diriger. Nous perdons beaucoup de temps et gâchons beaucoup d'énergie tout au long de nos vies — et pas seulement à l'école — en essayant de dominer nos pensées. « Voici — disons-nous — une bonne pensée, je dois y revenir souvent ; en voici une mauvaise, je dois l'éliminer. » Ce sont, tout le temps, des batailles entre une pensée et l'autre, entre deux désirs, ou entre un plaisir et tous les autres qu'il veut dominer. Mais si l'on a conscience de la façon dont se forme la pensée, il n'y a plus, en celle-ci, aucune contradiction.

Lorsque vous entendez des assertions telles que « la pensée est toujours vieille », ou « le temps, c'est la douleur », votre pensée commence à les traduire et à les interpréter. Ces traductions et ces interprétations sont basées sur les connaissances et les expériences d'hier, de sorte qu'invariablement vous traduisez selon votre conditionnement. Mais si vous considérez ces affirmations sans les interpréter, simplement en leur accordant une attention totale (qui n'est pas un état de concentration), vous verrez qu'il n'y a ni observateur, ni observé, ni penseur, ni pensée. Et ne demandez pas lequel a commencé. Cette argumentation habile ne mène nulle part. Vous pouvez observer par vous-mêmes que tant qu'il n'y a pas de pensée (ce qui ne veut pas dire être dans un état d'amnésie, de vide), je dis que tant qu'il n'y a pas de pensée provenant de la mémoire, de l'expérience, des connaissances, c'est-à-dire du passé, il n'y a aucun penseur. Ce n'est pas une affaire philosophique ou mystique. Nous parlons de faits réels et vous verrez, si vous m'avez suivi dans ce voyage, que vous répondrez à une provocation non plus avec le vieux cerveau, mais d'une façon toute neuve.

14

*Les fardeaux d'hier. La tranquillité d'esprit. Les com-
munications. La réalisation. La discipline. Le silence.
Vérité et réalité.*

Les vies que nous menons comportent, en général,
très peu de solitude. Même lorsque nous sommes seuls,
elles sont encombrées par tant d'influences, de connaissances, de souvenirs, d'expériences, de soucis, de chagrins, de conflits, que nos esprits s'alourdissent de plus
en plus, deviennent de plus en plus insensibles dans
leurs routines monotones. Ne sommes-nous jamais
seuls ? Sommes-nous toujours surchargés des fardeaux
d'hier ?

Il y a une assez jolie histoire de deux moines qui
marchaient de village en village. Ils rencontrèrent une
jeune fille assise au bord d'une rivière, et qui pleurait.
L'un des moines s'approcha d'elle et lui dit : « Pourquoi pleurez-vous, ma sœur ? » Elle répondit : « Vous
voyez cette maison sur l'autre rive ? Ce matin j'ai tra-
versé facilement la rivière à pied, maintenant elle a
enflé, je ne peux pas rentrer chez moi, il n'y a pas

de barque. — Qu'à cela ne tienne », répondit le moine. Il la prit sur ses épaules et la déposa sur l'autre rive. Or, deux heures après qu'ils eurent repris leur chemin, l'autre moine lui dit : « Frère, nous avons fait le vœu de ne pas toucher une femme. Tu as commis un péché terrible. N'as-tu pas éprouvé un plaisir, une intense sensation en touchant cette femme ? — Eh quoi ! répartit le premier, je l'ai laissée il y a deux heures ; tu la portes encore, n'est-ce pas ? »

Et c'est ce que nous faisons. Nous portons toujours nos fardeaux, nous ne mourons jamais au passé, nous ne le laissons jamais derrière nous. Ce n'est que lorsqu'on accorde une attention totale à un problème, et qu'on le résout immédiatement, sans le prolonger jusqu'au lendemain, ni même jusqu'à la minute qui suit, que l'on se trouve dans un état de solitude. Alors, même si l'on vit dans une maison encombrée, même lorsqu'on est dans un autobus, on peut être dans cette solitude, qui indique que l'on a l'esprit frais et innocent.

Il est très important d'avoir cette solitude et cet espace intérieurs, car cela comporte une liberté d'être, d'aller, de fonctionner, de s'envoler. Après tout, le bien ne peut fleurir qu'avec de l'espace, de même que la vertu ne peut fleurir qu'en liberté. On peut jouir d'une liberté politique et n'être pas libre intérieurement, donc n'avoir pas d'espace. Aucune vertu, aucune qualité valable ne peut fonctionner et grandir sans ce vaste espace en nous-mêmes. Il nous est nécessaire, ainsi que le silence, car nous ne pouvons avoir de contacts avec le neuf qu'étant seuls, sous l'emprise d'aucune influence, d'aucune discipline, d'aucune expérience.

Nous pouvons voir immédiatement que seul un esprit

silencieux a la possibilité d'être clair. L'unique but de la méditation en Orient est d'engendrer un état d'esprit capable de dominer la pensée, procédé qui s'apparente à celui de répéter des prières pour se calmer l'esprit, dans l'espoir de résoudre ainsi les problèmes psychologiques. Mais si l'on n'établit pas de vraies fondations à cet effet, qui sont l'affranchissement de la peur, de la douleur, de l'anxiété et de tous les pièges que l'on se dresse à soi-même, je ne vois pas comment il serait possible d'avoir un esprit réellement au repos.

Cette compréhension est des plus difficiles à transmettre. Communiquer entre nous veut dire non seulement que vous devez comprendre mes mots, mais que vous et moi, ensemble, soyons dans un même état d'intensité, au même moment, sans un instant d'intervalle, afin que, nous trouvant au même niveau, nous puissions nous rencontrer.

Une telle communion est impossible tant que vous interprétez ce que vous lisez, selon vos connaissances, votre plaisir ou vos opinions, ou tant que vous faites de terribles efforts pour comprendre.

Il me semble qu'une des principales pierres d'achoppement dans la vie est ce perpétuel effort pour parvenir, pour réaliser, pour acquérir. On nous entraîne à cela depuis l'enfance, et les cellules mêmes de nos cerveaux créent ce besoin d'accomplissement, en vue d'obtenir une sécurité physique. Mais la sécurité psychologique échappe à cette sphère d'action. Nous aspirons à une sécurité dans nos relations, dans notre comportement, dans nos activités, mais, ainsi que nous l'avons vu, rien n'existe au monde qui se puisse appeler sécurité. Nous rendre compte par nous-mêmes que la sécurité n'existe dans aucune de nos relations, que rien n'est permanent dans le monde psychologique, modifie totalement notre façon habituelle de vivre. Il est essentiel, évidemment, d'avoir une sécurité physique : un abri, des vêtements, de la nourriture ; mais cette sécurité est détruite par notre demande de sécurité psychologique.

L'espace et le silence sont nécessaires pour aller au-delà des limitations de la conscience. Mais comment un esprit si constamment actif dans son intérêt propre peut-il être calme ? On peut se discipliner l'esprit, le contrôler, le façonner, mais de telles tortures ne le tranquillisent pas : elles l'abrutissent. Poursuivre un idéal qui consiste à avoir un esprit calme n'a évidemment aucun effet, si ce n'est que plus on agit sur lui avec vigueur, plus il devient étroit et stagnant. Exercer un contrôle, sous quelque forme que ce soit, ou une répression, c'est engendrer un conflit. Ces disciplines appliquées ne sont pas plus la bonne voie que n'a de valeur une vie indisciplinée.

La plupart de nos vies sont disciplinées par les pressions extérieures de la société, de la famille, de nos souffrances, de notre expérience, par notre conformisme à une idéologie ou à ses structures. Ces disciplines sont mortelles. C'est sans contraintes, sans répressions, sans aucune forme de crainte qu'il nous faut nous discipliner. Mais comment nous y prendre ? Il ne s'agit pas de se discipliner d'abord et ensuite d'acquérir la liberté. Celle-ci doit se trouver au tout début, pas à la fin. Le comprendre c'est se libérer des conformismes en matière de disciplines, et cela, c'est une discipline en soi.

L'acte même d'apprendre est discipline (après tout, la racine de ce mot veut dire apprendre) ; l'acte même d'apprendre devient clarté. Pour comprendre la nature et toute la structure des impositions, des refoulements, et aussi de l'indulgence, il faut y mettre beaucoup d'attention. Pour étudier une discipline, on n'a guère besoin de se l'imposer, car le seul fait d'apprendre engendre sa propre discipline, qui ne comporte pas de contrainte.

En vue de rejeter l'autorité (je parle de l'autorité psychologique, pas de celle de la loi), en vue de dénier toute autorité aux organisations religieuses, aux traditions, à l'expérience, on doit voir pourquoi l'on a une tendance habituelle à obéir, et l'on doit étudier ce penchant. Pour ce faire, on doit se libérer de tout ce qui est condamnation, opinion, acceptation. Il est impossible d'accepter l'autorité tout en l'étudiant. Pour étudier en nous-mêmes toute la structure psychologique de l'autorité, nous devons en être dégagés. Cette étude comporte une négation de toute cette structure, et lorsque nous la nions, cette action est la lumière de l'esprit qui s'est libérée de l'autorité. Nier, dans ce domaine, tout ce à quoi on a attribué de la valeur, la discipline imposée, les maîtres, l'idéalisme, c'est les étudier, et cette action n'est pas seulement discipline, mais sa négation, qui est un acte positif. Nous nions ainsi tout ce qui a été considéré important en vue de provoquer ce silence de la pensée.

Nous voyons donc que dominer la pensée ne la rend pas calme et paisible. Avoir l'esprit tellement absorbé par son sujet qu'il s'y perd, n'est pas non plus un état de silence. L'enfant à qui on donne un jouet qui l'intéresse s'y absorbe et devient très calme. Mais lorsqu'on lui retire le jouet, il redevient turbulent. Nous tous avons nos jouets qui nous absorbent et nous nous imaginons être très tranquilles, mais on peut se dédier à une activité, scientifique, littéraire ou autre, sans, pour autant, être du tout dans un état de silence.

Le seul silence que nous connaissions est celui qui se produit lorsqu'un bruit s'arrête. Ce n'est pas cela, le silence. C'est, comme la beauté, comme l'amour, quelque chose de tout différent. Ce n'est pas le produit d'un esprit au repos. Ce n'est pas l'effet d'un arrêt de certaines cellules cérébrales, lorsque ayant compris tout le processus de l'agitation, elles en ont assez et veulent qu'il se taise, car alors ce sont elles, les cellules, qui produisent un silence. Ce n'est pas la conséquence d'un état d'attention où l'observateur est l'observé : là, il n'y a plus de frottements, mais ce n'est pas le silence.

Vous attendez que je vous dise ce qu'est ce silence, afin de le comparer à ce que vous pouvez en penser, de le traduire, de l'emporter et de l'enterrer. Il ne peut pas être décrit. Ce qui peut se décrire n'est jamais que du connu, et l'on ne peut se délivrer du connu qu'en mourant chaque jour à lui, aux blessures, aux flatteries, à toutes les images que l'on avait formées, à toute l'expérience ; qu'en mourant chaque jour, afin que les cellules du cerveau redeviennent fraîches, jeunes, innocentes. Mais cette innocence, cette fraîcheur, cette qualité de gentillesse et de tendresse n'engendrent pas l'amour. Cette qualité n'est pas celle de la beauté ou du silence.

Ce silence-là, qui n'est pas celui où s'arrête un bruit, n'est encore qu'un petit début, comme si l'on passait par un petit trou vers l'énorme, l'immense étendue de l'océan, vers un état immesurable, intemporel. Mais cela, vous ne pouvez pas le comprendre verbalement si vous n'avez pas compris toute la structure de la conscience, la signification du plaisir, de la douleur, du désespoir et si vos cellules cérébrales ne se sont pas mises d'elles-mêmes au repos. Alors, peut-être, rencontrerez-vous le mystère que personne ne peut vous révéler et que rien ne peut détruire. Un esprit vivant est un esprit silencieux qui n'a pas de centre et, par conséquent, ni espace ni temps. Un tel esprit est sans limites, et c'est la seule vérité, la seule réalité.

*Les expériences vécues. La satisfaction. La dualité. La
méditation.*

Chacun de nous veut vivre certaines catégories d'expériences, qu'elles soient mystiques, religieuses, sexuelles,
ou celles de posséder beaucoup d'argent, d'exercer le
pouvoir, d'avoir une situation, de dominer. En vieillis-
sant, nous pouvons ne plus avoir d'appétits physiques,
mais nous avons le désir de vivre des expériences plus
vastes, plus profondes, de plus grande portée, et nous
cherchons à les obtenir par toutes sortes de moyens
tels que l'élargissement de notre conscience par exemple
— qui est tout un art — ou l'intensification des sensations par des drogues.

Cet usage des drogues est un artifice qui existe depuis
des temps immémoriaux. On mâche un morceau de
feuille ou on absorbe le produit chimique le plus récent,
pour obtenir, au moyen d'une altération temporaire
de la structure des cellules cérébrales, une plus grande
sensibilité, des perceptions plus élevées, qui ont un
semblant de réalité. Ce besoin de plus en plus répandu

d'expériences de ce genre, révèle la pauvreté intérieure de l'homme. Nous nous imaginons qu'elles nous permettent d'échapper à nous-mêmes, mais elles sont conditionnées par ce que nous sommes. Si nous avons un esprit mesquin, jaloux, inquiet, nous pouvons prendre la drogue la plus récemment inventée, nous ne verrons que nos propres créations à notre mesure, nos projections émanant de notre arrière-plan conditionné.

La plupart d'entre nous aspirent à des expériences durables, que la pensée ne peut détruire, susceptibles de nous satisfaire pleinement. Ainsi, sous-jacent à cette aspiration, est un désir de satisfaction qui détermine la nature de l'expérience. Il nous faut donc comprendre à la fois ce désir et les sensations que l'expérience procure.

C'est un grand plaisir que d'éprouver une grande satisfaction. Plus une expérience est durable, profonde, vaste, plus elle est agréable. C'est ce plaisir qui dicte la nature de l'expérience à laquelle nous aspirons, et qui nous donne sa mesure. Or tout ce qui est mesurable est dans les limites de la pensée et susceptible de créer des illusions. On peut vivre des expériences merveilleuses et être dupé. Les visions qu'une personne peut avoir sont déterminées par son conditionnement. Vous pouvez voir le Christ ou le Bouddha ou tout autre personnage objet de votre culte, et plus vous serez croyant, plus intenses seront vos visions : ces projections de vos désirs.

Si, à la recherche d'une notion fondamentale telle que celle de la vérité, nous voyons que sa mesure — pour nous — est notre plaisir, nous projetons déjà l'idée de ce que serait cette expérience, et elle ne serait plus valable.

Qu'entendons-nous par vivre une expérience ? Existe-t-il rien de neuf, d'originel, dans ce que l'on éprouve au cours d'un tel événement ? Il n'est que la réaction d'un paquet de mémoires, en réponse à une provocation. Ces mémoires ne peuvent répondre que selon leur arrière-plan, et plus on est habile à interpréter l'expérience, plus cette réponse se développe. Vous devez donc non seulement mettre en question les expériences des autres, mais aussi les vôtres.

Si vous ne reconnaissez pas une expérience, c'est que ce n'en est pas une. Chaque expérience a déjà été vécue, sans quoi vous ne la reconnaîtriez pas. Vous la reconnaissez comme étant bonne, mauvaise, belle, sainte, etc., selon votre conditionnement, donc sa récognition doit inévitablement être vieille.

Nous voulons vivre l'expérience du réel — c'est ce que nous voulons tous, n'est-ce pas ? — mais vivre le réel c'est le connaître et dès que nous le reconnaissons, nous l'avons déjà projeté et il n'est plus réel parce qu'il est dans le champ de la pensée et du temps. Ce que l'on peut penser au sujet de la réalité n'est pas le réel. Nous ne pouvons pas « reconnaître » une expérience neuve : c'est impossible. On ne reconnaît que ce que l'on connaît déjà, donc lorsque nous déclarons avoir eu une expérience nouvelle, elle n'est pas du tout neuve. Chercher des expériences nouvelles au moyen d'une expansion de la conscience, ainsi qu'on le fait avec des drogues psychédéliques, c'est encore demeurer dans le champ limité de la conscience.

Nous découvrons maintenant une vérité fondamentale, qui est qu'un esprit à la recherche des expériences vastes et profondes auxquelles il aspire est très creux et obtus, car il ne vit qu'avec des souvenirs.

Si nous n'avions pas d'expériences, que nous arriverait-il? Nous avons besoin de leurs provocations pour nous tenir éveillés. S'il n'y avait en nous ni conflits, ni perturbations, ni changements, nous serions tous profondément endormis. Donc ces rappels sont nécessaires pour presque tout le monde. Nous pensons que sans eux nos esprits deviendraient stupides et lourds, par conséquent nous avons besoin de provocations et d'expériences pour nous faire vivre plus intensément et pour aiguiser nos esprits. Mais en vérité, cet état de dépendance ne fait qu'émousser nos esprits. Il ne nous tient pas du tout éveillés.

Je me demande donc s'il me serait possible d'être éveillé totalement, non en quelques points périphériques de mon être, mais totalement éveillé, sans provocations ou expériences. Cela exigerait une grande sensibilité, à la fois physique et psychologique. Cela voudrait dire qu'il me faudrait être affranchi de toute aspiration, car je provoquerais l'expérience dès l'instant que je l'appellerais. Pour être débarrassé de mes exigences intérieures, de mes désirs et de mes satisfactions, il me faudrait reprendre une investigation en moi-même et comprendre toute la nature de mon désir.

Toute demande intérieure provient d'une dualité : « Je suis malheureux, je voudrais être heureux. » En cette aspiration : « Je veux être heureux » est un état malheureux, de même que lorsqu'on fait un effort vers le bien, en cette vertu est le mal. Toute affirmation contient son opposé, et tout effort renforce ce que l'on veut surmonter. Lorsque vous désirez l'expérience du vrai ou du réel, cette demande émane de votre manque de satisfaction au sujet de ce qui « est », et crée, par conséquent, son contraire. Et dans ce contraire se trouve ce qui « a été ». Nous devons nous libérer de ces incessantes demandes, autrement il n'y aurait pas de fin au couloir de la dualité. Cela veut dire se connaître soi-même si complètement que l'on ne cherche plus.

On a, en cet état, un esprit qui n'appelle pas l'expérience ; qui ne veut pas être provoqué ; qui ne connaît pas la provocation ; qui ne dit ni « je dois », ni « je suis éveillé » ; qui est complètement ce qu'il « est ». Ce ne sont que des esprits frustrés, étroits, creux, conditionnés, qui recherchent le « plus ». Peut-on vivre en ce monde sans le « plus », sans ces sempiternelles comparaisons ? Assurément, c'est possible. Mais on doit l'apprendre par soi-même.

Mener une enquête dans toute cette sphère, c'est méditer. Ce mot a été employé, en Orient et en Occident, d'une façon malheureuse. Il existe différentes écoles et différents systèmes de méditation. Certaines écoles disent : « Observez le mouvement de votre gros orteil, observez-le, observez-le, observez-le », d'autres recommandent que l'on s'assoie dans certaines postures, que l'on respire régulièrement, ou que l'on s'exerce à être lucide. Tout cela est purement mécanique. Une autre méthode consiste à vous donner un certain mot et à vous dire que si vous le répétez très longtemps, vous aurez une expérience transcendantale extraordinaire. C'est une absurdité. C'est de l'auto-hypnotisme. Il est certain qu'en répétant indéfiniment Amen, Om, ou Coca-Cola, vous aurez une certaine expérience, parce qu'au moyen de répétitions on se calme l'esprit. C'est un phénomène bien connu en Inde depuis des milliers d'années, que l'on appelle Mantra-Yoga. Avec des répétitions vous pouvez inciter votre esprit à être aimable et doux, mais il n'en sera pas moins un petit esprit mesquin, misérable. Vous pourriez aussi bien placer sur votre cheminée un morceau de bois ramassé dans le jardin et lui présenter tous les jours une fleur en offrande. Au bout d'un mois vous seriez en train de l'adorer, et ne pas lui offrir une fleur serait un péché.

La méditation ne consiste pas à suivre un système ; ce n'est pas une constante répétition ou imitation ; ce n'est pas une concentration. Une des méthodes favorites de certaines personnes qui enseignent la méditation est d'insister auprès de leurs élèves sur la nécessité de se concentrer, c'est-à-dire de fixer leur esprit sur une pensée et d'expulser toutes les autres. C'est la chose la plus stupide, la plus nocive que puisse faire n'importe quel écolier, lorsqu'on l'y oblige. Cela veut dire que pendant tout ce temps on est le lieu d'un combat entre la volonté insistante de se concentrer et l'esprit qui vagabonde, tandis qu'il faudrait être attentif à tous les mouvements de la pensée, partout où elle va. Lorsque votre esprit erre à l'aventure, c'est que vous êtes intéressé par autre chose que ce que vous faites.

La méditation exige un esprit étonnamment agile ; c'est une compréhension de la totalité de la vie, où toute fragmentation a cessé, et non une volonté dirigeant la pensée. Lorsque celle-ci est dirigée, elle provoque un conflit dans l'esprit mais lorsqu'on comprend sa structure et son origine — que nous avons déjà examinées — elle cesse d'intervenir. Cette compréhension de la structure de la pensée est sa propre discipline, qui est méditation.

La méditation consiste à être conscient de chaque pensée, de chaque sentiment ; à ne jamais les juger en bien ou en mal, mais à les observer et à se mouvoir avec eux. En cet état d'observation, on commence à comprendre tout le mouvement du penser et du sentir. De cette lucidité naît le silence.

Un silence composé par la pensée est stagnation, une chose morte, mais le silence qui vient lorsque la pensée a compris sa propre origine, sa propre nature et qu'aucune pensée n'est jamais libre mais toujours vieille, ce silence est une méditation où celui qui médite est totalement absent, du fait que l'esprit s'est vidé du passé.

Si vous avez lu ce livre attentivement pendant une heure, c'est cela, la méditation. Si vous n'avez fait qu'en extraire quelques mots et que rassembler quelques idées afin d'y penser plus tard, ce n'est pas de la méditation.

La méditation est un état d'esprit qui considère avec une attention complète chaque chose en sa totalité, non en quelques-unes seulement de ses parties. Et personne ne peut vous apprendre à être attentif. Si un quelconque système vous enseigne la façon d'être attentifs, c'est au système que vous êtes attentif, et ce n'est pas cela, l'attention.

La méditation est un des arts majeurs dans la vie, peut-être « l'art suprême », et on ne peut l'apprendre de personne : c'est sa beauté. Il n'a pas de technique, donc pas d'autorité. Lorsque vous apprenez à vous connaître, observez-vous, observez la façon dont vous marchez, dont vous mangez, ce que vous dites, les commérages, la haine, la jalousie — être conscients de tout cela en vous, sans option, fait partie de la méditation.

Ainsi la méditation peut avoir lieu alors que vous êtes assis dans un autobus, ou pendant que vous marchez dans un bois plein de lumière et d'ombres, ou lorsque vous écoutez le chant des oiseaux, ou lorsque vous regardez le visage de votre femme ou de votre enfant.

Comprendre ce qu'est la méditation implique l'amour : l'amour qui n'est pas le produit de systèmes, d'habitudes, d'une méthode. L'amour ne peut pas être cultivé par la pensée ; mais il peut — peut-être — naître dans un silence complet en lequel celui qui médite est entièrement absent. Un esprit ne peut être silencieux que lorsqu'il comprend son propre mouvement en tant que penser et sentir, et, pour le comprendre, il ne doit rien condamner au cours de son observation.

Observer de cette façon est une discipline fluide, libre, qui n'est pas celle du conformisme.

16

La révolution totale. L'esprit religieux. L'énergie. La passion.

Notre objet, au cours de tout ce livre, a été de provoquer en nous-mêmes, et par conséquent dans nos vies, une révolution totale qui n'a rien de commun avec la structure de la société telle qu'elle est, car telle qu'elle est, elle est horrible, avec ses interminables guerres d'agression, que l'agression soit défensive ou offensive.

Ce dont nous avons besoin c'est de quelque chose de totalement neuf : une révolution, une mutation de la psyché elle-même. Le vieux cerveau ne peut absolument pas résoudre le problème des relations humaines. Le vieux cerveau est asiatique, européen, américain ou africain. Nous nous demandons, en somme, s'il est possible de provoquer une mutation des cellules cérébrales elles-mêmes.

Demandons-nous encore une fois, maintenant que nous sommes arrivés à mieux nous comprendre nous-mêmes, s'il est possible à un être humain qui vit quotidiennement une existence ordinaire dans ce monde brutal, violent, cruel — dans ce monde qui devient de

plus en plus efficient, donc de plus en plus cruel —
s'il lui est possible de provoquer une révolution, non
seulement dans ses rapports extérieurs, mais dans le
champ de son penser, sentir, agir, réagir.

Tous les jours nous lisons que des actes épouvan-
tables sont commis dans le monde, comme conséquence
de la violence de l'homme. Vous pouvez dire : « Je
n'y peux rien » ; ou : « Comment pourrais-je influencer
le monde ? » Je pense que vous pouvez l'influencer
considérablement si, en vous-mêmes, vous n'êtes pas
violents, si vous menez réellement, chaque jour, une
vie paisible, non compétitive, une vie sans ambition ni
envie, qui ne crée pas d'inimitiés. De petits feux
peuvent devenir un brasier.

Nous avons réduit ce monde à un état de chaos par
nos activités égocentriques, par nos préjugés, nos
haines, nos nationalismes, et lorsque nous disons que
nous n'y pouvons rien, nous acceptons le désordre en
nous-mêmes comme étant inévitable. Nous avons brisé
ce monde en morceaux et si nous-mêmes sommes
brisés, fragmentés, nos rapports avec le monde le seront
également. Mais si, dans nos actions, nous agissons
totalement, nos rapports extérieurs subiront une for-
midable révolution.

En somme, tout mouvement valable, toute action
ayant une vraie portée doivent commencer en chacun
de nous. Je dois, pour commencer, me changer moi-
même. Je dois percevoir la nature et la structure de
mes rapports avec le monde, et dans le fait même de
les « voir » est le « faire » ; dès lors moi, en tant qu'être
humain vivant dans le monde, j'engendre une nouvelle
qualité, une qualité qui, à mon sens, est celle d'un esprit
religieux.

Un esprit religieux est totalement différent de celui qui croit en une religion. On ne peut pas être religieux et en même temps hindou, musulman, chrétien, bouddhiste. Un esprit religieux n'est pas à la recherche de quelque chose, il ne peut faire aucune expérience avec la vérité, car elle n'est pas une chose qui puisse être dictée par le désir ou la souffrance, ni par un conditionnement, hindou ou autre. L'esprit religieux est un état d'esprit en lequel il n'y a aucune peur, donc aucune croyance d'aucune sorte, mais seulement ce qui « est », ce qui est, en tout état de fait.

Dans l'esprit religieux est l'état de silence que nous avons déjà examiné. Il n'est pas engendré par la pensée, mais par une lucidité qui est méditation, lorsque celui qui médite est entièrement absent. En ce silence est un état d'énergie en lequel aucun conflit n'existe. L'énergie est action et mouvement. Toute action est mouvement et toute action est énergie. Tout désir est énergie. Tout penser est énergie. Tout vivre est énergie. Toute vie est énergie. Si l'on permet à cette énergie de s'écouler sans contradictions, sans résistances, sans conflits, elle est sans limites et sans fin. Lorsqu'il n'y a pas d'opposition, elle n'a pas de frontière. Ce sont les résistances qui la limitent. Lorsqu'on voit cela on se demande pourquoi l'être humain introduit toujours des résistances dans l'énergie, pourquoi il les crée dans le mouvement qu'on appelle vie. Est-ce que la pure énergie, l'énergie sans limitations, n'est, pour lui, qu'une idée ? N'a-t-elle pas de réalité ?

Nous avons besoin d'énergie, non seulement pour provoquer en nous une révolution totale, mais aussi pour nous explorer, pour voir, pour agir. Tant

151

qu'existent des conflits quelconques dans nos rapports humains — entre mari et femme, entre homme et homme, entre une communauté et une autre, un pays et un autre, une idéologie et une autre — des résistances intérieures ou des formes extérieures de conflit, quelque subtiles qu'elles soient, il y a perte d'énergie.

Tant qu'existe un intervalle de temps entre l'observateur et l'observé, il crée un frottement, donc il y a perte d'énergie. Cette énergie est à son plus haut degré de concentration lorsque l'observateur est l'observé, sans aucun intervalle de temps. Alors se manifeste une énergie sans motif qui saura canaliser son action, parce que le « Je » n'existe pas.

Il nous faut une quantité énorme d'énergie pour comprendre la confusion dans laquelle nous vivons, et le sentiment : « je dois comprendre », engendre la vitalité nécessaire à cet effet. Mais explorer, chercher, exige du temps et, ainsi que nous l'avons vu, se déconditionner graduellement l'esprit n'est pas le bon moyen. Le temps n'est pas la voie à prendre. Que nous soyons vieux ou jeunes, c'est « maintenant » que tout le processus de la vie doit être élevé à une autre dimension.

Rechercher le contraire de ce que nous sommes n'est pas non plus le moyen, ni aucune des disciplines artificielles imposées par des systèmes, des maîtres, des prêtres, des philosophes — tout cela est si puéril ! Lorsque nous nous en rendons compte, nous nous demandons s'il est possible de transpercer immédiatement ce lourd conditionnement des siècles, sans entrer dans un nouveau conditionnement, s'il est possible d'être libre de telle sorte que l'esprit soit tout entier neuf, sensitif, vivant, conscient, intense, efficient. Voilà notre problème. Aucun autre problème n'existe, parce qu'un esprit libre peut les résoudre tous. Voilà la seule question que nous ayons à nous poser.

Mais nous ne la posons pas. Nous demandons qu'on nous instruise. Une des caractéristiques les plus curieuses de la psyché est ce désir de se faire instruire, conséquence de dix mille années de propagande. Nous voulons que notre façon de penser soit confirmée et corroborée par autrui, tandis que poser une question c'est se la poser à son propre sujet.

Ce que je dis a très peu de valeur. Vous l'oublierez aussitôt que vous fermerez ce livre, ou vous vous souviendrez de certaines phrases, ou encore vous comparerez ce que vous avez lu ici avec ce que contiennent d'autres livres. Mais vous n'affronterez pas votre propre vie. Pourtant, c'est la seule chose qui importe : votre vie, vous-mêmes, vos petitesses, votre existence creuse, votre brutalité, votre violence, votre avidité, votre ambition, vos affres quotidiennes, votre douleur sans fin. C'est tout cela qu'il vous faut comprendre et personne sur terre ou au ciel ne vous en délivrera, si ce n'est vous-mêmes.

En voyant tout ce qui a lieu au cours de votre existence quotidienne, de vos activités quotidiennes — lorsque vous prenez votre plume en main, lorsque vous parlez, que vous sortez en voiture ou marchez seuls dans les bois — pouvez-vous, d'un seul souffle, d'un seul regard, vous connaître très simplement tels que vous êtes ?

Lorsqu'on se connaît tel que l'on est, on connaît toute la structure des entreprises humaines, les illusions, les hypocrisies, les recherches de l'homme. Pour se connaître, on doit être honnête à l'extrême vis-à-vis de soi, jusqu'au tréfonds de l'être. Lorsqu'on agit selon des principes, on est malhonnête car on agit tel que l'on pense qu'on « devrait » être, et non tel qu'on « est ».

Il est brutal d'avoir des idéaux. Si l'on a des idéaux, des croyances, des principes, de quelque nature qu'ils soient, on ne peut pas se voir directement. Pouvez-vous donc être complètement négatifs, complètement calmes, sans penser, sans rien craindre, et pourtant être extraordinairement, passionnément vivants ?

L'état d'esprit où l'on n'est plus capable de faire des efforts est l'état religieux, et en cet état on peut rencontrer la chose que l'on appelle vérité, ou réalité, ou félicité, ou Dieu, ou beauté, ou amour. Cette chose ne peut être invitée. Veuillez comprendre ce fait très simple. Elle ne peut pas être invitée, elle ne peut pas être recherchée, car les esprits sont trop stupides, trop petits, vos émotions sont trop faibles, votre façon de vivre trop confuse, pour que cette énormité, cet immense quelque chose, se laisse inviter dans votre petite maison, dans le petit coin de votre existence sur lequel on a piétiné et craché. Vous ne pouvez pas l'inviter. Pour l'inviter il faut le connaître. Peu importe qui l'affirme : dès qu'une personne dit « Je connais », elle ne connaît pas. Dès l'instant que vous dites l'avoir trouvé, vous ne l'avez pas trouvé. Si vous dites que vous en avez fait l'expérience, vous n'en avez jamais fait l'expérience. Toutes ces déclarations sont des façons d'exploiter les autres : vos amis ou vos ennemis.

On en vient à se demander s'il est possible de rencontrer cette chose sans l'inviter, sans l'attendre, sans chercher, ni explorer, de sorte qu'elle puisse simplement se produire comme pénètre une fraîche brise lorsqu'on laisse la fenêtre ouverte. On ne peut pas inviter le vent, mais on doit laisser la fenêtre ouverte, ce qui ne veut pas dire être en attente : ce serait une autre forme d'illusion. Cela ne veut pas dire que l'on doive s'ouvrir pour recevoir : ce serait une autre forme de pensée.

Ne vous êtes-vous jamais demandé pourquoi cette chose fait défaut aux êtres humains ? Ils engendrent des enfants, ils ont des rapports sexuels, de la tendresse, la qualité qui consiste à partager les choses dans une vie en commun, dans une amitié, dans une confraternité, mais cette « chose », pourquoi ne l'ont-ils pas ? Ne vous l'êtes-vous jamais demandé, paresseusement, à l'occasion, en marchant seul dans une rue sordide, ou assis dans un autobus, ou en vacances au bord de la mer, ou en vous promenant dans un lieu plein d'oiseaux, d'arbres, de ruisseaux et d'animaux sauvages ? Ne vous est-il jamais venu à l'esprit de vous demander comment il se fait que l'homme ayant vécu des millions et des millions d'années, n'ait pas cette chose extraordinaire, cette fleur immarcescible ?

Comment se fait-il que vous, en tant qu'être humain, qui êtes si capable, si habile, si rusé, si compétitif, qui avez une si merveilleuse technologie, qui allez dans les cieux et à l'intérieur de la terre, et sous la mer, et qui inventez des cerveaux électroniques extraordinaires — comment se fait-il que vous n'ayez pas cette unique chose qui importe ? Je ne sais pas si vous avez jamais affronté sérieusement la question de savoir pourquoi votre cœur est vide.

Quelle serait votre réponse si vous vous posiez cette question, votre réponse directe, sans équivoque ni artifice ? Elle serait selon l'intensité avec laquelle vous auriez posé la question, et son urgence. Mais vous n'êtes ni intenses ni urgents, et c'est parce que vous n'avez pas d'énergie, l'énergie étant passion. Et vous ne pouvez pas trouver la vérité sans passion, sans une passion avec une fureur derrière elle, une passion en laquelle n'existe aucun désir caché. La passion est une chose assez effrayante, parce que, lorsqu'on l'a, on ne sait pas où elle vous mènera.

La peur est-elle peut-être la raison pour laquelle vous n'avez pas l'énergie, la passion qu'il faut pour découvrir par vous-mêmes pourquoi cette qualité d'amour vous fait défaut, pourquoi il n'y a pas cette flamme dans votre cœur ? Si vous avez examiné de très près votre esprit et votre cœur, vous saurez pourquoi vous ne l'avez pas. Si vous êtes passionnément à la découverte de ce pour quoi vous ne l'avez pas, vous saurez qu'elle est là. Ce n'est que par une complète négation, qui est la plus haute forme de passion, que cette chose, qui est amour, entre en existence.

De même que l'humilité, vous ne pouvez pas cultiver l'amour. L'humilité naît lorsque cesse totalement la vanité ; alors on ne sait pas ce que c'est qu'être humble. L'homme qui le sait est vaniteux. De même, lorsque vous vous adonnez avec votre esprit, votre cœur, vos nerfs, vos yeux, avec tout votre être à la découverte du processus de la vie, afin de voir ce qui réellement « est », et d'aller au-delà, en niant complètement, totalement, la vie que vous vivez maintenant, en cette négation même de la laideur, de la brutalité, « l'autre » entre en existence. Et vous ne le connaîtrez cependant jamais.

L'homme qui se sait silencieux, qui sait qu'il aime ne sait pas ce qu'est l'amour, ni ce qu'est le silence.

Table des matières

REFLECTIONS FROM DAVID

Other books by the same author:

REFLECTIONS
FROM DAVID

Hugh B. Black

NEW DAWN BOOKS
GREENOCK, SCOTLAND

First published 1992 by
NEW DAWN BOOKS
27 Denholm Street, Greenock PA16 8RH, Scotland

ISBN 1 870944 13 5

Unless otherwise stated, biblical references are
to the Revised Version.

Cover photo: Pauline Anderson

Production and Printing in England for
NEW DAWN BOOKS
27 Denholm Street, Greenock PA16 8RH, Scotland by
Nuprint Ltd, Station Road, Harpenden, Herts AL5 4SE.

To Drew Greenwood

*without whose encouragement, or perhaps I should say
pressure, this book and my last one,* Christian
Fundamentals, *might never have been written.*

Acknowledgements

I am grateful to my daughter Alison for editorial assistance; to my wife Isobel and to Miss Pauline Anderson, Mr Alistair Duff, Miss Jennifer Jack and Mr George Marshall for proof-reading and helpful contributions; and to Miss Ina Thomson, Alison, and Miss Irene Morrison for their respective parts in the processing of the material, much of it from tape-recordings.

My thanks are also due to the various authors and publishers whose works have been quoted.

Contents

PART THREE: THE LAST TIMES

Foreword

I have known the author for over fifteen years. His ministry and love for Christ have profoundly affected my own life.

It was through his ministry that I first received the baptism in the Holy Spirit. The first time I heard Mr Black preach, I was left with the distinct impression of one who was waiting on the unction of the Holy Spirit for his every word. Many times I had heard preachers speak enthusiastically, but for the first time I met one who transmitted the living Christ as he spoke.

Over the years Mr Black has stood with me through many mountain-top and deep valley experiences. I have found his ministry dynamic, but also clothed with tremendous wisdom and wealth of experience.

This book is about David, who happens to be my favourite Bible character. His gentleness and strength I have always found particularly attractive. I pray that this study will draw you closer to the One who is so strongly emanated through the author's ministry.

Diana Rutherford

Preface

In recent years a pattern has begun to develop at our annual camps in July and August. There are two distinct thrusts: one teaching, leading to an understanding of spiritual principles; the other preaching, designed to produce immediate action. Material from the first may be very easily adapted for publication and' very objectively presented. The second has in it a degree of intimacy, and its inclusion has led to the idea of taking readers into the conferences rather than attempting to take the conferences out to readers. The idea was exploited in my last book, *Christian Fundamentals*,[1] and I have followed the same pattern again. This explains the inclusion of occasional prayers, prophecy and linking material. The camp from which many of the present book's addresses are taken was held in July 1989 at the YMCA Conference Centre at Wiston Lodge, Lanarkshire. Material is also drawn from the August camp of the same year and from other sources.

The first part of the book examines specific events in the life of David and spiritual principles which emerge from that life. The second part speaks of God's plan for every life, His provision for His people in delivering from the power of the enemy in all of his manifestations, and testimonies to deliverance and healing in the lives of people in our own day.

The third part deals with the coming again of Christ.

Note

[1] Hugh B. Black, *Christian Fundamentals* (New Dawn Books, 1991).

PART 1

REFLECTIONS FROM DAVID

Introduction

The life of David presents us with extremes of sunshine and shadow. From triumph over Goliath to defeat over Bathsheba, we pass from heights of achievement to depths of tragedy. From wise behaviour under Saul's extreme provocation, we pass to the folly of numbering Israel. Veritably a life of contrasts! Well might the glory notes reverberate in wondrous psalms. Well might the chords of deep contrition move the hearts of men through the ages. He rejoiced in His God as a favoured son—a man after God's own heart. He wept before Him as a guilty adulterer with bloodstained hands.

Not only do we see contrasts in David; in God's dealings with David and people associated with him, we see age-abiding spiritual principles which many find difficult to understand. There seem on the surface to be almost irreconcilable opposites. God was a God of compassion who loved and constantly guarded His chosen son as he walked in righteousness before Him. The same God smote him with an exceeding bitter rod in his waywardness and sin. The God who cared for David and forgave him allowed the consequences of his sin to affect his family. David committed adultery with Bathsheba in secret and virtually murdered Uriah. His wives, God said, would be publicly defiled and the sword would not depart from his house. The God of love exacted retribution. Abiathar the

15

priest knew the curse that lay on Eli's family. Adonijah, Joab and Shimei all died violently. The consequences of sin fell upon them all. David's numbering of Israel was forgiven; yet many thousands died as a result of it. Veritably a God of justice—a God of unsurpassed love—but a God of iron firmness with whom there is 'no variation, neither shadow cast by turning': surely to many in our age still 'an unknown God'.

It is hoped that spiritual principles of age-long significance will be learned and obeyed as they unfold in the following pages.

1

The Backdrop

The first delivery of the material in this book began thus:

'In presenting the first of a series of studies on the life of David, may I say that I have not prepared erudite addresses, but rather I look to the Holy Spirit to open up particular issues and give His own illumination. I am aware that sometimes camp preaching is the foundation of a later book, but I have no intention of deviating from what God would have for the conference for the sake of a future book. I know, however, that the possibility may have its influence on my subconscious—and I will exercise care.'

There are tremendous lessons to be learned from the lives of men and women of old. Before going in depth into the life of David, let me sketch first the general, then the more immediate background. The backdrop of the ages, from Eden up to David's day, shows us the battle that goes on incessantly between God and the wicked one. Man was put out of the garden through sin, but God planned his redemption. Satan moved in opposition, and actually the whole of human history may be viewed as a commentary on the ensuing conflict between good and evil. In the plan of God and in His redemptive purposes there was going to be born in due time the Christ—the seed of the woman—

17

and through that seed salvation would come to mankind. There would come redemption. There would come restoration. The 'paradise lost' would be regained and the gates of glory opened wide. The gates to Eden closed with man on the outside, but the gates to life and glory were one day to open through Christ. A great part of the Old Testament is really the story of the preparation of a nation to contain that seed and the preparation within that nation of a family from whom the Christ would come. We find that in the line through which Christ was to be born there are seeming anomalies. Rahab, for example, was in that line: although she had been a harlot, grace found her. Ruth the Moabitess was in it too, although she belonged to a nation whose members were excluded from the congregation of Israel for ten generations—in other words, more or less for ever—and this because of the attack of Moab on Israel on her way into the promised land after the bondage of Egypt. Yet Ruth was allowed into Israel, not under strict law, but under grace. The Messianic line comes down through Ruth, Obed, Salmon, Jesse, David. David would become a progenitor of Christ. All this was in the plan of God. Through this line the Christ-child would be born—He would be prophet, priest, and king—the Messiah, the Saviour of the world. Through Him Eden's tragedy would be reversed. And all this was opposed of Satan.

We move now from the general to the particular—to the more immediate background of the life of David. A generation before David's day the people expressed their dissatisfaction with theocracy. The rule of God had come through judges and prophets, but the people wanted a change. At the time, they were under a wonderful prophet, Samuel by name, a man called and anointed of God, indeed one of the greatest of the prophets of Israel. He had come into his office after the death of Eli, who had been rejected of God. Although a good man, Eli had been

remiss in training his family and in punishing them as he should have done when they sinned.[1]

Samuel judged and led Israel, and fulfilled his role particularly well, but even so the people preferred to have a king as their ruler. This must have been painful to Samuel—in some degree for his own sake but more particularly for God's. Not only was his leadership rejected, but so in a sense was God's. The people said by their action, 'Samuel, we are not content with your leadership. We want to be like the nations round about us. We want to have a king to lead us out to battle.' They had a prophet. They had God. They had theocracy: but they wanted monarchy. And you know, it's an interesting principle: God sometimes gives a person the desire of his heart with accompanying leanness of soul. The thing desired may not be God's perfect will and may not be in the person's own best interest, but he persists and ultimately gets his own way. It reminds us of a child who craiks* and goes on craiking until father or mother says, 'All right, if you are so determined, go that road. It's the wrong road and you'll learn that at the end of the day, but I'm tired listening to you. Have your own way.' That is putting it in blunt terms. The Israelites were determined to have a king and God said, 'All right, have a king.' They ought never to have rebelled against the divine rule and lusted for something of their own. The day would come when the full consequences of their choice would come home to them. Under intolerable taxation and autocratic rule, monarchy would seem much less attractive.

At this point we face an intriguing kind of conundrum, perhaps of particular interest to those of you who are philosophically inclined. It seems that God had planned to have David and David's line from the beginning; but does this necessarily imply a monarchy? And if so, how can it be reconciled with the fact that there should never have been a monarchy? And what is the bearing of this on the

* An old Scots word meaning, 'requests wearisomely'.

earlier selection of Saul? Had he no chance from the beginning of ever establishing his dynasty?

We can apply a similar thought-process to God's redemptive plan for mankind. Man should never have sinned, but God knew that he would. He planned redemption from the beginning. Ideally should there never have been a Saviour, a Redeemer, an atonement? Christ could still have been Lord, and perchance an unfallen race would have become His bride—but still deep mystery remains, and unresolved philosophic questions.

Back now to more straightforward matters.

Note

1 Eli's sons were evil men and they went unjudged. For this failure Eli was rejected. There are lessons to be learned from the fate of Eli. Always remember that in the kindness of grace we carry the responsibility to be true to the deep law of God, which involves the exercise of discipline where this is necessary. We must be firm as we represent God. Let all leaders know it. In leadership you may sometimes find that God expects you to extend almost infinite grace where you are dealing with certain of the weaknesses of mankind. You can forgive again and again and hold out the offer of grace. But when you are dealing with wolves who come into the flock, in sheep's clothing or otherwise, and you find that they are harming the flock, you may require to be very severe indeed. Sometimes you may have to say to a trouble-maker, 'For your own wrongdoings I have great patience and compassion, but in so far as you destroy the flock of God you must be cut off— even although you are personally loved and wanted. We cannot allow you to harm others, because the flock must be shepherded.' Eli should have looked beyond the personal and human and seen what his sons were doing to Israel, and ended it. God would have been with him. But he neglected to discipline his own family, and it was particularly serious because of the position which they occupied in the nation.

2

First That which Is Natural

The first king, Saul, was in his beginnings a humble and a good man. When he was chosen to be king of Israel he was so backward and self-effacing that instead of going boldly to his crown he was found hiding amongst some baggage. He was duly anointed king and was told by Samuel that there would come a time when the Spirit of the Lord would come upon him and he would become 'another man' (1 Sam 10:6).

For a time he ruled well, and then we come on another very strange spiritual principle. Very often the first in a series is rejected and the second is selected. Cain is rejected and Abel is received. Esau is rejected and Jacob is chosen. Saul will be rejected and David will be chosen. There comes first that which is natural and then that which is spiritual (1 Cor 15:46)—and I give you a hint here. Watch a somewhat similar principle being out-worked in your ministry. Often you will lose the first-fruits—I don't know why—and the next fruits remain. For those of you who are studiously inclined, I recommend the writings of Norman Grubb on this topic.[1] You find that God was scrupulously fair with Saul. He was with him and gave him every opportunity. Samuel was at his right hand to help him—but Saul failed and was

21

rejected by God. There came two major incidents in Saul's life, and I would draw attention to both of them.

Amalek had attacked Israel as she travelled from Egypt to Palestine. Moses interceded, and while his hands were upraised Israel prevailed; when his hands came down Israel began to know defeat. Aaron and Hur, one on each side, then supported Moses' arms, so that Amalek was ultimately defeated and Israel passed on her way safely. But Amalek was not forgiven of God, and He gave orders that she was to be utterly destroyed. Saul was selected to do this, and when he went against Amalek he won a glorious victory. But he preserved the best of the flock 'to sacrifice to the Lord', and he preserved the life of king Agag although he had had very strict instruction to destroy all that pertained to Amalek. Now, evangelical preachers have long equated Amalek with the flesh. The instruction came to destroy, to be absolutely ruthless in dealing with Amalek. When Samuel came to the camp of Israel Saul said, 'Yes, I've obeyed the word of the Lord. I did what the Lord commanded.' Samuel said, 'What meaneth then this bleating of sheep in my ears?' 'Oh, they were preserved for another purpose.' In other words, Saul took the law into his own hands and disobeyed the word of the living God. Agag had been preserved—and Samuel took a sword and hewed him in pieces. Again, it is interesting to speculate. Haman, who tried to destroy the whole of Israel at a later stage, was an Agagite prince. I suggest that we see in Haman's plot the fruits of Saul's failure to exterminate the Amalekites, a remnant of whom survived until Hezekiah's reign.

There were two particular acts of disobedience on Saul's part. He appears to have been a carnal man who did not understand deep spirituality. He judged very largely by the seeing of his eyes and the hearing of his ears and by the laws of the natural world that was all around him. These were very important things to Saul. There came a time when he was impatient for the arrival of one in the

priestly office to offer sacrifice, and he usurped the function of the priest, saying, 'I'll do it myself.' He stepped
into a role that was never his, and thus committed sacrilege. His attitude was casual, careless, arrogant. He broke
God's law—but it was just God's law! I wonder if I could
pause at this point.

Get into your deep being an awe of the divine. Let me
explain what I mean by this in terms that all may understand. You read in Jude about the danger of railing against
dignities, which a man of God should never do. Even an
archangel did not bring a railing accusation against Satan,
but said, *The Lord rebuke thee* (v.9). How careful then
should we be not only to avoid railing against Satan and
spiritual dignities, but even more to avoid speaking against
God or any of His works or His anointed servants?

I have been shocked through the years when people
who may not totally agree with a preacher pass from fair
comment on the sermon to an attack on the servant of
God. You commit murder in the spiritual world by doing
that, because your opinion may influence the minds of
others who in turn influence a widening circle—and the
ministry of God's servant may be cut off from many
because of your carnal judgment. I remember listening to
a young preacher in his very early days as an evangelist—
and, oh dear, he did a number of things in ways that I
would not have done them (and no doubt there were many
things that I did which he would not have done). I could
have criticized this and that . . . but my lips were sealed.
My mouth was shut. God was using that man; He was
saving souls through that man; His anointing was on that
man. What had I to do with pointing a finger at the Lord's
anointed? Let me tell you a story that has had a profound
effect on me all my life and which I very frequently
repeat—quite deliberately.

Sandy Peden, a saint and outstanding prophet,[2] was a
very popular preacher amongst the Covenanters. One day

there came over from Holland a young man named Renwick—evidently a brilliant preacher and an outstanding man of God. I don't know whether the east wind got into Sandy's soul—and remember, the east wind, the wind of jealousy, can get into souls not only at the beginning of Christian experience but in mature years. You might be surprised at just how many, and how much, men and women of God can be touched by the east wind. It soils the spirit, it colours the judgment and it can colour words spoken. One day, maybe a year or so after Renwick arrived in Scotland, Sandy met him and, being a very honest man, didn't go round about the subject making excuses, but said in effect: 'Young man, I want to shake your hand. When you arrived in Scotland I spoke a few words against you, and things have never been the same again between God and me. I have wanted to meet the man whose relationship with God was such that this could have happened.'

The point I am after is this. That saint of God, like Moses in an earlier age, spoke inadvisedly with his lips. He was a mature man of God when he did it, and he suffered the consequences. In my own case, I have known myself start to say something that offended the Spirit and have felt a reaction and stopped immediately. I have never forgotten Sandy Peden and Renwick. I believe the story absolutely. I believe that something wrong happened in Sandy and through all that intervening time his relationship with God was not the same again. Friends, I take spiritual things as seriously as that. Keep your tongue off the anointed of God, and come very quickly to the second lesson: keep your tongue off the children of God—keep it off each other and off outsiders as well. Dwell in love, radiate love. I don't mean that you should be foolish and accept everybody as wonderful, but don't let viciousness and evil-speaking and malice ever proceed from your lips or your heart, because you will find that you have to deal with God. If you are opposed, even wrongly and cruelly

opposed, commit your cause to God. Don't take up cudgels on your own behalf—and don't think that it makes things easy for your enemies when you commit everything to God. *Vengeance is mine,* says God, *I will repay.* It is a fearful thing to fall into the hands of the living God. I consistently and deliberately refuse to take up cudgels. I leave my causes with God. Leave your cause always with God—always.

Saul was not a deeply religious man. I think it meant very little to him to take the sacrificial knife and stand in the place of the priest—after all, it was only God who might be offended... only God. And God looked down and saw a rebellious and disobedient heart, and He rejected Saul from being king of Israel—rejected him totally. Oh, I do ask you to study the Old Testament to imbibe divine principle. Samuel was a mighty prophet and he loved Saul. He had been used in anointing him, and he grieved over what God said about Saul. He pled with God for him until God said to him one day, 'Don't speak to me again on this matter. Saul is rejected and there is no road back.' It was not that the nation would no longer have him to be their king. There was no road back, because the King of Heaven decreed it.

I am reminded of the watchers in the story of Nebuchadnezzar: *The sentence is by the decree of the watchers, and the demand by the word of the holy ones* (Dan 4:17). I have great regard for the watchers. If I found myself in a situation where I had deliberately sinned, I would be much afraid of the watchers, the holy ones. You say, 'What are you talking about? I don't know anything about the watchers or the holy ones.' There are those who do, and I suggest that you learn something about them. Please listen carefully. If on an issue you are opposing God and you go too far in your opposition, the watchers make a decree and the decree is, I believe, like the laws of the Medes and the Persians: it does not alter. When the word has gone forth that judgment will fall, fall it surely will. I

will tell you more. I believe that were you to recruit thousands of the most devoted prayer warriors in all the world, they could pray endlessly without altering that decree by a hairbreadth. I have as deep a conviction of the place of the watchers and the holy ones as that. You say, 'I don't like this.' I hope you don't. Don't get to like it either. Remember that the angel of the Lord is to be feared: God's Name is in him and God has so ordained things that He rules His universe and rules His spiritual world with an absolutely fair but firm hand. I have never known that there is any rescinding of such a decree as went forth regarding Nebuchadnezzar.

I believe that if every prophet of the Old Testament with the greatest men of the New Testament had been gathered together to set aside a time of prayer and fasting for a month to have Saul restored, they would have wasted their breath and wasted their time. Now that may not be the kind of thing we want to believe. It speaks of an unchanging principle, an unchanging God, whereas we try to repair, we try to mend, we try to sort. But though that can be done at one level, when the watchers, the holy ones, have decreed, there is no alteration, but a fearful finality.

Sometimes people come into a camp like this and wonder at the depth of blessing. I will tell you two things that go together: the depth of teaching of absolute obedience to the living God and the flood of the glory of God. These two things are linked. If we departed from the fundamentals that you are hearing expounded, from utter reality as God has revealed it, the meetings would be very different. God honours and blesses when His conditions are met. Then He sets people free. Often it is not more prayer meetings or more intensive Bible studies that are required: it is often just simply more obedience, more reality, more simplicity, more close walking with God—simple things which can be very easily understood and really can be practised.

I don't think Saul had a notion of the seriousness of his situation. A spiritual way had opened to him and he neg-

lected to go that road. He became careless—like many of you who come for ministry because you have grown careless. You may not have set out deliberately on an evil course, but you have been overtaken by evil because you did not walk carefully with your God.

Note that next a strange thing happens. An evil spirit comes and troubles Saul and, as is so typical of evil spirits, its influence was not the same at all times. Saul's was not an absolute possession driving him as an insane man. An evil spirit came upon him from time to time and troubled him. No individual with an evil spirit is ever untroubled. There is nowhere you can fly for peace when you are troubled by an evil spirit. It will trouble you anywhere in the world; it will trouble you in the belly of hell, it would trouble you if you could reach the ramparts of Heaven— wherever you go it will trouble you. It will be there in the dark watches of the night, or in the midst of your everyday business.

Saul discovered a young harpist, David, whose playing brought God into Saul's chamber. There came in that glorious music the emanation of God, and the evil spirit departed, leaving Saul free for a period. But the spirit would come back, time and time again. Not only was Saul to lose his crown, to lose the dynasty, but he was losing peace in his ordinary life, and the day was to come when he would lose life itself as he suffered defeat at the hands of the Philistines.

I want to show you one more picture of Saul, and oh, it is a fearful picture. The hosts of Israel are gathered and the hosts of the Philistines are over against them in the valley. The Anakim ('sons of the giants') are there, particularly Goliath of Gath—and day by day this mighty champion comes out from the army of the Philistines and thunders his challenge to Israel: 'Choose you a champion, that he may come out and fight with me, that all the people be not engaged, and the issue will depend on his fight with me.' A wonderful idea from his point of view. He was standing

some nine feet tall and he had the breadth to go with his height. He had also a strong armour-bearer going before him. Goliath was thirsting for a fight, and it is not at all surprising that there weren't too many Israelites jumping to take up his challenge. There was one man for whom I can feel sorry—Saul, who was head and shoulders above the people physically, a man who had known divine power upon him at an earlier stage but who has lost God. He is like Samson shorn of his hair; he has lost God, he is out of touch, and now day after day he has to endure the jeering and taunting of Goliath, that gigantic Philistine. No doubt he suspects that all the nation knows that he is skulking in his tent—he knows that he is now no champion of Israel, he has no strength, no fight in him. So day by day he has to endure these fearful taunts. There had been an earlier day when he could have taken up the challenge and emerged victorious—a day when he walked with God and knew His power. Oh, the derelict condition of the fallen man of God—weak and powerless; the opportunity is there for glorious victory that might have resounded down through the centuries—but he cannot go with sword in hand; he cannot even unsheath the sword.

Let me draw your attention to a spiritual principle that is worth your while considering and remembering. I have observed its operation through a lifetime. Often an hour of opportunity comes into our life, an hour of which we may have no expectation, because God's opportunities often come on us without our having any forewarning of them. Suddenly a door opens, and before its opening there comes quite violent satanic assault. Now I don't mean that Satan appears with horns and hooves, but a darkness comes down upon us. There comes discouragement, fear—a sense of opposition, an unrest. Something may occur which causes us to lose our temper. We may fall out with someone close to us, and the waters become ruffled. Or temptation comes into life, very subtle and pleasant, very appealing. It draws us and we succumb and, like Samson,

are left metaphorically without our hair. Then, in our weakened condition, we suddenly notice that the door of opportunity is open. We instinctively know we can't go through it, and if we try, we are not successful. The attempt is not fruitful and things fall apart. As the writer J. McConkey put it, often when God is about to make princes of us we make fools of ourselves.

Go backwards for a moment. There was coming a glorious day when Goliath would thunder his evil words at Israel, a day on which, had Saul been in proper condition, he would have gone down into that valley and slain the uncircumcised dog of a Philistine—but he couldn't do it. He didn't have what it took in the hour of opportunity—and I am speaking now to leaders in particular. Watch the outworking of these principles.

And further, in addition to guarding your spirit prior to the opening of the door of opportunity, never allow yourself to be ruffled by any action of Satan; never pay too much attention to what Satan is doing or suggesting. There is only one thing to know in every situation: the will of God. There is nothing you need to know but the will of God. You look at the mess that Satan may be creating and you say, 'What has God got to say? What does the word of God say? What is the word of God in my ear?' Pay no attention to the word of Satan, ever. He will tell you a whole lot of truths and you will go along nicely, and then he will slip in a great black lie and you will swallow it along with the rest and be like a foolish fish caught on a hook. He is a liar from the beginning, and he knows the kind of lie that you will believe. Never listen to Satan; never give him any place in your life. As Billy Bray said: 'His 'pinions bain't worth a docken.' Don't consider the opinions of Satan—don't listen to the opinions of Satan, and even if a demon is speaking through a person in the course of exorcism, don't pay attention to the suggestions that come from the demon—such as, 'Leave me alone and I'll depart quietly.'

I am reminded of Johnny Anderson, a Scottish preacher. When his ministry in exorcism was beginning, he found himself in such a situation. Unsatisfied with the effectiveness of his ministry, he had sought the face of God with fasting and praying. The ministry of exorcism was about to be given of God, and on the night that his fasting ended, the illegitimate and deeply clairvoyant daughter of a medium came to his meeting for ministry. On being prayed for, she fell to the floor and was carried into an adjoining room. But the racket was fearful, and ultimately some of his deacons went with Johnny and the woman in a car to the open country. (I know exactly how they felt. I've had to do it myself many times.) As it happened, they arrived at the very field in which the notorious Peter Manuel had committed the last of his murders. There Johnny proceeded to minister to the woman. The demons in her were very arrogant and confident. They spoke to Johnny, not in the least afraid. Then suddenly the mantle of the Holy Spirit came upon His servant. This was the very beginning of Johnny's ministry in this realm, and he maintains that the demons knew the moment of the change. Immediately they changed their tune and became cringing, pleading for mercy. They wanted to be left where they were, on the ground that they had never harmed Johnny. They desperately did not want to be cast out. Johnny, who at this early stage probably did not have much finesse, refused to listen or compromise, but cast them all out. By this time his collar and tie were off, and his elders had run for their lives (understandably, when people are experiencing these things for the first time). I don't know how far away they were, but Johnny was left in the field without a collar and tie, with a woman covered with a blanket for decency's sake. The Holy Spirit came down and she was gloriously baptized in the Spirit. Evidently she came through singing, 'I'd rather have Jesus than anything this world affords today.'

By this time the police had arrived. It was a famous

field, and Manuel, I imagine, had still not been apprehended. They approached Johnny and said, 'Who are you?'

'I'm a Pentecostal preacher.'

'Well, you don't look like one!'

Johnny moved to put his hand on one of the officers, who moved backward saying, 'Don't touch me—I saw what happened to that woman!' People have various introductions to exorcism. Some of you are coming into this ministry, but you are coming in a lot more quietly than Johnny did. In his case a wonderful and effective ministry developed. You can't get into that kind of ministry without the anointing; for its development you will find that you must be careful in your walk with God. Spiritual things are extremely real.

Notes

1 Norman Grubb has been a wonderfully gifted teacher of some of the deep things of God. You will find in certain of his books insights into spiritual principles expressed in a way I don't find so clearly laid out elsewhere. He has been prepared to face up to difficult problems. Take, for example, his *Rees Howells, Intercessor* (Lutterworth Press, 1973). Rees Howells had a tremendous ministry—he moved both men and nations and affected, I believe, the outcome of the Second World War. He was a man signally used in prayer, and when he broke into the realm of healing the first person for whom he committed himself, and whose recovery he predicted, died and left him looking a fool to the whole community. To many he probably still looks a fool over that case; but read Grubb's account of the incident before you form too quick a judgment. Rees Howells was a man who came into a wonderful ministry. A succession of glorious healings followed. The first person died, and Howells' reputation in one sense died with her. There are strange, strange things in the working of inner spiritual law that don't lie on the surface of life. Grubb draws on Howells' experience to reveal the law of the sacrifice of the firstborn. In some of Grubb's writings there are real riches for

those who are minded to contemplate the deep things of God. I would refer you to the same theme dealt with in some depth in *Yes I Am* (Christian Literature Crusade, 1982), by the same author.

2   See the author's *Reflections from Moses: with the Testimony of Dan McVicar* (New Dawn Books, 1991), p. 73, note.

3

Then That which Is Spiritual

So Saul, who had been chosen of God and anointed of God, failed in his walk with God and was rejected (1 Sam 15). There was no road back for Saul. God did not say, as the Philistine was thundering defiance, 'I will save Saul's face in front of Israel.' He did not say, 'My Name is being dishonoured by this matter. I will help Saul back.' Saul metaphorically died the death. But there was another man, a mere youth at the time of the challenge: the youngest of a large family. Being myself a youngest child, I tend to empathize with youngest children—such as David and Joseph (youngest in his earlier days). A youngest child can see the world very differently from older children: life is different for the youngest. As a stripling David was out on the hillside watching his father's sheep. That was a wonderful background. Many of you, being town-born, may not understand this. It is possible to have deep intimacy with nature. You get to know individual animals, horses, cows, sheep. They have separate identities. You feel the country itself and in a peculiar sense you know it. I remember passing through one part of Britain and feeling, 'This is alien soil. I would need to live here for a time to get to know the hills, the fields, the mountains, the waters—it's not my land.' Some of you may think that

33

this is unreal. But I assure you that I could take you to where I was born and speak to you in depth about every part of the land. I knew every field, every one separately; I knew the streams; I knew almost every inch of that place. You develop an intimacy with nature. And out there on that hillside David played his harp and learned of God. There came a day when Samuel was sent by God to anoint one of the sons of Jesse without being told which of the sons it was. He was in difficulty because Saul was not likely to be very pleased about this. Samuel had been reluctant to turn from Saul, but the word of God was explicit. The sons of Jesse were brought in to be seen by the great prophet. In came Eliab the firstborn, a mighty man of valour, great in strength. Abinadab, the second, was similar, as was the third, and so each came in and all were rejected until Samuel said, 'No, he is not here. Have you no more sons?' This is the kind of situation a prophet can find himself in: apparently all have been seen, yet none is chosen. 'Are there no more sons?'

'None but a youth—just a boy out watching the flocks. He's only a lad—only a stripling.'

'Only a stripling.' Never have that attitude. Of course I may be prejudiced. I have always opposed that attitude! In early days I suffered from it—'Och, he's only a cullan,* not fit to be heard'—seven years younger than the nearest brother, and who would want to listen to his opinions? Who would think his opinions worth considering? Growing up that way and being told very adamantly, 'You'll never be half the man your father was,' did not instil confidence. To be honest, I do not carry deep wounds from this kind of issue from the past. The words may have ruffled but they never really got too deeply under my feathers. But I tell you, I have to deal with so many people nowadays who do carry deep wounds. They come for ministry and sometimes the amount of hurt and pain and

---

* Scots term for 'youth'.

damage that has been done in their lives in their earliest years is almost incredible. Let me give you an example of the kind of thing I mean—I won't identify anyone, so don't be worried. A child is treated unfairly within a family situation and others are preferred before him—but 'it isn't anything to worry about—he'll grow out of it.' Do you know that injustice can go right into the heart of that child and stay there for a lifetime? A sense of unfairness, bringing resentment and dislike, can sprout from what are comparatively small things, and the person may be bound as with iron bands. Through all a lifetime such individuals may be bound; they may be converted and baptized in the Spirit and still find these bondages remaining deep within them. To be set free they not only have to forgive, but they have to love those who caused the damage. There is a terrible depth to which hurts go in children. Never think, 'Oh, he's only a wee fellow. He'll not remember anyway when he gets up a bit. He'll forget this.' Don't you believe it. These things can go in and rankle to an awful depth. Again and again there needs to be ministry to set people totally free.

So I imagine that his family had little regard for this stripling David, the youngest of them all. He was good enough to watch a few sheep in case they got lost, but who would ever think of him as being the anointed of the Lord or king of Israel? But the Lord does not look on the outward appearance. He looks on the heart—and here he saw a heart that was spiritual. This was going to be a man after God's own heart, a spiritual man. Now David's spiritual career did not start on the day Samuel came to the house, although there was a very particular empowering at that point. Nor was David anointed of God to make him a man of God. He was anointed with oil because he *was* a man of God, albeit still a young man.

I can imagine the faces of the brothers as they looked at this stripling: 'Him the king! *Us* having to obey *him*!' Like Joseph's brothers—'Not on your life!' Little is recorded

as having been said. I think the meeting disbanded quickly. Nobody wanted word to get to Saul at all, and you can imagine young David going back out to the hillside. I am not certain, but I imagine it may have been between the time of the anointing and the Goliath incident that he slew the lion and the bear that came against the flock. He began to know the power of the living God. When the anointing of the holy was upon him, he would not be afraid of either the lion or the bear. He had a knowledge of the divine. He knew God, and his knowledge of God was not solely based on what he may have learned from others. I think he learned deeply of God in the loneliness of the hills. The school of God is often found in absolute aloneness. There is a time for the gathering of the saints together—oh, yes, we know this and have long acknowledged it—but there is also a time to be alone with God in the solitude of the night, or on the hillside if you are able to go there, or alone in your car. There is no other voice, no other personality present—none but the living God. He will speak to you, He will empower you, He will give you drive and initiative, and He will cover you with Himself in the aloneness.

The time comes when the battle lines are drawn and David is called. 'You're only a stripling. You don't go to battle—but you'll be good enough to carry the sandwiches to your brothers who are engaged in war. Here are some provisions—so leave your sheep and attend to your brothers' needs.' What an inglorious role for God's chosen man! God, I may say, sometimes gives his chosen man very inglorious roles. I know that in the early days of WEC (Worldwide Evangelization Crusade), when young men and women volunteered to be missionaries, probably sometimes thinking that they were doing very well and giving up a lot for God and that the red carpet should be rolled out, they went down to headquarters and were given the lavatories to clean and the drains to attend to. They were observed as they were engaged in these menial tasks,

and if they were not fit for these tasks they were not fit for the mission field. God often starts mighty men with very ordinary jobs, and I reckon there wasn't much glory for David in carrying bread out to his brothers. For a young man like David, a man born for war, what a humble role! The warrior carrying bread to brothers who had no doubt tormented him in his earlier days and caused him trouble as older brothers often do to younger.

And so David arrives at the battle field. It is a wonderful story. I really love this story—I find it one of the best in the whole Bible. He hears the giant thundering his defiance and he is absolutely amazed and shocked. He has been so long with God on the hillside that he can see nothing but God. He has so communed with God that he can hear none but God. These others have not been with God on the hillside, and they can see nothing but Goliath, and cannot shut out his roaring. David is seeing God and they are seeing Goliath. David is hearing God, and they are hearing Goliath. David is scandalized, and thinks, 'How is it possible that this is being allowed to happen in the armies of Israel—why is this uncircumcised dog of a Philistine being allowed to do this? Why doesn't somebody go out and kill him?' I can understand his reaction totally. But he is still only a stripling—he is looking around at all these big men, his own brothers, and he knows that Saul, though maybe not a giant, is still a very big man—and yet Goliath is allowed to challenge and insult the armies of Israel. Word ultimately comes to Saul: 'There's a young man so exasperated that he wants to go against the giant himself.' Oh, what a terrible thing for Saul to hear—a terrible and humiliating thing. 'Bring in the stripling.' Yes, the stripling wants to go out and fight. He is not afraid of Goliath. He had seen what God did to the lion and the bear, and he is not afraid of Goliath; he is desperate to go.

So Saul said, 'Well, we'll at least give him armour.' (David had nothing with him, no sword, only a sling and

his shepherd's staff and pouch—no armour.) You can imagine the position. David had probably never been in armour in his life. Have you ever seen armour hanging in a museum? It must often have been very cumbersome, and sometimes a man might have been better without it. In any case, David knew that he couldn't go this way and he got rid of the armour and went out in the Name of the Lord alone. People have got used to this story and they don't always appreciate the wonder of it, the miracle of it: a boy and a sling and a terrible man, one of the most fearsome men in all the world's history, gigantic, roaring his wrath. He saw this boy coming against him, and his anger was probably increased tenfold. 'Are they mocking me? To send out this boy against me! Are they trying to treat me as a buffoon?'

There is the armour-bearer out in front. How does David feel now? You know what it can be like, when you have decided that you are going to take the plunge and you are up on the high diving board. You were quite definite when you were down at the water level, but when you get up there you think, 'Oh, why did I ever get myself into this position?' I imagine that that skier they called 'The Eagle' wondered many a time how he got himself into the positions he did, and he may well have wished he was far from the place of danger. But it is not like that with David. You don't get the feeling at all that David said to himself, 'I was rash, but I'll have to go on with it. I'll seem a fool if I turn back now—but I'll go quietly—maybe something will turn up.' Not for a moment! He runs, and I am reminded of my daughter Grace's dog Tara. I remember the first time she got into a fight and I thought I'd rescue the poor wee soul. She was wild at me. She wanted to pursue the fight—she wanted to get back into the battle! She was a high-spirited animal. I might say, 'You're a fool of a dog, Tara. That dog will eat you.' Tara never realizes that—she doesn't have the sense to realize that. Actually Tara is a very nice and friendly dog, but not above being

annoyed by dogs of her own sex. Should she ever take exception to an Alsatian or a Rottweiler, or even a pit bull terrier, I just hope it's her master that's with her at the time and not me. On the other occasion on which I got involved I stretched my length on the pavement holding on to her tail; my shirt was all dirty and I had an appointment to keep with the manager of a bookshop, in this state. I had to explain, 'I fell in the gutter—you see, I got involved in a dog fight.' My friend solicitously enquired, 'Oh, and is the dog all right?' 'The dog? Never you mind the dog,' I said. 'What about me?'

So David goes rushing down into that valley to get at Goliath. He can't get at him quickly enough. This is true. Just picture it; picture the masses on both sides watching the scene. The excitement that there is at Wimbledon just now* is nothing to what was in the vale of Elah. I would love to have been there; I would love to have seen it. I have no love of cruelty or violence for its own sake. I have no desire to see a bullfight—I deplore that sort of thing; but I'd like to have seen this event. David goes right down and tells Goliath that he has come in the Name of the Lord and by the power of the living God. He tells Goliath that he will have his life that day and will give his flesh to the birds of the heavens. Oh, the trumpet note is sounding now. This man has been under the anointing oil. He has such a conception of God that Goliath is a dwarf so far as David is concerned. He fits the stone in the sling, which is the kind that is swung round the head and one cord is released. Now a real expert could sling a stone with great accuracy, but it is a very, very difficult art. I remember trying to do it, and the stones went about ninety per cent in the wrong direction. You are liable to break a window at your back, or somewhere else. It is, however, very effective in the hands of the expert. In David's case, the stone just finds a

* The Wimbledon tennis tournament normally coincides with one of our annual camps.

chink in Goliath's armour and lodges in his forehead.

Down he goes like a log and the armour bearer, wise man, flees for his life. He isn't waiting for any more. David goes—oh, the ignominy of the matter for the dead giant, were he able to realize it. David pulls Goliath's mighty sword out of its sheath and he cuts his head off. Imagine getting your head cut off with your own sword by a boy who had hit you with a stone from a sling! It is a tremendous story, and there David goes dancing back up, carrying the head of the dead giant. The lips that thundered the fearsome challenges are silent—the mouth forever closed in death.

What a terrible day for Saul when the enthusiastic crowds began to sing, 'Saul has slain his thousands, but David his tens of thousands.' David the stripling was a greater man than Saul—and Saul envied him in his heart. Deep enmity was born.

In David's case, there was the preparation of a man of God in the aloneness with God. He was in the right condition and the right position in the hour of opportunity and need, and he fitted into the plan of God. God has a plan for every life. He had a plan for Saul's life, but Saul broke it. He has a plan for your life, and a plan for mine. God grant that we will all fit into the divine plan.

4

The Hour Brings Forth the Man

PRAYER: *Lord our God, we sense the overshadowing of Thy presence and we pray that the hand of Thy power, the hand of Thy love, shall be upon us. We pray that illumination regarding Thy Word shall come very easily and that there shall be no impediment. We pray for open ears and understanding hearts. We ask in the Name Lord Jesus Christ and for His sake. Amen.*

I come now to the next in our series of studies. We ended the last with a very glorious episode in the life of David. David had gone down into the valley to fight Goliath. You may remember that earlier I indicated that there was first a general and then a more particular background to the story of David. I want to take you again for a moment to the more general background. God was interested in the line of David—the Christ would be born of that line—and Satan was interested in seeing that that line would be destroyed and that the seed of the woman would not eventually bruise the head of the serpent, nor would all the nations of the earth be blessed in that seed. One might almost say, if judging from a natural point of view, that God took terrible risks. Consider for a moment, for the same principles as operated in the case of David will come into your life and mine. God was minded to bless David, and Christ would be born of David's line. There came

times on the hillside, probably not just once or twice but from time to time, when a lion or a bear would steal a lamb of the flock, and David could say that he went and caught the marauder by the hair and slew him. He learned to know God on the mountainside. I want you again to view that dramatic scene where the mighty Philistine is standing and hurling his challenge to Israel. The hour comes when David goes down against him—a stripling, unarmed. The Philistine tells him that he will give his flesh to the birds of the air and the beasts of the field, and the young champion of God hurls the challenge back: *I will give the carcases of the host of the Philistines this day to the fowls of the air, and to the wild beasts of the earth; that all the earth may know that there is a God in Israel* (1 Sam 17:46).

Beyond the familiar features of the story, what interests me is this: Your fate, my fate, and the fate of all the ages, in one sense, is hanging on a very slender thread: it is dependent on the victory of David. Millions of people, if asked to judge David's chances, would have said that he had no chance. I am sure that whether you are sports fans or not there come times in life when a major boxing championship, for example, catches your attention. All the world, even the ladies, get to know. In the old days it might have been Joe Louis or Mohammed Ali who was the focus of attention. Tyson is the character at the moment. When it comes to one of the major title fights, people are very interested. They begin to judge the chances, and opinion polls are taken. Normally it might be a sixty-forty chance, or fifty-fifty—but just calculate the chances of the boy David killing that mighty great giant. You would find that voting would be millions to one against David. He just had no chance—no chance—in the eyes of humanity in general. Do you realize what is hanging on this? In a sense the birth of Christ—your salvation and my salvation—is hanging in the balance, down there in the valley of Elah. If you get that into your mind, you will read the story from a very different point of view. Your eternal

destiny is hanging on a thread in that valley, and all the chances from a human point of view are against David being victor—but God—but God!

You might say that was the most dangerous place in all the world on that particular day. You know, I believe that on the contrary it was one of the safest places of all on that particular day, because down into that valley with David went the Lord God of Hosts, and David smote the giant and lived to found the dynasty from which the Christ sprang. Look a little now behind the scenes, to the power of the Eternal, the power of Almighty God: in spite of the seeming chances and hazards of life, God is in the background, God is in the hinterland. Consider the action of God. It seems to me that men play their parts like pygmies on the stage of life: while they boast themselves that they will do this and that and they will not do the other, it is as though there is a smile on the face of God as he looks at the little men with all their proposals and ideas.

There is a lovely part in the testimony that Rosemary McAuley gives regarding one of the crisis times in the life of her severely crippled daughter Lisa. Rosemary and her husband Robert were sitting listening when a group of physicians were having a consultation about Lisa. Rosemary seems to have gone out of the body for a little time and had audience with God. Men were discussing Lisa's case when Rosemary suddenly felt that God smiled to her and said, 'And they think they are the ones making the decisions!'[1] They thought they were in control—*but God*. This conference will have been worthwhile if you learn nothing else than the significance of '*but God*'. *God is*. And not only is it true that God is, but God is all-powerful, all-knowing, all-loving. When your life and affairs are in the hand of God you are totally safe—as safe as the life of David was in the valley that day when hell's champion came against the Lord's anointed. Had you forgotten?— *the Lord's anointed*. I do not think David forgot. The anointing of David was very different from what happens

to a crowned monarch in our own day. It was done quickly and privately. There was no great blaring of trumpets or heralding of the fact across the land. David was anointed, Samuel disappeared, and the matter was kept, I imagine, very quiet. But there was one heart in which there would be little quietness. There was one young man who had been called in from watching his father's flocks, and the anointing oil had come down on him; he was very well aware of what that signified. He knew he was the chosen king of Israel. He went back out to his sheep. There were no laurels, no banquets. It was back out to the hillside— but he never forgot.

There was someone this morning telling us that after anointing oil had come upon her on the occasion when God miraculously and instantaneously healed her, for days she would not touch or wash her forehead because the anointing oil had been there—the anointing oil! I believe that David for all the rest of his life never forgot that the anointing oil had come upon him—symbol of the Holy Spirit coming upon him. Have you not got it in your heart to be almost sorry for Goliath? David went down into that valley knowing the anointing of the living God—knowing the power of the divine that was in him. By the power of the Holy Spirit, he ran down to destroy the Philistine that day. He knew God. The anointing had been upon him. The deed is done, and he is famous throughout all Israel— from the north to the south his name is known: David the conqueror of Goliath.

You might expect that in the preparation of a man of God things will now be made very comfortable. People will be very careful to see that no accidents happen to David. This man is called of God, chosen of God, anointed as king of Israel for a future day. You might naturally expect God's chosen to have a very easy and sheltered path. I suggest that if you have a very easy pathway you are not God's chosen in any deep sense of that word. I have noticed that the chosen of the Lord often have very rough

roads to walk. I am not suggesting you should go and look for rough roads—if you just follow the Lord you will get your rough road without any special petition. All you need to do is stand for Christ in every circumstance and you will have a great part of the world against you. As someone said, any dead fish can be carried downstream, but it takes a living fish to swim against the current. I tell you, you will have adversity; you will have your problems. There are times of course when our problems are of our own making, but there are other times when they simply result from our being true to Christ.

Recently I have been again deeply impressed with this spiritual principle. On reading *Lords of the Earth*[2] by Don Richardson, I was reminded of Bruce Olson's book *For This Cross I'll Kill You*,[3] and again I was compelled to consider the degree of sacrifice that some of the choicest saints are called to make for Christ. Sometimes the suffering is beyond our comprehension. In Richardson's story, the details of Stanley Dale's fearful eight-hour journey after having been pierced with five arrows are almost incredible. His final martyrdom, along with that of Phillip Masters, beggars description. There he was, still on his feet with perhaps a hundred arrows in his body as though refusing to die, to the amazement and consternation of his killers. God allowed it. God did not send legions of angels in this instance to rescue him. God accepted the sacrifice and the blood of two new martyrs again became the seed of the church. In a remarkably short time the gospel swept the area and the kingdom of darkness was toppled. Habitations of great cruelty were cleansed. Fear and bondage were routed. Christ was triumphant—but never forget the way of sacrifice. In earlier days I used to preach a sermon under the title 'The Unreasonable God'. From a normal earthly viewpoint, the ways of God can seem very unreasonable. His dealings with men can seem unreasonable, and perhaps the most unreasonable of all were His dealings with His own Son at Calvary. Never forget that, in

judging what is reasonable and what is unreasonable. Our eternal salvation flows out from His 'unreasonableness'. Perhaps it is time for us to revise our outlook?

Notes

1   For further detail, see the author's *Reflections on the Gifts of the Spirit* (New Dawn Books, 1988), pp. 104–7.
2   Don Richardson, *Lords of the Earth* (Regal Books, 1977).
3   Bruce Olson, *For This Cross I'll Kill You* (Lakeland, 1977).

5

Waters of Affliction

Now David landed in a sea of trouble. David, that mighty monarch-to-be, that great man of God, that man who was described as a man after God's own heart, drank the water of affliction. It happened almost immediately. From the very beginning, as they sang in their dances, 'Saul has slain his thousands and David his tens of thousands,' the scene was set. Saul was jealous of David and he marked the reaction of the people. He marked David from that hour, but even for the king it was not the easiest thing in the world to slay the popular hero—that would have brought great criticism upon him. He moved initially with subtlety. Remember that he had promised that the conqueror of Goliath would have his daughter for his wife, but Saul did not give David the daughter who had been promised. He gave her to another. This may have suited David very well, for Saul's second daughter, Michal, loved David and wanted to marry him. Saul thought, 'I know how I can snare him'—for David had said to those who had been talking to him about marriage to a daughter of Saul: 'I have no money, no wealth, no dowry. How can I be the king's son-in-law?' He did not jump at the chance, because he did not have the substance to support the position. So Saul quietly said to the people, 'Tell David that he doesn't

need to worry about the idea of paying for my daughter. I tell you what I would be perfectly pleased with: evidence that he had slain one hundred Philistines. Tell him to bring back a hundred of their foreskins—that will do for payment.' And he said in his heart, 'I'll not kill David myself, but I'll get the Philistines to kill him. By this plan he'll lose his life and I'll be rid of him.' Now David was a mighty man of war: he went out with his bands and, for good measure, instead of bringing in a hundred foreskins he brought in two hundred and almost threw them at Saul's feet. He married Michal, and she loved him.

Saul was not finished. He saw that David showed great wisdom and sagacity, and that he was highly regarded by all Israel as he moved in and out amongst them; and Saul bided his time. From the beginning, David was consistently successful. Never once, either then or in all his years as the warrior king, did he suffer defeat at the hands of his enemies. He won every battle which he ever fought, and before he went into battle he enquired of the Lord and obtained the word of the Lord. If he had the word of the Lord to stay, or to go in by a kind of back way, he obeyed, and never knew defeat.

Let me just take a teaching point from this. When we move on our own initiative, when we make up our mind and decide what we will do, again and again we suffer defeat. But the men of God who learn to know the voice of God and who move with God know victory as men like Hudson Taylor and George Müller knew it. You will be amazed at how successful men of that calibre were—how God honoured them, spoke to them, communed with them, instructed them, and how victorious they were in the affairs of God. Learn to move with God, to enquire of the Lord, to have the Lord's blessing in the project in your hand.

Saul was not finished. He did not find that he was able to take the life of David in the way of his first devising. We read that an evil spirit had come upon Saul. Again and

again as David harped before him, Saul found relief and the evil spirit departed, but burning hatred remained deep down in his heart, and twice he tried to kill David by pinning him to the wall with a spear. David evaded the spear and fled for his life.

Now David had become very friendly with Jonathan, Saul's son. Jonathan loved David and realized that the hand of God was with his friend. These two made a covenant and Jonathan warned David from time to time of the danger in which he stood. Fleeing from Saul, David found himself at the head of a band of outcasts in the cave of Adullam. Unable to continue there permanently he went into the wilderness and was relentlessly pursued by Saul, who was determined to kill him. But God was with David and on two different occasions he was able to come to where Saul was and even take of his possessions. David could hail Saul from a distance and say, 'Now look! Your life was in my hand, but I spared you,' and Saul would be temporarily ashamed of what he was doing and would desist for a time—but the deep burning hatred continued.

I believe that Satan had begun to use Saul, and this is an awful thing to happen to a man. Here is a man who had known the power of the Spirit of the Lord: a man of whom it was said, *And the Spirit of the Lord will come mightily upon thee, and thou shalt become another person* (1 Sam 10:6). It is this man who is trying to kill the Lord's anointed—trying to kill the man through whom the Christ will ultimately be born. I believe he became an instrument in the hand of Satan, and from this we must learn a lesson.

You may say that it is a terrible thing for a person to become an instrument of Satan, and to that I say, 'Indeed, yes.' You may look out and see a Stalin or a Hitler and say, 'These men were very obviously servants of Satan.' You may come nearer home. You may come into religious circles and say, 'Well, that person is not really serving God. He is serving the cause of Satan.' And, you know, it can come very near home. You may find that certain lives

are used of God and then something happens and they take a turn and become emissaries of Satan—not necessarily wilfully or intentionally; but because they have followed a wrong course and come under a delusion they think they are serving the living God when in fact they are serving the cause of Satan. It is comparatively simple to sit and look out and make your judgments and be pleased with them. You are not so much judging, you feel, as making reasonable assessments. You are clearly aware of this and that. It may do you good one day if God suddenly says to you, 'You yourself are an emissary in a particular matter in the hand of Satan.' Don't say, 'Never me, Lord.' I have known myself pursue a course, thinking it was right, and God suddenly bring me to my senses and show me, 'This is not serving God. This is wrong.' There is a word that I would point out to you. It is a word that is perhaps not sufficiently preached on or understood: *Watch and pray, that ye enter not into temptation.* Christ does not just say, 'Pray.'

He says, 'Watch!' Guard your spirit. Never treat Satan as an easy foe. I shiver at times when I hear folk, particularly young folk, say, 'Oh, I have the measure of Satan. I can handle Satan.' *I* don't know how to handle Satan and *I* don't have the measure of Satan. The only one I know who has the measure of Satan is Christ. We don't have that measure. Satan is exceedingly subtle and he can fool us. I know he has fooled me. I think the only way to avoid being fooled is to obey that commandment of Christ to *watch*—watch very carefully that you act under the hand of God and that there is no touch of the dark one in your actions or attitudes. Saul ultimately became very, very deeply an emissary of that wicked one, and I am not sure that he ever really knew it. He pursued David and tried again and again to kill him. Behind Saul was Satan, and Satan's devices were foiled in relation to David. I wonder if one of his stratagems was to get David to lift his

hand to defend himself against the Lord's anointed? Spiritually, this might have ruined him.

David had a sister called Zeruiah who had three mighty sons: Joab, who became the captain of the host, Abishai, one of David's three mightiest men, and Asahel, who was particularly fleet of foot and who died ultimately by the spear of Abner. Abishai pled with David to let him kill Saul, and from a natural point of view we may well understand Abishai: David and his men were fleeing over the deserts and mountains and were having a desperate time. On two occasions Saul was at their mercy and they could have killed him. On one occasion Abishai said in essence, 'Let me take a spear—I'll finish this. I'll pin him to the earth'—brave man that he was. To kill a king is no light matter. 'Don't lift your hand against the Lord's anointed': David saw beyond the man Saul. He saw the anointing oil that had been on that man. Saul too had been the Lord's anointed and David had such a regard for the divine, for the holy, for God, that he would never touch Saul—and I suggest that had he touched Saul and slain him he himself might have been rejected because of what God might have regarded as tantamount to sacrilege. Satan's plan was thwarted: neither was Saul able to kill David, nor was Saul's conduct such as to enable him to get David to sin against the living God.

Ultimately David fled down to the land of the Philistines and presented himself to Achish, king of Gath. I think that Satan had a wonderful strategy concerning David in the land of the Philistines. By this time David was a notable warrior. He had never been defeated in any skirmish or raid or battle in which he had engaged. I am sometimes reminded of the Arthurian legend. Of Arthur they said that in the jousting and in the tournament Lancelot, for example, could overthrow him, but none could do so in battle. In time of battle he was indomitable. He was a tremendous commander in time of war, and it looks as though David was an exceptional commander with

exceptional strength. The Bible seems to give a pointer to this. On an occasion when he was without sword and without food he presented himself at Nob the town of the priests and obtained bread there, and asked, 'Is there no weapon here?' They said, 'No weapon save the sword of Goliath of Gath, and it is wrapped in a sheet behind the ephod.' 'Ah,' said David, 'Give me that one. There is no none like it. There is no sword in the world like the sword of Goliath of Gath.' I reckon it was a mighty sword and could only have been wielded by a very strong man, and David evidently greatly desired it. I have always been interested in the sword of Wallace the Scottish hero and have at different times tried to get a sight of it. It too was a mighty sword and could only have been handled by a mighty man. So David really wanted to get a grip on Goliath's sword, probably the biggest in all the ancient world. 'There is none like it. Give me that one.' I think that gives you some indication of the strength of David when he went to war. He wasn't just a young captain who had been lucky in a personal encounter with Goliath. It was as a warrior leader that he went down to Gath and was welcomed there.

Now I believe that Satan was again minded to ruin David. There is one thing that a nation will normally not tolerate: that is, one of their leaders fraternizing with the enemy or going to war against his own people. David found it expedient to go with his band from the land of the Philistines on raids from day to day. I must explain to you that the rules of morality in the ancient world where lying was concerned were somewhat different from the rules of Christian morality as understood in our day. In old times Israelites used language often intentionally to deceive one another, and they might do it very light-heartedly. Jacob was very skilled in the art and David indulged in it with the Philistines. He would go out raiding non-Israelite tribes close to Philistine territory and he would slay everybody in a locality so that nobody could report his action to

the king. When David came before the king he would say, 'Oh, yes, I raided today in the southern parts of Israel.' And Achish thought that David was putting himself absolutely beyond the pale where Israel was concerned because he was raiding their borders and killing their people, whereas in fact he never killed a single Israelite. He killed only the enemies of Israel, and concealed the truth from the Philistines. In spite of this, when the time of major battle came between the Philistines and the Israelites, the lords of the Philistines (and I believe God was in this) would not allow David to go to battle alongside them. They said, 'Look, when the battle is joined, he'll turn against us and it will be disastrous for us. Don't let David and his men come with us to this battle at all.' The king wanted him to come and supposed David wanted to go. The fact that David didn't go meant that his sword was never wet with the blood of his own people, and his own people knew it—never one of them died at the hand of David. And that day was a dreadful day for Israel. It was the day on which both Jonathan and Saul fell on Mount Gilboa: it was the day when Saul took his own life. He had been told very shortly before that he would be with his sons where Samuel was in the afterlife. Saul and Jonathan both died and a new day dawned for David. David was clearly in no way guilty of Saul's blood. From a national point of view he had behaved wisely and conducted himself properly. Mark the subtlety of Satan. If David had been involved in action against his own people they might never have accepted him later as king.

As it turned out, Judah very quickly wanted David as their king. Abner, Saul's captain, supported Ishbosheth, Saul's son, and the latter became king of the tribes of Israel. Long war ensued between the two houses, but David's power grew stronger and stronger while the house of Saul grew weaker until ultimately the two parts of the kingdom came together under David. David then went to war with almost every nation round about and subdued

them all—absolutely subdued all his enemies. He was victorious in his every battle. He ruled with a rod of righteousness—a victorious king, God's anointed, God's appointed, God's man. The road to glory opened before him, and you might think it would be gilded all the way and he had nothing to do but roll on in triumph. He had fought his battles. He had slain his Goliath. He had defeated the dark one, the prince of darkness—he had foiled him again and again. He was God's man in God's hour in God's appointed place: all would be well.

But let me tell you this: never underestimate the devil. David was a man who was prepared to die for God, and he risked his life on a hundred fields with never a shimmer of fear—but would he find it as easy to live consistently for God and emerge victorious in personal conflict with the devil? Joseph in an earlier day never fought a battle, but he was prepared to do something greater than dying for God. He proved to be a man who could live for God. It is sometimes easier to die for God than to live for God. A brave man may face death and death may be instantaneous: the crack of a bullet and eternal glory. On the other hand, you will find that there are men and women who live through a long lifetime faithful in their obedience to the living God. Is not this often a greater achievement than sudden martyrdom?

6

Defeat

David has come through the early stages so victoriously, so gloriously, so free of blemish. He obtains the kingdom and wears the crown—but Satan is not dead. Satan saw him there and knew very well that there was a time in the year when the kings went out to war. National activities in those days were different from ours; but there is a certain similarity. In our day there is a time when the tennis players and public seem to go mad; there is a time when a temporary insanity falls on the golfing world; there is a season for football and another for cricket. When we were children, there was a time to play peevers,* a time for skipping ropes, a time for yo-yo—these things came round in their cycles. Thus in a similar but more serious way in the ancient world there was a time when the kings went out to war.

David was king now and there came an occasion when he did not go out to war. We do not know why he stayed at home—maybe he thought he was getting old and felt in need of a rest. He wasn't really getting old and he didn't need a rest. In his early days David was ever in the forefront of battle. He was the leading captain, right there

---

* Scots children's word for hopscotch.

55

in the midst of the action—but this time he did not go out to war. He sent Joab and stayed at home. You don't get the impression that there was any planned wrongdoing, any evil, any wickedness in his mind. There is a saying that we do well to remember: 'Satan finds some mischief still for idle hands to do'. David's hands were not engaged in God's war, and as he looked out from his housetop he overlooked a lady bathing. It seems to have been as simple as that, and his eye was caught. His carnality was touched and he lusted—he failed to meet the high standard that Christ was later to set: *Every one that looketh on a woman to lust after her hath committed adultery with her already in his heart* (Mat 5:28). He also broke the commandment which forbade him to covet his neighbour's wife. But he was king and perhaps to some extent kingship had gone to his head. It can be dangerous when a person has very great power. He was used to having his own way and giving orders by this time. There is a saying, 'All power tends to corrupt and absolute power corrupts absolutely.' David wanted that woman and, being king, he sent for her and committed adultery with her. He knew very well in his heart what he was doing. It was adultery and could not be defined as anything else, and this was a very serious sin in Israel—punishable, indeed, by death. David did not want to be caught—oh, no—he did not want his sin to be known, and he sent for Bathsheba's husband Uriah to come back from the battlefield so that he might sleep at home, and if as a result of David's adultery a child should be born the world would assume that the child was Uriah's. Given that he had the king's permission to waive normal military practice, we do not know why Uriah refused to sleep at home. Someone may have known of David's behaviour or at least been suspicious and given Uriah warning, or it may be that God intervened and gave Uriah direct illumination. The reason he gave was that the ark of the covenant was out on the field of battle where Joab and the hosts were engaged in war—how could he

sleep in an ordinary house while they were pitched in the field? He would not go into his house, and David realized that there was now real trouble. When a person falls and begins to try to cover up the fall, he is often led from one entanglement to another. David wanted Uriah dead, and committed murder in his heart.

It is fearful to think how wicked the human heart is. Here is David, a prince amongst men, a man after God's own heart, so pressed of evil that even murder is contemplated. When we think of his wonderful early days and remember his glorious psalms and feel the reality of his love for God, we stand almost awestruck at the nature of evil and the vulnerability of our race.

So David reasoned: 'I'll marry Bathsheba.' He then wrote to Joab as follows: 'Put Uriah in the forefront of the battle and when the enemy comes out tell the others to withdraw, but leave Uriah standing so that he might be slain.' We don't know what Joab thought, but he followed his orders, and so Uriah the Hittite was slain by the enemy—but in reality murdered by David.

David thought that it was all over now. All was covered, and he married Bathsheba, who was in fact already with child by him. But oh, the revelation of the living God, and the uncovering of sin. I remember an evangelist giving a powerful illustration of this. As my memory goes, a girl in a family of boys was given a present of a doll. It was a big doll, and it was stuffed with corn (although this was not known). Now boys don't tend to look on dolls in the same light as girls do—and one day these boys cut the doll's head off. They knew better than to be caught by their parents; the doll had to be got rid of, and they buried it in the garden. That was fine. There was no evidence of the crime. They weren't there; they didn't know anything about it; they didn't do it. But, you know, the seasons changed. Spring and summer passed to autumn and a glorious crop of corn in the shape of a doll grew in the garden. The crime was covered—but it wasn't covered!

Be sure your sin will find you out. *Man looketh on the outward appearance, but the* LORD *looketh on the heart*— comforting words when David was anointed for kingship, but less comforting when sin as well as potential for good is under the scrutiny of the all-seeing eye of God.

There comes a time of uncovering. David thought he was quite safe, but God spoke to His prophet, and Nathan came to David. It is a wonderful story. He told the king a very sad story about a poor man whose one ewe lamb was killed by a rich neighbour in order to entertain a visitor. The host could have killed many a lamb of his own without feeling the lack; there was no need to covet the poor man's ewe lamb. David was appalled. He was absolutely indignant and declared that the person who had done this fearful thing in Israel deserved to die. When he had thoroughly taken the prophet's bait and still had the hook in his mouth, Nathan drew in the line and said, 'You are the man. That's exactly what you have done. David, you had plenty of wives and concubines, and Uriah the Hittite had one wife, one ewe lamb: you lusted for that one, you took that one, and you slew Uriah by the sword of the enemy.'

David is now exposed before all Israel. The thing that he had done in secret is cried from the housetops of the nation from the north to the south. David, the man after God's own heart, the glorious warrior king, is a common adulterer and a murderer. There is your king, O Israel. How sad—how fearfully sad! A man of God who had so opposed Satan and had been so victorious, to crumble in this dread hour and to be exposed to a whole nation—and that exposure carries on right to our own century. I remember in my school-days one agnostic teacher jibing about 'godly' David. David's sin has been remembered through all the centuries.

What a pass for David to come to! What a situation for God's anointed and appointed servant to find himself in. Let us learn from the incident our own need to watch and pray, lest we too enter into temptation. Let us always be

aware of the exceeding sinfulness of sin and the fickleness of human nature. If we are confident in ourselves we are in danger of falling. We must put the doctrine of death to self into practice and have our whole confidence in God. In our flesh dwelleth no good thing. *Wherefore let him that thinketh he standeth take heed lest he fall* (1 Cor 10:12).

7

A Second Defeat

There are two main sins of David's recorded in Scripture, and we should perhaps consider them together. Similarly there were two notable sins of Saul, as a result of which Saul was rejected. In David's case, he is not rejected. The sin of David that we have been considering is one which you will understand very well and you will appreciate something of its enormity. The other sin you may not understand so easily. There was a commandment that Israel was never to be numbered, nor was she ever to multiply horses. The multiplication of horses was forbidden to prevent her having an easy way to return to Egypt, from which she had been delivered. The numbering of Israel may have been because of the danger of Israel's depending on her own strength rather than on the power of God and saying, 'We have 300,000 warriors (or whatever), and we'll do this and that.' Perhaps in pride of possession David wanted to know the number of his people. Joab tried to restrain him from his course of action, but David persisted. The message of God came that punishment would fall upon him for his sin. The Bible is a wonderful book. It does not gloss over the sins of great men, and it shows that they do not escape punishment because they are great. Indeed, they may suffer more

severely because they have known God at deeper levels
than their fellows. God gave David three options: three
years of famine, or three months of fleeing from his
enemies, or three days of plague in the land. David reasoned, 'God is merciful; I would rather fall into His hands
than into the hands of my enemies.' Then comes devastat-
ing plague upon Israel. Seventy thousand die, until the
destroying angel is over Jerusalem, where he stays his
hand and comes down on the threshing floor of Ornan the
Jebusite. There the plague is halted.

David is punished and Israel suffers for the sin of the
leader. Sins of leaders frequently bring repercussions not
only on themselves but on their people, and the whole of
Israel suffered through David's sin, thousands of them
dying.

In the other major sin, relating to Bathsheba, the end
was not yet. The child that was born was ill, and David
besought God for his life—but the child died. David
broke his heart over that child, but God did not grant his
request. Do you realize that it was from Bathsheba's line
that the Christ would come? It was in the plan of God that
from the woman whom David saw and for whom he lusted
the holy seed would come, but not in David's way. David
put a human plan into action where God had His own
plan. In due time Bathsheba would, I believe, have legit-
imately become David's wife if he had waited. The child of
lust died, but it is from Bathsheba's later seed, Solomon,
that the line ultimately sprang. Wonderful are the ways of
God with men. Abraham in his day, man of faith though
he was, anxious about the future and about his seed, gave
up hoping that Sarah would ever have a son and took her
maid, and Ishmael was born. God had to tell him, regarding the chosen seed: 'It won't come through Ishmael but
through Isaac and Sarah.' It seems to me that Abraham
tried in a natural way to bring into being the plan of God,
and he failed. David actually sinned, while God had His
own plan in the background ready to unfold at the

appointed time. The precise details of this who knows?
Uriah might have died naturally in battle, leaving David
free to marry Bathsheba. The first babe died. There could
have been time for Solomon to be conceived exactly as he
was. It would have paid David to wait for God.

Learn from these things. In our hurry and our rush and
our taking of our affairs into our own hands, we do not
assist the plans of God. Begin to trust God. Learn to leave
your affairs in His hands. Obey the voice of God, and you
will find that God will make you fruitful in His kingdom.
Learn the laws of God—the connection between sin and
punishment, the need for the uncovering of sin whether
publicly or privately, that there may be forgiveness and
cleansing.

I remember something that Miss Taylor[1] once said,
with which I very deeply agreed. She was speaking of the
coming of revival and of the devastation that would come
with it—the uncovering of sin. She said something like
this to the people: 'Get right with God now. Put away your
sin now when it can be put away quietly, because if you
wait until that day God will come like devouring fire and
you will not be able to deal with sin quietly and privately.
It will come pouring out and be publicly exposed.' Let us
get right with God now in comparative privacy. Don't wait
until the thunders of God are on the streets of earth and
men are crying for fear and their sins well up and out like a
ghastly tide.

PRAYER: *Lord, Thou who searchest the hearts of men and knowest
the intents of the heart and hast shown us so clearly in the lives of
men like David that Thou hast no favourites and sin meets its due
reward, and whether it be a Moses or a David who sins on a vital
matter, the sins are not concealed or covered but they are brought to
book—Lord, give us a healthy fear of sin and its consequences,
that we may serve the living God wisely and obediently, for
Christ's sake. Amen.*

Note

1 A leader of our church who has since passed on. Her story is in the author's *A Trumpet Call to Women* (New Dawn Books, 1988), Part 2.

8

Judgment Pronounced

PRAYER: *Lord our God, there is an anointing present, and we pray that nothing shall be lost of all that Thou wouldest say to Thy people tonight. We come, Lord, to one of the most serious parts of the Old Testament, and we pray that as we listen to Thy Word and learn from it nothing shall be lost, but it shall be applied, O God, in a way that shall be remembered for a lifetime—and no man can do this. It has to be done by the power of the Holy Spirit. We pray that that power may be mightily upon us, upon preacher and hearer. We ask it in the Name Lord Jesus Christ and for His sake. Amen.*

In this series of addresses no attempt has been made to go exhaustively into the life of David. There are many things that are of tremendous interest in that life, but I am seeking to emphasize those parts that the Holy Spirit Himself would bring to our attention. This has led to a concentration on certain episodes in depth rather than to a general survey.

David was what would be called in our day a very charismatic figure. From an early stage it could be observed that he was blessed of God in his going out and his coming in. He seemed to be unusually wise for his years. What his hand touched prospered, and it seemed to be known through all Israel that God was with him. In his

early training as a man of God you might have expected an easy road, but instead we find adversity piled upon adversity. He was in the training school of God and he graduated with very high honours from that school.

Then came temptation and sin. Adultery and virtual murder are followed by an unsuccessful attempt at concealment. David's sin is exposed to the eyes of the whole nation. The mills of God grind slowly but they grind exceeding small. The hour of judgment has come. Nathan has pronounced the fateful words: *Thou art the man.*

> *Thus saith the LORD, the God of Israel, I anointed thee king over Israel, and I delivered thee out of the hand of Saul; And I gave thee thy master's houses, and thy master's wives into thy bosom, and gave thee the house of Israel and of Judah; and if that had been too little, I would have added unto thee such and such things. Wherefore hast thou despised the word of the LORD, to do that which is evil in his sight? thou hast smitten Uriah the Hittite with the sword, and hast taken his wife to be thy wife, and hast slain him with the sword of the children of Ammon. Now therefore, the sword shall never depart from thine house; because thou hast despised me, and hast taken the wife of Uriah the Hittite to be thy wife. Thus saith the LORD, Behold, I will raise up evil against thee out of thine own house, and I will take thy wives before thine eyes, and give them unto thy neighbour, and he shall lie with thy wives in the sight of this sun. For thou didst it secretly: but I will do this thing before all Israel, and before the sun. And David said unto Nathan, I have sinned against the LORD. And Nathan said unto David, The LORD also hath put away thy sin; thou shalt not die. Howbeit, because by this deed thou hast given great occasion to the enemies of the LORD to blaspheme, the child also that is born unto thee shall surely die. And Nathan departed unto his house* (2 Sam 12:7–15).

Now the church generally remembers that the prophet said, *The LORD . . . hath put away thy sin; thou shalt not die.* The fact that there is forgiveness with God that He may be feared, greatly appeals; Psalm 51 is oft quoted. David has been at the gates of hell: he has sinned and known terrible

conviction. The word of the Lord has come to him, and now he is truly contrite. But there is another side which is often bypassed in our reading: the firmness of the divine judgment and the consequences of sin.

First let us look at Psalm 51, which David wrote after Nathan's visit to him. We shall want to consider now two matters: David's outlook and God's—or the normal church viewpoint and the divine viewpoint. Oh, what wonderful compassion is shown here, and how men have empathized with the cry of a convicted David through all the centuries:

> *Have mercy upon me, O God, according to thy lovingkindness: According to the multitude of thy tender mercies blot out my transgressions. Wash me thoroughly from mine iniquity, And cleanse me from my sin. For I acknowledge my transgressions: And my sin is ever before me.*

I believe that David's sin had been before him from the moment of his adultery. Indeed, I believe that the very act of adultery would be little more than complete before an awful sense of guilt would be almost overwhelming.

> *Against thee, thee only, have I sinned, And done that which is evil in thy sight: That thou mayest be justified when thou speakest, And be clear when thou judgest. Behold, I was shapen in iniquity; And in sin did my mother conceive me. Behold, thou desirest truth in the inward parts: And in the hidden part thou shalt make me to know wisdom. Purge me with hyssop, and I shall be clean: Wash me, and I shall be whiter than snow. Make me to hear joy and gladness; That the bones which thou hast broken may rejoice. Hide thy face from my sins, And blot out all mine iniquities. Create in me a clean heart, O God, And renew a right spirit within me. Cast me not away from thy presence; And take not thy holy spirit from me. Restore unto me the joy of my salvation: And uphold me with a free spirit. Then will I teach transgressors thy ways; And sinners shall be converted unto thee. Deliver me from blood-guiltiness,*

—it is as though his spirit is springing up every now

and again and he sees the light, and then with a bump he remembers it all again and suddenly, 'Oh, I am guilty of murder!'—

> *O God, thou God of my salvation; And my tongue shall sing aloud of thy righteousness. O Lord, open thou my lips; And my mouth shall shew forth thy praise. For thou delightest not in sacrifice; else would I give it: Thou hast no pleasure in burnt offering. The sacrifices of God are a broken spirit: A broken and a contrite heart, O God, thou wilt not despise.*
>
> *Do good in thy good pleasure unto Zion; Build thou the walls of Jerusalem. Then shalt thou delight in the sacrifices of righteousness, in burnt offering and whole burnt offering: Then shall they offer bullocks upon thine altar.*

The cry of a wounded spirit: the cry of a broken heart: the cry of a man who has been down in the vestibule of hell; and, very contrite, he raises his eyes and he raises his voice to the living God, for the prophet has said, *The LORD also hath put away thy sin.* So all is over, the scene is ended and, David, all you have to do now is to get up and get on with your life and follow the Lord your God....

You know, that is what one might suppose much of the church thinks and teaches and preaches. Let me make this very clear. When God finds a person in the depths of sin and saves his soul, he has a wonderful way of wiping the record clean. But let a person who is called of God, knows Christ and has gone on with God, turn to folly, and he will find it is a very different matter. Here you have a man of God, who knows Him perhaps more deeply than any other man in Israel, and he has turned to folly. I want to show you something of the eternal law of the eternal God which operated in David's life and will operate in yours.

I thank God for some of my early religious training. Although there were aspects of it that God had to undo, I remember with gratitude one man of God who used to indicate very clearly in his preaching that sin has consequences: personal sin has personal consequences,

national sin has national consequences, and while God forgives sin there are times when the consequences even of forgiven sin are horrendous.

There may be some of you who do not want to come to grips with this. You may want to argue in your hearts with it. Indeed, you may want to argue with me—and I warn you that on some matters you may not find me the most comfortable person to argue with. I remember preaching a series of addresses in school when I was a headmaster. The whole senior assembly was there, with many of the staff, and I came in the natural course of things to the doctrine of hell. This I preached as bluntly there as I would preach it here or as I teach it in one of my books that deals with it in detail.[1] You know, the staff were angry—some of them were really angry. I got on very well with my staff normally, but some of the very best of them were, I think, enraged at this doctrine—that a God of love would allow any of His creatures to be eternally condemned and in the heart of hell. I said that you might not find me the most comfortable person to argue with, as you may judge when I tell you how I dealt with this. I sensed that they were angry and just ready to attack me, in thought if not in deed, and so just as I closed the sermon I said, 'Now if any of you are otherwise minded and you don't agree with this doctrine, I want you to know I did not formulate it. I am not responsible for the doctrine. I have nothing to do with the doctrine. I am merely telling you what Jesus Christ said when he was on earth. If you have any argument, your argument is with the Son of God: I have nothing to do with it. You don't need to fight with me about it because I am merely a transmitter of what is written in the Bible.' And none of them ever came to me. I know they went to each other, but they didn't come to me.

At the end of this sermon I will not say, 'I have been expressing an opinion, giving you one possible viewpoint on Scripture.' It is not like that; I will say, 'This is what God said, and not only is this what God said, but this is

what God allowed to happen. He predicted: and that which he predicted was fulfilled—fearfully fulfilled.'

Now listen to what God said to David: three predictions after the pronouncement, 'You killed Uriah with the sword of the enemy and you took his wife to be your wife: you slew him by the sword of the children of Ammon.'

First: *The sword shall never depart from thine house, because thou hast despised me, and hast taken the wife of Uriah the Hittite to be thy wife.* 'Lord, but you've forgiven me.' Yes, David, your soul is safe for eternity, but the sword is loose in your house and there is nothing you can do about it now or through all your lifetime: it will follow—it is the word of the Lord. Could I say again—there is given a word from the watchers and the holy ones: it has been decreed in the heavenlies.

Second: *I will raise up evil against thee out of thine own house, and I will take thy wives before thine eyes, and give them unto thy neighbour, and he shall lie with thy wives in the sight of this sun.* 'You did it secretly; I will do it before all Israel, not in darkness but in full daylight.'

Third: *Because by this deed thou hast given great occasion to the enemies of the Lord to blaspheme, the child also that is born unto thee shall surely die*—and Nathan walked away.

'Oh, this is not the God I know. This is a terrible God. This is not the nice love and kindness that I associate with Christianity! This is fearful—I can't come to terms with this. Could we not get somebody to pray for poor David? Why not get the sons of the prophets to intercede for David?'

Let me say to you again in this connection: I believe that if every holy man in Israel or in all the world, of that age and earlier ages, had interceded, it would have been of no avail. If Abraham himself had been there, with Isaac and Jacob, and they had all with fastings and prayers and intercession spent month after month after month to alter any of these three decrees, not by a fraction would any one of them have been altered.

Have you ever been in a position where God has said to you: 'If you pass that point, things will never be the same with you again'? If God says that to you, you may think, 'Oh, well, I'll go to some of the great-name healers or preachers, and I'll be all right.' You won't, you know. If God makes that kind of decree there will be no alteration of it for you through all time.

That is the God I know, and if some of you want to know why there is such blessing in these meetings, it is at least partly because the leaders of the movement know *that* God—that God of severity. There have been people from outside who have come into our midst and spoken of what they could do if they had control of this company—to 'set them free', as they put it. In a matter of weeks, I imagine, if they were given scope, sanctification would go out the window and people would be jumping around, shouting hallelujah, and I don't know what all.[2] At the heart of this movement is the iron of God, this God. The reason that the demons come screaming out is because they meet this God, the God of iron, the God who is of purer eyes than to behold iniquity. This knowledge of God is fundamental to this particular work of God. We are not the only work God has. He has many works here and across the world—but let us attend to our own allotted part of the vineyard. Let us realize and teach God's severity. When God says, 'I will bring a particular judgment,' He does just that.

Notes

[1] Hugh B. Black, *The Incomparable Christ* (New Dawn Books, 1989), chap. 9.
[2] Not that there is anything wrong with movement and praise, provided it is God-inspired and God-controlled. This we strongly encourage.

9

Judgment Outworked

Let me take you quietly, step by step, to the focal point. Uriah is dead. Take the birth of the child first. David loved that boy, and he fasted and prayed and interceded before God to spare the life of the child, the beloved child—but the child died. There was no hope for that child, and it was in connection with that child that David uttered the ever memorable words: *I shall go to him, but he shall not return to me* (2 Sam 12:23). When the child died David arose and dressed himself and took food. People said, 'Why are you doing that? The child is dead.' 'Oh,' he said, 'I fasted before the child died, while there might be hope; but now that he is dead there is no more hope.' And so he resumed normal life.

David had sons and daughters, one of whom was a girl born of a foreign princess, extremely beautiful; her name was Tamar. She was a full sister of Absalom, who himself was a man of great personal beauty and charm. Another son, by a different wife, was Amnon, who was thus a half-brother of Tamar. Now Amnon fell in love with Tamar, although she was his sister.

It is a strange world in which we live, and we can sometimes view its strangeness with interest—not necessarily in a macabre way, but quite objectively. Most people

71

know about the normal failings of humanity in sexual
matters; but then beyond the normal there is the abnormal
and the perverted, and people generally do not know a
great deal beyond the groups with which they mix and
work. But if you worked in the realm in which I am called
to work, you would reach a stage where you would cease to
be shocked. You do not become contemptuous: you do not
look down on human frailty, not for a moment, but you do
realize that the inclinations of humanity are desperately
affected by the Fall, and you treat people with love and
kindness. Now here in Amnon's case we meet one of these
abnormalities. Incest is not uncommon, but it is unusual
for a man actually to fall in love with his sister as this man
did. He was so deeply in love that he went off his food and
began to go into a decline.

I think I will digress for a moment at this point on the
whole subject of love. The remarks of a recent speaker
struck me, and I would like to underline them. In his early
days he had formed a relationship with a young woman
which was not of God. My advice to him at the time met
with some annoyance, as I remember! But the relationship
ended, and he ultimately married another. Last night in
giving testimony he underlined the point that marriage
should be in God. Tonight I am going a little further than
he did. Of all the relationships which you are likely to
form, the love relationship can be one of the most dangerous because of the depth to which emotions are
involved. Recently one of you spoke to me of a case where
a person was saved, baptized in the Spirit, and involved in
such a relationship. She was unclear as to whether God
was in it or not, but was so involved that she found it
difficult to get guidance. What should she do? Let me
explain to you quite precisely what we teach on this matter. If, for example, a young man seeks help or advice, he
is almost uniformly advised to commit himself fully to
God—to put his whole life into the hands of God before
allowing any such relationship to come into life, because if

he gets deeply involved in love with another and Christ is not first in his heart (even though he is a saved person), he will find it very difficult to put things right later. If, on the other hand, Christ is first and another comes into life in a proper way, they meet in Christ, the deep relationship with God is not disturbed, and marriage can be wonderful and should be totally encouraged.

Normally a person looks and is attracted, not realizing that he or she could be attracted to many another in other circumstances. 'Oh no,' says the romantic, 'she's the only one, born out of eternity into time specially for me!'

Very seldom do we give advice to people who do not ask for it. We are not marriage brokers, and even if we are asked for advice we are very careful about any particular and personal detail, but the following general line of instruction is given because it is totally spiritual and not at all personal.

Never become involved in a love relationship before you know the will of God. If you are walking with God, He will make His will as clear as daylight. Do not assume that the married condition is the perfect condition for you. Do not assume that the unmarried condition is the perfect condition for you. The will of God is the perfect condition, and if He leads you into marriage it can be perfect: if He does not lead you into it, do not go, because it ought not to be entered outwith the will of God.

There are people who teach otherwise, who teach that you should endeavour to get married. Totally resist it: lives may be blasted by that doctrine. Sometimes we have to wipe up afterwards because the consequences can be quite tragic. A mistaken and unhappy marriage may result—and marriage is one relationship which is lifelong and is so important that it should be entered into by a Christian only in the express will of God. If you want a low-level, carnal life it may not matter so very much. Sometimes a leader, in dealing with a particular situation, may judge that in view of the kind of life a person is living, it is not

going to make a great deal of difference if the individual concerned takes his own way in this matter. But those who have aspirations for the highest should be most careful. Do not enter marriage outwith the will of God. Now I know quite well those who are present tonight, and I know to whom I am speaking. I am not one of those preachers who say I'm not referring to anybody in particular. I am saying quite pointedly: If this shoe fits you, put it on, and if it hurts you badly it means you have needed the teaching more than most. You say, 'If I am hungry, am I not allowed just to go and have a meal? If I have a desire for marriage am I not allowed in the same way to go and make my own arrangements?' Well, the ill effects of a meal, even of a bad one, are usually thrown off shortly; a mistake in the other only lasts for a lifetime! You say, 'There is always divorce.' God says He hates the 'putting away'. Don't take matters to an extreme point in either direction. If God is leading you into marriage and there is a person for you and you are resisting God, you will have no happiness. You will not have the blessing of God until you obey Him. Always remember, God may forbid a marriage: He may also ordain it, and if He does, you will desire it and find happiness in it, so long as both partners continue in God's will. Never take the law into your own hands in this matter and do not influence others unless you have the guidance of God. If you do, they are liable to come back to you and accuse you of advising them wrongly.

PRAYER: *Lord, we pray that this word shall find a deep lodgement in the hearts of thy people. Help us to realize that for one person the way to the highest is through marriage and for another it is by bypassing marriage. We must not interfere; if we do, it can be to lifelong harm and eternal loss. Lord, let Thine anointing be upon this part of Thy word, and if and where wrong advice has been given, we pray it shall be blotted out, rubbed clean as from a slate. We ask it very simply in Christ's Name and for His sake. Amen.*

Just to finish this diversion. There are times when I

have had to rectify wrong advice on this theme—and you say, 'Who are you, to rectify other people's advice?' Leaders under God have not only the right but the duty to act in these matters. Authority is vested in them by God himself, and they will give an account to God one day for the way they have dealt with the souls He has put in their care.

Amnon fell in love with Tamar. You say, 'Could he have done anything about that?' Yes. People say, 'But I was in love; I couldn't help it.' Now it can be very difficult to deal with love after it has gripped you, but you can help falling in love. It has even been said, 'Love is an act of the will.' I don't say you can help the first attraction, but you can help what you do with it. You are early aware of the attraction, and Amnon knew perfectly well that marriage with Tamar was forbidden by the Mosaic law. It was within prohibited degrees and Amnon needed to have no doubt about the will of God; but his eye was attracted and his carnal sexual nature was aroused. When a man lets that grip him, a situation can develop which he feels is beyond his power to handle. Sex can become a driving obsession and it can lead men to rape, adultery and murder. The grip of sex is incredibly strong, and perhaps especially where there is no likelihood of a consummation. As Amnon regarded Tamar she was forever outwith his reach; she was his sister. Many a day I suppose he said, 'O God, why was she not born further out: why did she have to be born within the household of my father? She is lovely, she is beautiful!'

If you are attracted by a person's beauty, the more you look at it the more attracted you will become until it may grip and drive you. If you want to be free of it, you stop looking at the beauty, you stop being where the beauty is, you get out of the proximity of the temptation. You do not put yourself in a position where it is going to grow upon you, because that way lies disaster. Amnon, instead of being wise in that and saying, 'Lord, I have got this

obsession, help me get rid of it,' pursued his own course and took matters into his own hands. God might well have brought someone else into his life, and he could have known the 'expulsive power of a greater affection.' I am quite sure that Tamar was not the only lovely-looking girl in Israel. As the old saying has it, and as many a broken-hearted swain has comforted himself: 'There are better fish in the sea than ever came out of it.' It is a very healthy philosophy if you are heartbroken. I am not unfeeling about this kind of thing. I can understand how deeply these matters can cut into a person's life, but I would not subscribe to the idea of pining for ever as a result of forbidden or unrequited love. Amnon failed to get out of temptation's way. Oh no, he didn't get out of temptation's way—rather he conspired with a cousin and they set a trap. He had been somewhat sick to begin with, but that was just love-sickness. Now he feigned real sickness and went to bed, and sought his father's permission to have Tamar come and keep house for him. Unsuspecting David allowed this, and at a suitable time Amnon got everybody else out of his apartment and clearly revealed his love to his sister.

Tamar, I believe, was a good woman, but very unwise. I think women often are very unwise in dealing with men in sex matters. Instead of saying to Amnon a firm, 'No, not on your life—not now, not ever. I'd rather put a dagger in myself than go that road,' she said, 'No, this isn't right, we shouldn't do this: this isn't allowed in Israel—but if you ask my father I am sure he won't keep anything from you.' In other words, 'Amnon, I do not find you unacceptable. I have no basic personal objection to what you are suggesting but I don't want to do it, because it's wrong.'[1] Immediately, I believe, Amnon knew that he was not unacceptable to Tamar. With her spoken response the position became one hundredfold worse. Any girl who by the slightest action lets a boy know of even a slight degree of acceptance in a forbidden liaison is normally

asking for trouble and frequently gets it. To that extent she brings it on her own head and is at least partly responsible for the consequences. Amnon then just used his physical strength to rape his sister.

Can you hear David say: 'Amnon, that is a fearful thing that you did! Amnon, that is sin against the living God.'

Hear Amnon: 'Father, do you remember Bathsheba? Do you remember what you did to Uriah the Hittite? I didn't kill anybody; I didn't commit adultery with anybody's wife. I took a virgin. Father, my sin's not half as bad as your sin, and, father, you just keep your mouth shut.'

The sword shall never depart from thy house—it shall never depart from thy house. Absalom, Tamar's full brother, loved her, and Absalom was a deeply designing character. He did not say a word to Amnon. He simply took Tamar into his own house and shielded her. He acted like a perfect gentleman, but he murdered his brother in his heart. He was the kind of man who was able to wait for his revenge. He was not the kind who had to go storming immediately: he could wait with patience, and he waited for a week, and he waited for a month, and he waited for a year, and he waited for two years—without doing a thing about it.

I imagine there were many in Israel who wondered that Absalom, who was a man of exceptional charm and ability, a resolute and strong man, did nothing. The day came, however, when he arranged to have a sheep shearing to which all of the king's sons were invited. They would have a party, there would be drinking, and they would have a great time. David said, 'Why do you want Amnon to come up?' 'Well, all the king's sons are coming.' David was obviously a little reluctant; David was never anybody's fool. However, they were all going; it seemed fair enough. Nothing had happened between Absalom and Amnon over the years. Perhaps the trouble was buried.... Absalom waited until he had them all there and then he just quietly

killed Amnon—he thrust him through, and he died in the midst of his brethren.

'Thy sin, David, is forgiven.' Now, David, although your sin was forgiven, the consequences of it are coming home to roost. One of your sons is a rapist, one of your daughters has been violated, the rapist is now murdered and the murderer is another of your sons. David, it has come into your own house. You murdered Uriah: your son is murdered. You committed adultery with Bathsheba: your daughter is violated by your son. O God, O God. The ways of the wicked are hard. 'Lord, let it depart from my house.' No, David, it will never depart from your house. 'Lord, is it not enough? Lord, all right, I was a murderer; all right, I was guilty of adultery: now my son is a rapist, now there is incest, now there is murder and my son is a murderer. Is it not enough? Can the curse never lift? Can the curse not depart from me and from my house?' *The sentence is by the decree of the watchers, and the demand by the word of the holy ones*—as with Nebuchadnezzar, so with David. Not only did David have a murdering son, but he lost that son because he could not overlook his guilt. Absalom fled and was in exile for years—back at the court of his mother's people. The time came when there was a desire to have Absalom back again in Israel and matters were set in motion. David loved Absalom deeply and may indeed have spoiled him in earlier days. I think David was very typical of many of us. He was a godly man, but he was very human. He had a high degree of spirituality but also a depth of ordinary humanity in his make-up. Absalom, I believe, was a bad man from the beginning, an emissary whom Satan planned to use in his purposes. David was emotionally deeply attached to Absalom, maybe more so than to any other son he had. He longed to have him back, and permitted his return. Absalom still was not free to come to court, but a little plot was managed. The king's secret desire was known, and Joab with another engineered a way whereby the banished son came

home again. And now starts horrible treachery. The consequences of David's sin are now deeply in his own house.

Note

1 Tamar may, on the other hand, merely have been trying to keep Amnon at bay. If so, her evasive answer was no less damaging.

10

Insurrection

'David, in your early days you knew the hand of God, the blessing of God. Everything you touched prospered, and no plot that was formed against you had any hope of success. Now you are a fallen David—a forgiven but a fallen David. And a plot is hatched against you. Absalom's eye is on the throne: he wants leadership.' And oh, he is wonderfully subtle. 'What I would do were I in power!'

Those of you who listen to political broadcasts may have noticed that when a government is in power it has to do with the realities of situations, but the Opposition can shout and trumpet to the country: 'Oh, if only we were in power, what we would do for you! If we were in power, there would be a fair tax system. If we were in power, everything would be happy in the educational services and in the health services, and it would be a wonderful world. Inflation would come down, the bank rate would come down. Mortgages would fall. Unemployment would fall.' When the tables turn—because they do with great regularity—things may not be just quite so. When the Opposition becomes the Government it may suddenly find that there is not enough money to do this, and, well, yes, we did promise that, but there is not enough money, and we may go to the International Monetary Fund, and these

nasty people may say, 'Not until you put a rigid economic policy into operation are we going to give you any money.' So it isn't really the new government to blame: it's these bad people out there. In the meantime the new Opposition are saying, 'If we were in power we wouldn't do this and we wouldn't do that, and we wouldn't do the next thing. It would be a wonderful world.' It is always easy when you are not in government to show just how much better things would be if you were in charge, and how good you would be to the people. As for that other lot, they are very bad to everybody!

Now I am a-political. Historians are apt to become very cynical of political parties, whether of left or right or centre . . . I'll just leave it at that. I am not speaking against any one party in particular—I tend to keep politics right outside the church in any case. I am speaking in general terms.

So Absalom sits at the gate of the city where he will be in contact with all the people coming in and going out. 'Oh, you have a case? What is it—what is your problem? Oh, you've got trouble with your neighbour. Let's just hear what the position is. Oh, yes, justice is on your side, friend. You know, I wish I was judging Israel; it would be wonderful for you because you would win this case, but I am not a judge.' And the next one comes up, and the next one; and Absalom is sitting at the gate, talking to them and winning their hearts subtly. Can you hear them say, 'Oh, if Absalom was king it would be wonderful: he's got a real sense of justice, that man—he would decide in my favour.' You know how just people seem who side with you! And Absalom subtly won the hearts of Israel. 'Wouldn't it be fine if Absalom was king? And he is such a good-looking man! Why, he's got hair way down to yonder: he could sit on it.' It was a wonderful mop! He could have masses of it cut and sold for many shekels every year. It was so thick that he had to have it regularly polled. Yes, he was truly fine to look at, a handsome fellow. A

king in the making, everything but a throne, the finished article. And he insinuates himself. He gets in to see the king and he says, 'You know, when I was an outcast I made a vow that I would do certain things and sacrifice to the Lord and obey Him. Now, father, would you let me fulfil my vow? I would like to go down to Hebron to do this.' How could David, a man of God, a man after God's own heart, possibly say no? Subtle!

Away Absalom goes and he has many men under his hand. He sends out spies through all Israel and gives notice of the time of his planned insurrection. The shout would rise all over Israel—'Absalom is King!' Insurrection began. It began first in the heart of Absalom. Then practical steps were taken until a point was reached where many of the chief men of the country, including Abiathar the priest and Ahithophel the counsellor, joined the rebellion. So great and so widespread was the support for Absalom that David had to flee for his life from his own city. There he left ten of his concubines in charge of his house and he fled from the face of Absalom with a handful of men. And oh, the pain that David had to bear. As he was going, there was a wretched man, Shimei, a son of Belial, of the house of Saul, who saw David in flight. As David moved along one hillside, Shimei moved along another, and he cried his curses on David. 'O you man of blood, you are a cursed person, rejected!'—and he cast up dust and threw stones at David. As he shouted his curses in the moment of David's deep distress, Abishai the brother of Joab said, 'Let me go and kill this dog.' David said, 'No, don't, the Lord has bidden him curse me. The hand of God is in this: it is part of the cup I have to drink.' It reminds us of a later day: 'Simon, put up your sword into the sheath: don't kill that man.' David knew that it was Shimei's hour; he was allowed to curse and revile and blaspheme, and David the great king of Israel took it as he went, with never a murmur. In one aspect he was beginning to reflect his greater son Christ who, when He was

reviled, reviled not again. And he went all the way down to the depth of his valley.

Meanwhile Absalom arrived in Jerusalem and Ahithophel the counsellor gave him two pieces of advice. Now Ahithophel was an exceptionally wise counsellor, whose word had never been known to fall to the ground. Absalom sent for him and said, 'Have you anything to say?' 'Yes,' he said, 'two things. Spread a tent in the eyes of all the people, put the ten concubines in there and go in and have sexual intercourse with them. All Israel will then know that you are really committed against your father and that he will never forgive you — you will be an outcast for ever. They will trust you then to carry this war to its conclusion.' And Absalom did it. David, you sinned in secret with Bathsheba; this thing will be perpetrated on your wives in the eyes of all Israel. O God—O God—how fearful are the consequences of sin.

I am not sparing you tonight; we have passed the day of soft speaking. In my earlier days I would never have touched some of these things in this way, but we are in an age and generation where sexual morality is flouted all around, and we will be quite blunt. David's concubines were violated by David's son, and the foul sin is committed in a blaze of publicity, and deliberately so.

Ahithophel's second piece of advice was this: 'David is exhausted just now and sorely grieved, and he has few people who are with him. Let me quickly choose twelve thousand men and catch David before he recovers. I will take him while he is dejected and in despair. If we kill him but don't touch the others, the whole country will rally to you.' Absalom thought the advice was good.

Now Hushai the Archite, a friend of David, had wanted to be with him but David had said, 'Look, Hushai, don't come with me—go back and offer your services to Absalom, but in reality act on my behalf.'

Hushai went back, and Absalom said, 'Tell me, you who are a friend of David: why are you here?'

'Oh, I was a friend of David, but I am a friend of David's son. I stand with the king of Israel and all the people.' (Don't ask me to justify the way this was done; I am just telling you the facts of the case.)

Absalom said, 'We have heard the counsel of Ahithophel. Let us hear the counsel now of Hushai.'

God was with Hushai and he said, 'You know that David is a great warrior—doesn't all Israel know of the prowess of David?—and you know he has with him his mighty men. [They included the greatest warriors in Israel.] They may be few in number, and you may out-number them in your first assault, but I tell you that David and these men will be like bears robbed of their whelps—they will be like animals—and they are powerful men. Ahithophel's counsel is very unwise, Absalom. If you follow it and immediately attack and are forced to retreat, the people will say that God is on the side of David. The rumour will spread fast and the people will melt away through fear of the great warrior king. That is not the way to do it. What you want to do is wait: gather the host from all Israel, and when you have a mighty host then you can give chase and catch David.'

Absalom took Hushai's advice, thus giving David a breathing space. It was God's way of counteracting the influence of Ahithophel, who was so upset that he went home and hanged himself. It is never wise to get on to the wrong side in these deep spiritual battles. Ahithophel died the death—just as simple as that.

David managed to get people together, and in due time the irreligious Absalom, the proud usurping tyrant, lusting for the throne of Israel, was to meet his fate. He was proud in his beauty, perhaps a worthy representative in some ways of the wicked one himself. He was certainly an emissary. Satan had a plan: Get David off the throne, get a carnal man in his place—bring Israel back to idolatry, no doubt.

David set his army in battle array and gave one-third to Joab, who was an outstanding commander. Joab has

always been a favourite of mine in certain respects (not in all). He was a great soldier. The next third of the army was given to Abishai, who also was a mighty man of valour. The men were brothers—nephews of David. A third brother Asahel, who was as fleet of foot as a roe on the mountains, had been killed earlier by Abner, and Ittai got the third part of the army. The commanders refused to let David go out in front as he wanted to do. They said, 'No, we can't risk your life—you are more important to us than ten thousand men. You stay at the gate of the city,' and out they went without him.

Battles are always with the Lord. The greater numbers may have been with Absalom, but the hand of the Lord was with David's men, and the battle went strongly against Absalom and his forces. He eventually tried to escape from the field on a mule, and it may be that his great pride became his great downfall. As he rode, his head with its massive crown of hair caught in the boughs of an oak tree, and the mule—as mules would do—went on and left him hanging there. Animals are like that. I don't know whether many of you ride or not, but in your early stages, especially if you are riding bareback, you will find that you can be going along merrily, trotting or galloping—and if you don't know how to control your horse, suddenly it decides it is going to the right, and you just go straight on. You learn with experience. Well, Absalom's mule just went straight on and left him caught (by his hair, most likely) on an oak tree.

When Joab learned of it he criticized the young man who brought the story for not killing Absalom. The young man replied, 'It's all right for you to say that, but I heard David giving you orders, and the other two commanders also, that you were to deal kindly with the young man Absalom.' Joab more or less said, 'Get out of my road,' and he went and killed Absalom as he hung from the tree.

The word came back to David, 'Yes, your forces are victorious.'

'And is it well with the young man Absalom?'
'God grant that all the enemies of the king will be as the young man Absalom today.' Absalom is dead and a heap of stones is over him.

> O my son Absalom, my son, my son Absalom! would God I had died for thee, O Absalom, my son, my son!

And David broke his heart over his second dead boy. Joab, who was a very tough character, came in and said to David, 'You are showing more fuss over that dead treacherous son of yours than you are about all the people who have supported your cause. If you don't quit it and come out and welcome and congratulate the people, there won't be left a man beside you tonight; we'll desert you and leave you to it.' David the mighty king is dictated to by the commander of the host, and he has to go out and speak to the people. David had sung, *How are the mighty fallen and the weapons of war perished!* in connection with Saul and Jonathan. But there is another song that could now be sung:
'David, David, conquering prince with whom God was always present—how through this fearful sin thou art fallen; and there are consequences that ride beside you all along life's road... right along, David. The day is to come when you will be an old man stricken in years, you will be unable to get warm no matter how many blankets you wrap around you. You will be cold, David, as you draw near to the gates of death.' What is this sound in David's ears? The sound of merriment and acclamation! David, while you are lying there on your deathbed, another of your sons is usurping the throne.

Adonijah, so like Absalom, wanted to be king and made his preparations. David's friends quickly took action and prevailed on Bathsheba (Solomon's mother) to intervene. David had sworn to Bathsheba that Solomon would sit on his throne although Adonijah was an older brother. David gave orders, and Solomon was anointed.

11

Final Retribution

Solomon is proclaimed king—and Adonijah is suddenly afraid; Joab, who had supported him, is afraid; and Abiathar the priest is afraid. They had been guilty of insurrection. It is ever dangerous to be involved in insurrection against the work of God. God is powerful on behalf of His chosen and His anointed. The guilty men now face the consequences of their wrongdoing. David is lying there—lying back in bed, so old that he is cold and dying. Solomon is anointed and appointed, and David speaks to him.

'You are a wise man, Solomon' (obviously even at this early stage wisdom was noticeable in Solomon), 'and I have some charges to give you.' Some of the charges that followed were fearful. I want you to consider the mild attitude of many fine Christian people who teach that it is always right to forgive your enemies and deal with them kindly. I want you to realize that it can be equally right to deliver them into the hand of God for the punishment that comes on earth in consequence of their sins. You can forgive them totally at a personal level but still deliver them into the hand of the Lord for His judgment. 'Mr Black, do you mean that?' Yes, I do. I mean that. There is an iron in God and an iron of God. Most of you have no

idea of the strength of the iron that casts out demons, or of the strength of God to execute judgment—no idea.

'Solomon: Joab, my nephew, brought blood guiltiness by the murder of Abner in time of peace. He killed Amasa, a better man than himself. See that his grey hairs do not come down to the grave in peace. You will know how to deal with the matter.'

'But, father, Joab has journeyed with you through your whole life; he is your nephew. He has been an outstanding man of valour; he has led the hosts of Israel. He has been one of your mightiest men—Joab, the son of your sister Zeruiah.'

'Yes, a great warrior. He was loyal to me in the time of Absalom's defection, but then he disobeyed my command and killed Absalom. He slew Abner with treachery and Amasa in jealousy. Now he has supported Adonijah in rebellion. See that his grey hairs do not come down to the grave in peace.'

'Father, father, do you really mean it?'

'Yes, I mean it. Have him put to death.'

You say, 'What a God is this? Do you mean that God marks iniquity to this extent?' Yes, I believe that. I have always believed it, and the experiences of life have deepened my belief in it.

'Solomon, there was a man called Shimei: in the day when the Lord afflicted me he cursed me with a deep and grievous curse, and he stoned me; I was not allowed to lift a hand in my own defence. Solomon, you are a wise man and you will know how to handle the matter. See to it that his hairs do not come down to the ground in peace.'

'David, are you really a very loving man? Are you really a man after God's own heart, David?'

To which David might have responded, 'What are you talking about? This is not personal vengeance. I have forgiven these people long since. I have held nothing against anybody. I am now speaking as a servant of the

living God. See to it that a full retribution is visited upon these men.'

After the fall of Adonijah, Joab fled to the tent where the ark was housed and he gripped the horns of the altar—perhaps thinking, 'Nobody can kill me here—this is a holy place, this is the house of God.' Word was taken back to Solomon and he sent Benaiah the captain of the host to fall upon him and kill him by the altar where he stood.

'Shimei, you met me', I can imagine David saying, 'when I came back after my exile, and you pled for mercy, and I gave you mercy.' Personally David had forgiven, but now he is acting as God's messenger, and Solomon was given his instructions. To Shimei Solomon later said, 'You may build yourself a house in Jerusalem and live there, but the day you leave that city your life will be forfeit.' In due time two of Shimei's slaves escaped to Gath and he went after them. Word came to Solomon, and he then sent Benaiah, who slew Shimei. Shimei's curse on David was reversed.

Although Adonijah had been dealt with lightly after his insurrection, he still had a plotting heart. He wanted that throne—oh, yes, he wanted the throne. He had been told that if he proved himself worthy all would be well with him; but if wickedness was found in him, that would be a different matter. Adonijah was a subtle man—very like his full brother Absalom.

There was one young lady who had been favoured by David at the very end of his life: Abishag the Shunammite, beloved, I believe, of Solomon himself and probably the lady spoken of in the Song of Solomon—more beautiful, perhaps, than all the women in Israel. Because of her association with David, there was the possibility that if Adonijah could marry her he would strengthen his position in a bid for the throne. He was Solomon's older brother, and Adonijah may have felt, 'Although my earlier attempt at the kingdom failed, there is always tomorrow. If I get Abishag for my wife, it will be a step in the right

direction.' He wanted her, and very astutely he did not make a direct approach, but went to Bathsheba, the king's mother, who might be expected to be influential with the king. He said, 'There's something I'd like you to do for me.' Many people are flattered right away when they're put in the position, 'There's something you could do for me ... I'd like you to do this for me....' Immediately the person feels important—and Bathsheba said, 'What is it? Say on.'

'Well,' he said, 'it's about the Shunammite. Could you intercede with Solomon the king for me that I might have her to wife?'

Solomon was a wise man. You may remember that when God came to him in a dream shortly afterwards and invited him to name his request, he asked for wisdom. It was a wise man who made that later choice, and he was wise from the beginning. He seems to have seen right into the heart of the plot that was fermenting in the heart of Adonijah. The gift of discernment did not start after Pentecost. It was in operation in earlier days as well. Often God's man and God's woman see right into the heart of treachery in its earliest stages—sometimes almost before the person concerned is fully aware of the treachery that is moving within. God knew Adonijah's heart and his plot, and Solomon had perhaps knowledge from Heaven. He said, 'It would be as well for Adonijah to ask for the throne itself. I know what is in his heart. I know quite clearly and absolutely what Adonijah is after, and it is very unfortunate for him. Benaiah, on you go—kill him.'

This is the third of the sons of David to die violently. *The sword shall never depart from thine house.* 'You committed adultery with Bathsheba privately; your wives will be violated in the sight of all Israel. You have murdered and committed adultery; rape, murder and death will come into your house and never depart from it.'

Do you know this God? I imagine I hear some hearts saying, 'I don't want to know Him.' That is unfortunate.

If you don't know Him now, you will know Him as you stand in the eternal judgment, for this is a God of judgment as well as mercy. This is the God who walks with me. This is the God, full of great compassion, who heals the sick, baptizes in the Holy Ghost, casts out demons, brings the lost to salvation. He is the same God. My word to those of you who know Jesus Christ as Saviour and as Lord is quite blunt. I am telling you, you have a responsibility to live right. You may not be called to the throne as David was, but you are called to your own position, your own place in the living God, and you will give an account of every deed that is done in the body. It is time that the church was preaching contrition and repentance and holiness as loudly as she preaches salvation and forgiveness. Then might we have a holy church and a people who fear God. Did you think you would dance forgiven into Heaven having played the fool for years? I have eyes that see deeply, and just as they moved across this company they fell on one who shall be nameless who is playing the fool and has played the fool for quite a time, and probably thinks that all will be well. Indeed, no, it will not be so! There are people who will go through the portals of hell having thought, 'All will be well.' Without holiness no man shall see God—and let me emphasize this also. Nobody ever changes God. In so far as I misrepresent Him tonight, it will not change Him. In so far as any man delivers a soft message that is not wholly true, it in no way changes God. Take wrong advice from someone, and it will in no way change the truth of the living God. It will alter nothing in your favour. There is no escape from God. There is no alteration in the laws of God. With our God *there can be no variation, neither shadow cast by turning* (Jas 1:17).

Christ came to fulfil the law—and, you know, if there is greater severity than is seen in God's dealings with David, it is seen through Christ Himself. I think the greatest severity of all comes through Jesus. I have never fathomed

why people misunderstand Him. I have never been able to misunderstand Jesus. I find that His code, His laws, wound me, pierce me. I have never come to absolute terms with some of the commands of Jesus.

They are so high, so searching, so deep. Some of you have, I know, read my book *The Incomparable Christ*, and I recommend that those of you who have not at least borrow one and read the chapter on hell. It shows the awfulness of the teaching of Jesus, the severity of the Son of God. The soul that lands in hell is in it forever. There is no way out. There is no way through. There is no way over the gulf. The person who is in it is in eternal torment. *Send Lazarus*, said the rich man in torment,

> *that he may dip the tip of his finger in water and cool my tongue, for I am in anguish in this flame.... Son, remember that thou in thy lifetime receivedst thy good things, and Lazarus in like manner evil things: but now here he is comforted and thou art in anguish. And beside all this, between us and you there is a great gulf fixed* [fixed for all eternity] *so that they which would pass from hence to you may not be able, and that none may cross over from thence to us* (Lk 16:24–6).

'You are in an eternal agony. Son, remember!' There is memory in hell. Any of you who are here tonight, and land in it, may remember tonight. *Son, remember*—an eternal remembering in the midst of an eternal torment from which there is no escape through all endless ages. Who could teach such things? What manner of person could ever enunciate such a doctrine? The kindest, gentlest, most loving man who ever trod the roads of earth—who had compassion on the sinner, who healed the blind, who raised the dead, who fed the multitudes. The words are the words of Jesus the eternal Son of God.

'Lord Jesus, has God changed? Is the milk and water doctrine that we have been fed for years not true? Will you really see any of your creatures eternally lost?'

'My child, I cared so much, I loved so deeply that I died

on Calvary that it might never happen to any. But if in spite of Me, in spite of God, men carry on in their hell-bent way, they will find hell as their destination.'

And I saw a great white throne, and him that sat upon it from whose face the heaven and the earth fled away; and there was found no place for them. And I saw the dead, the great and the small, standing before the throne; and the books were opened: and another book was opened, which is the book of life: and the dead were judged out of the things which were written in the books, according to their works...And if any was not found written in the book of life, he was cast into the lake of fire (Rev 20:11–15)

—the lake that burns with fire forever. Thank God, there is a book of life. The God whom you meet in Revelation with His rebellious creatures going into eternal damnation, and the character of God, have not altered by a hairbreadth from Eden to the eternal glory. God is God, and in Him there is no shadow cast by turning. There is no wilfulness or unsanctification in the human heart, no desire for an easier way or a lower standard, that will by one iota alter the Lord God of Hosts.

PRAYER: *Lord our God, we understand in some measure now what is meant when it is said, 'It is a fearful thing to fall into the hands of the living God.' Lord, forgive us our sins, our backslidings—and, O God, we ask simply, make the consequences of our errors as light as Thou canst possibly do, lest we carry them as a load to the grave. Lord, we remember that thou didst revive David and make him fruitful and prosperous, but there were consequences that walked with him. Lord, our sermon tonight, Thou knowest, is not to cause despondency and despair. It is to warn Thy people to tread the road that is holy and walk no other road and never be influenced by a lie or a suggestion of that dark one, for his dupes forever eat the fruit of their folly, and there is no escape. Lord, our God, be with us now.*

God is wanting very deep commitment in the hearts of

men and women—to absolute holiness without reservation, that we may become men and women of God. It is very easy to choose what one may imagine to be the highest when it is really only a second best. There can be a 'footering'* about in the kingdom of God, not becoming a sharp instrument—a sharp threshing instrument having teeth. Sharp instruments are what God wants. Blessed be His Name.

* A colloquial Scots expression meaning 'playing, trifling, wasting time'.

PART 2

THE ROAD
TO FREEDOM

Introduction

It is hoped that the selection of themes taken in this section will give a flavour of the camp gathering at which most of the addresses were given. Later material has been added to round out chapter 15 and to bring the testimonies in chapters 16–18 up to date.

12

For and about the Very Young

I remember that Roy Barbour once said something at a camp that I found really very interesting. He had been listening to his little boy Stuart, probably about four years old at the time. I imagine that the family had arrived for the second week of camp. During the first week the Tweedie family had been there and Tristan was just about the same age as Stuart. Roy overheard an interesting conversation between the two and realized that while there may be many worlds, there are certainly two which are quite distinct: the world of the adult and the world of the four-year-old. There were the adults, gathering for a time of spiritual activity—a holy convocation. Roy found Stuart leaning out the caravan window, talking to Tristan. The conversation was about birds' wings, birds' feathers, the length of the last worm found, a dead rabbit's paw and a whole world in which youngsters of four are interested. It is a very, very different world from the world of adults. You know, the treasures of a small boy's pockets are really quite remarkable. I am sure that many of you will have read the story of Tom Sawyer often found in school readers: Tom had offended very badly, I don't now remember exactly how—he did it fairly regularly—but he had earned his aunt's strong disapproval and was ordered

to whitewash the palings around the yard as his punishment.

In carrying out his punishment Tom wasn't allowed to consort with these other evil boys with whom he was friendly, but he had to work on Saturday morning of all mornings, when they were at play. Imagine the indignity of it. His friends would be running past where he was working, and they'd say, 'Ha, ha, what have you got to do that for, Tom? Poor Tom. Saturday morning, too. I'd hate to have to do that, Tom.' They would know he was being punished.

The first of them came down and began to jibe at Tom. Tom said, 'Well, it depends on how you look at it. It's not every boy who's got the chance to put paint on like this.' The other boy saw the point. 'That's right enough! Tom, could I get a wee shot?'

'Ah, well—no ...no, this is a very important job I've been trusted with. It's not everybody who could do it. Aunt might not be pleased.' 'Oh, go on, Tom—give me a shot.' One by one the boys gathered and for a suitable consideration each was allowed a turn. Tom got every treasure out of the boys' pockets: an old apple core, a bit of string, a bit of this and a bit of that. He was able to sit back and see the whole task completed—the fence painted, I think, three times over. He got all the treasures out of their pockets and it didn't add up to tuppence.

So there you are. I am quite sure that some of you young folk have come here with one idea in the back of your minds, and I am sure you will have a lovely time, particularly if the weather holds. We'll let you go now to your own meeting and not take you into heavier water tonight.

13

A Plan for Every Life

Christ said regarding John the Baptist, *What went ye out for to see?* In other words, Why did you go? What was your purpose? I would like to ask a similar question tonight— why are you here? Why did you come? What is your purpose? And you might say quite honestly, 'I don't really have a deep settled purpose. I had heard about the camp, I had heard that other people had enjoyed it in time past,' and so on. 'I had heard all these things and I am interested but, to be honest, really quite casual.' There are others of you who might say, 'Well, God met me here before and I am here hoping that He will meet me again. I come to meet God.' You can examine your own heart and answer the question in your own deeps: 'Why am I here?'

I feel that a week at camp is almost like the outworking of a spiritual play. The various acts come across the stage and the whole becomes one play. At the outset I want to sketch the background: reflect on God, God's desire, God's purpose, what God is looking for and expecting throughout this week, what God is wanting in our every life. For God has a plan for every life; we are the actors on the stage, and as the week progresses God will do various things to us and we will respond in various ways. We will change from the condition in which we are into something

101

nearer to His heart, or we may harden and move further away from what He wants us to be. Yes, God has a plan for every life.

This is a basic truth, although you may not find it particularly easy to believe. You will probably find that deep down in your subconscious there is the feeling that life is really quite casual and much is very incidental. You can be fortunate or you can be unfortunate in your circumstances, and the word 'chance' looms large in your thinking. I don't find that the Bible teaches that at all. Indeed, the Bible teaches the reverse—that God has a distinct plan for every life born. Now if the devil can convince you that this is not true, he will win a major victory. If God convinces you that it *is* true—that God is interested in you and has a plan for your life—you will begin to change immediately. Hope and anticipation will begin to rise in you, along with joy, a looking forward to what God has for you, and to what He will do in you. Hope will spring up. *God has a plan.*

You may say, 'You will find it difficult to convince me of this. I am not at all sure that God has a plan.' I would like to take you first of all to things natural. Look at a work of art. We see in it a picture, a design. And of course if there is a design there must have been a designer. Before that painting ever appeared on canvas, it began its existence in the mind of an artist who with a paintbrush gave it visible form. The fact that it is there argues for a designer. Look at the skies on a dark night when the stars are shining against that dark background. There they twinkle in their splendour, vast in number, far more numerous than your eye will ever see. As you observe them in that great, rolling infinity, together with the sun and the moon and the growing trees, mountains, hills and rivers, and the life of mankind and all his environment with the animals and all living things, don't you know really deep down that there must be a beginner of things, a creator, a designer? I

would find it much harder not to believe this than to believe it.

I came through a time in my own life, in my early teenage years, of deep doubt concerning much that I had been taught about the Bible. I was disturbed by the theory of evolution. I questioned much about human existence. It was an honest search, and it led me to the conclusion that it would be far, far more difficult not to believe in God than to believe in Him. There is an illustration I some-times use in this connection which I use again for the sake of those of you who may not have heard or read of it. A Christian astronomer was being troubled by fellow scien-tists, particularly one who was an atheist. Knowing that his atheist friend was very interested in astronomy, the Christian deliberately left a solarium lying on a table where the other would be sure to find it. A beautifully con-structed piece of work, it showed the planets going round the sun in their regular courses. In due time the atheist came in and asked him where it had come from. He was given no answer at first, but he persisted: 'Where did this come from? Who made it?' Ultimately the Christian replied, 'It didn't come from anywhere and nobody made it.' The atheist lost his temper, shouting, 'It must have come from somewhere. Somebody must have made it.' The Christian then took him to the door and, pointing to the heavens, said, 'Now listen: you have been shouting in my ear for a long time that "nobody made" this. It didn't come from anywhere—those planets in their courses around the sun, the vast mystery of the heavenly bodies. You went on declaring that the universe didn't come by design from anywhere; nobody made it. It was all chance, fortuitous circumstance. Yet for that little toy on the table in there you can't accept the possibility of any such rub-bish.'

I don't recollect the next stage of events, but I reckon that enough had been said to conclude the argument. I pondered these issues in my own early days, and now

recall much of my confusion and ultimate faith. I remember rejoicing in some of the writings of Aldous Huxley, who said (as best I recollect), 'If the theory of evolution is true, it means that somewhere in the infinitely remote past there was found floating on the primeval sea of ooze a single cell of protoplasm, coming from they [i.e., the evolutionists] know not where, they know not how.' In my imagination I stood with the steam of the swamp rising all around me, and saw the floating sea of primeval ooze. I didn't see the invisible cell of protoplasm, but I looked for it. I reasoned with myself: Do I really believe that if a man had stood there, knowing that he would live for millenia, he could believe that one day there would evolve from that one cell a living mate suitable for him to marry? You know, I just didn't believe it. I didn't believe it for one moment. Now there is no point in you saying I didn't want to believe it. Even if I had wanted to, I couldn't have done it. I hadn't enough faith to believe a thing like that. It seemed to me totally preposterous and it still seems to me totally preposterous. I find it much easier to believe that in the beginning was God and that God was the creator. Our entire surroundings argue for the proposition, '*In the beginning, God.*' And there is nothing illogical or unreasonable in believing that.

Now we move a little onwards: from the evidence of the design that you can see all around you, arguing for a designer, to the realization of your own smallness and the feeling of your own insignificance. This was one of my other difficulties in early days. How could the God who created the rolling spheres, who hung the stars in space, be concerned for me? Consider the vastness of the universe: we have seen over half as far into space as we ever will see, because even with more powerful telescopes we will reach a point at which the stars are receding from us at a speed equal to the speed of light. When we stand and think about the possible boundaries of space, infinity of space, infinity of time, we may well say, *What is man, that thou art*

mindful of him? (Ps 8:4). Suddenly we realize that we are as very small specks of dust in the balance. How can God possibly be interested in me? That kind of consideration worried me for a time, but I was fortunate enough to take botany as one of my science subjects in school, and in the study of botany there is quite a lot of work with transverse sections of plants. You take a very fine transverse section of a stem, a root, a leaf, and so on, and when you put these sections under the microscope they show up wonderfully: they are absolutely perfect. If, on the other hand, you were to put any part of this desk that I am perched upon under the microscope, you would see that at every man-made joint there is a roughness, a gaping irregularity, an unevenness. Increase the magnification and it looks worse. Take anything that God has created, and it is perfect under the microscope. Increase the magnification, and the perfection almost seems to deepen. Everything that He does is perfect. As we examine His work we realize the care He takes with His smallest creation. Every fingerprint is different and each perfect. No two blades of grass in all the universe are the same, but they all reflect perfect workmanship. He is the God of infinity! His work with the very small is as perfect as His work with the very great. As we realize that matter is inert and the whole vast universe is inanimate while man is alive and sentient, distinguished from other living creatures by his spirituality, intelligence, imagination and faculty of speech, it is not difficult to understand man's comparative importance. We are more important than all the inanimate natural things that are around us. We are alive, and livingness and spirituality and intelligence are of tremendous significance.

As we study the Bible, we realize that these things are of great significance to God. While He has made the galaxies, He has also made the tiniest blade of grass. He made man, and there is a difference between man and the rest of creation. The Bible shows us that man was made in the image of God Himself, and is special to God. He is not *just*

a star, he is not *just* a plant, he is a living soul, and he has in him something of the very life of God. God breathed into Adam the breath of life and man became a living soul. Man is unique—peculiarly important and peculiarly precious to God. And if that is true—and I cannot see how we can logically escape this conclusion—it follows that God who has ordered His universe will have a plan for our every life. By His drawing power we find Christ as Saviour, and Christ baptizes us in the Holy Spirit. I cannot believe for a moment that the God who does this is not interested in every further step of our way. To sum up, if God had a plan for the universe and a plan for earth life and earth creatures, He has a plan for you and He has a plan for me. It makes a tremendous difference to us to realize the truth of this.

One or two things immediately follow. If God has a plan for me, it is unwise of me to go out and live carelessly or casually, not worrying which way the wave takes me— Godward or manward, Heavenward or hellward, like flotsam or jetsam on the river of life. If God has a plan for me, it seems that the first logical thing for me to do is find out what that plan is, in so far as He is minded to reveal it. And again, if I may apply logic: in human affairs if the master of a firm has a plan, he will communicate it. It is essential for him to do this and for his workers to know the parts of the plan which apply to them. Details are revealed to everybody who needs to know them. There is no point in having a master plan in an architect's office if the plan is not communicated to the various people who need to have it to put the work into operation. While the plans are not posted for every Tom, Dick and Harry to see, they find their way into the hands of people who require to know them.

Now it is ridiculous to think of God concealing His plan when it is necessary for an individual to know it at least in part. Thus you can positively expect God to reveal His plan for your life in so far as you need to know it. You may

say, 'How will I find that plan? Where is the blueprint kept?' The careless teacher may immediately say, 'The plan is in the Bible,' and leave it at that. In your search, as likely as not you will end up at Leviticus, where for some reason many people who are just taking a dip in the Bible do land up—or alternatively in endless lists of genealogy—and you may say, 'I don't see much plan here.' You may read a lot of the Bible and not see a clear plan. I have to be much more specific than just say, 'Read the Bible.' God is our teacher; the Holy Spirit is the one who guides us into all truth.

One day there was an Ethiopian eunuch riding in his chariot and reading from the prophet Isaiah (Acts 8). God spoke to Philip and told him to join that chariot. Philip said to the man, *Understandest thou what thou readest?* And he said, *How can I, except some one shall guide me?* He was reading the Bible, all right, but he could not understand what he read. He needed to have it explained to him. Philip began to preach Christ from the Scriptures the eunuch had been reading.

In giving advice, I don't just say, 'Read the Bible and you will find God's plan for your life.' There are very many people who read the Bible very regularly and they don't necessarily find God's plan for their lives. If you obey the Bible and find Christ as your Saviour, and allow a relationship of love to develop between your soul and Him, you will learn to know His voice and will find that He speaks to you. There are some of you to whom He does not speak, for the very simple reason that when He spoke in the past you did not do what He told you, and He withdrew Himself and speaks no more: it is just as simple as that. Normally no soul to whom Christ speaks ceases to hear His voice except through disobedience. If you once knew that voice and you know it no more, get your life sorted out. Christ delights to speak to His people and He speaks to His youngest converts. Indeed, He speaks perhaps most clearly to young converts.

We of course tell new converts how to live their lives, and we give them a whole set of rules and regulations, and soon they listen to us and stop hearing the voice of God. Never let anybody choke out the voice of God in your life. Listen to good advice, but never let anyone get between you and Christ. He speaks to you, and He wants to speak directly to His own children. He speaks very gently; He does not always sound trumpets, nor does He always write in letters of fire, but very, very gently He drops into your consciousness the knowledge of what He wants you to know. And as you obey Him, light tends to brighten and your spiritual life deepens. He leads you from stage to stage, and He reveals His plan. You may be reading the Bible and suddenly find it speaks to you. Now there is a distinction between what is known as the general word of God and the *rhēma*, which is particular. The word of God may suddenly become alive to you in particular, by the power of the Spirit, and be applied to your life or to the lives of others. This is the *rhēma*.

In this connection I remember one wonderful experience in the island of Harris. I was due to preach in a house meeting, and as I read a particular portion of Scripture it was as though a star of light fell on the verse that God wanted me to speak from. This has never happened again. I remember the verse to this day: *As we have borne the image of the earthy, we shall also bear the image of the heavenly* (1 Cor 15:49). It is a glorious verse. Again and again God speaks specifically, you know the portion He indicates, you don't argue about it, you don't wonder if it may be this or that or the other—it is the word of the Lord, and you recognize it. Now you may say, 'I'm not hearing His voice like that.'

Dare I give an old illustration that I use many times? My illustrations often come from country life because of my early days there. You sometimes find a man out working in a field with a companion in an adjoining field. John might shout, 'Hey, Jimmy!' and Jimmy doesn't respond

because he doesn't hear. John goes nearer and gives another yell. Jimmy turns and says, 'I can't hear what you're saying.' John shouts, 'Come a bit nearer, then, and you'll hear me clearly.' Jimmy trudges over and has to get close to John to hear what he is saying. He is not going to hear half a mile away. He will only hear the sound of a voice, but not know what is being said.

It is like that with God. You may come into a good meeting like this and sense His presence. In a general way you may hear the voice of God, but your spirit is not near enough to Him to hear a particular word to you to come closer. He has a plan for your life and He desires to communicate that plan to you. Part of you may not really want to know that plan, because from the moment you know it you come under obligation to obey it. If you don't know it, you may feel you have an excuse and so you may not jump to know the plan. He might say 'no' to things you want to have or to do. He might give directions that you are not too keen to hear. You may deliberately hold back from knowing the plan of God. How foolish! Realize that you can never improve on this plan. No road in life you ever take will bring greater happiness than the road which follows His plan. There has to come a time of deep breaking inside—a breaking to God, a taking of Him in a deep sense as Lord, which you should really have done in the moment of salvation—a real bending to the will of God.

On one side the Holy Spirit is there to guide into all truth. But never forget, on the other side there is an evil and dark enemy who is not minded that you should ever know God's plan—Satan himself. You will find that he will obstruct you in many ways; he sometimes tries to prevent you getting to a critical meeting or to a significant camp. He throws up all kinds of obstacles and insinuates why the right way won't work out and why you would be much better, for example, to take another way. There are many things the devil is capable of putting in your path. I

suggest you deal with him as follows. Say, 'Look, I'll never find the plan of God through you: you are a liar from the beginning. What have you to do with the matter? Get out of my way. *Get thee behind me, Satan.* If I am ever to know the plan of God, I've got to hear from Christ. I've got to get close to Him. Get out of my way, Satan. Oh, I know you have a plan for my life, and I know that in so far as I've followed your plan it has been hell on earth. Oh, yes, I was told that drugs were wonderful—give you a great thrill; they nearly put me in hell. You told me that alcohol was a way out of stress and strain, and it brought greater stress and strain than I ever knew before I got hooked on it. Every situation that you've advised me in, Satan, has brought hell. *Get thee behind me.* I was fascinated with sex and I knew that what you were suggesting wasn't right, but it seemed so nice, and it was hell—I felt hell on my spirit. Everything you ever give me brings hell to me. I'm having no more of it, Satan. Stand clear—I want Christ.'

'If you have Christ, you are going to lose this and lose that, and you will have to do this and do that.'

You will never lose a thing that it will not be for your eternal good to be without, and you will never be asked to do anything that won't bring you ultimate joy and happiness. God is wonderfully just and benevolent. You will get absolute justice together with mercy. He will take you by the hand and He will begin to show you His eternal plan.

14

Observations on Deliverance

Oh that thou wouldest rend the heavens, that thou wouldest come down, that the mountains might flow down at thy presence; As when fire kindleth the brushwood, and the fire causeth the waters to boil: to make thy name known to thine adversaries, that the nations may tremble at thy presence! When thou didst terrible things which we looked not for, thou camest down, the mountains flowed down at thy presence. For from of old men have not heard, nor perceived by the ear, neither hath the eye seen a God beside thee, which worketh for him that waiteth for him (Is 64:1–44).

People have many different conceptions of revival, and there is one aspect which seems to be very quickly forgotten: the awfulness, the fearfulness, of the coming of God. *Oh that thou wouldest rend the heavens, that thou wouldest come down!*—we may say this in a very sanctimonious voice and very fervently pray that the mountains might flow down at God's presence, not realizing that the very first mountain that may flow will be a mountain that is in us, that separates us from God. When He comes, it is as when fire kindles the brushwood or causes the water to boil, and we have that inner feeling of awful boiling up. One of the most awesome things that we ever experience is the deep probing of God: *terrible things which we looked not for.*

111

I had thought to speak on principles from the life of David in the morning sessions of camp, but after Miss Black spoke last night I felt very clearly that I should take a very different theme today. I believe there would be many people here last night to whom the message that Mary brought would be very wonderful but also very awe-inspiring—and it would stir depths that they had not been aware of previously. I want to continue the theme this morning and give some explanation about various aspects of what I'll call deliverance.

Rather than preach too formally, I want to chat to you and share some of the things I have learned over the years both from reading and from experience, to make this whole subject perhaps a little more understandable than it sometimes is. Many of you come from evangelical backgrounds of one kind or other. Some have no church background, and with parts of the New Testament you may not be familiar. You may not have noticed, for example, that a great part of the ministry of Christ was connected with the exorcism of demons. We find that He would go into an area and the demons would cry out and would eventually be cast out. They couldn't stand the presence of the Holy One. They found that presence unendurable. We read again and again that He cast them out, and if you are an observant reader, you may ask, 'Why don't we see more of that today? Does it mean that there aren't any demons troubling people now? How does a demon get into a person?' and many more questions about the involvement of demons in the lives of men.

I want to start far back. The first conceptions that I would bring to you relate to our desperate ignorance of what God sees as our ultimate condition; what we were in the beginning when Adam was perfect; what God's plan for a human being was. You know that *God created man in His own image, in the image of God created He him* (Gen 1:27). God dwells *in light unapproachable, whom no man hath seen, nor can see* (1 Tim 6:16). He made man in that

perfect image—in the image of God. I believe that man was originally covered with light as with a garment. When Adam sinned and became naked and 'knew' that he was naked, he was in fact naked for the first time, because never before had he been without that glorious garment of light. He had been dwelling in light, living in light, moving in light. When man fell, how great was the fall! How deep and how awful the consequences!

When we view man strutting across the stage of life in our day, we may have that odd foolish attitude that this is all life is: that life as we know it is normal: that the general standard is the norm, when in fact it is not the norm at all. We step on to the stage as fallen creatures. Humanity is not in a normal condition from God's point of view, but is largely covered with darkness. *The whole world lieth in the evil one* (1 Jn 5:19). Satan is the prince of the air and we are, in the language of C.S. Lewis, denizens of a besieged planet. We are born into darkness and live in a dark kingdom, but we do have a measure of light, and we may mistake this half-light for full illumination. We see in a glass darkly. We may think that we see clearly when actually we are only having glimpses of the eternal— occasional glimpses of the glory that lies ahead. Perhaps none of us in this gathering today has a true conception of what God's norm for us is—because we live so deeply in a subnormal condition. I think it is necessary to understand this at the beginning of our study, for we tend to judge spontaneously that the position we are in is normal and that our condition and viewpoint are normal. If we study the Bible aright we will be disabused of these ideas.

God looks down on us in our present century. He sees us as we are in our various spiritual states. Sometimes He will see smugness, self-confidence and contentment, and a casual type of attitude. He will see some who have plunged through inborn barriers into deep darkness and are in a fearful condition, being led of the devil. He will see some with aspirations to holiness who have been reaching

upward into the glory land. He will see us in a whole set of different conditions—in different positions relative to Himself and to holiness. Now He is minded to bring us into the perfection of light; He is minded to bring us into deep contact with Himself, where we are like Christ, where we are holy, and from where we emanate holiness and light—light and holiness flowing out of His people as a body and as individuals—flowing out of you and flowing out of me.

I want you now to imagine a proficient dentist at work. He opens the door and brings in his first patient. He is quite shocked at the state of the teeth, shocked that any-one would let teeth get into that condition—it's almost a personal matter with some dentists. He then treats his first case and takes in the rest of the patients one by one and finds that they are all in different conditions. He sets about sorting all that needs sorting. If we take a doctor as our example, we will find that he too examines his patient thoroughly for general health. If he realizes there is some-thing wrong in various parts of the body, he will set about putting these things right.

Every patient is different, and it is exactly like that in your spiritual life and mine today. God looks down not simply to condemn, to list our sins and taunt us with them. Rather, He looks down and says, 'Because that sin or impediment is there you are not able to develop in the way you could. We'll need to get rid of that—and that—and that.' While He condemns sin and convicts us of it, His action is always in love; but even so, it is not every-body who enjoys the prospect of a spiritual operation any more than he or she enjoys the prospect of going to the dentist. The fact that the dental operation is for one's own good and that the dentist is acting with deep care and concern does not wholly alter the case.

I know of one young lady present who has to have really bad toothache before she visits her dentist. The pain has to be worse than the pain she associates with the dentist. The

consideration of how much a filling or extraction will hurt outweighs her knowledge that her dentist is a kind and caring person. With spiritual issues, we may know theoretically that God loves us and wants to set us free—but will the setting free hurt? That fear may be deep down in our consciousness and cause us to run from God. Some people have been known to ring the bell of the dentist's surgery and then literally run away. They get so near and then they think about it . . . and they turn and run.

Do you know, that is one of the signs I welcome in a conference or a meeting—when people rise and run. I remember one gathering where at an early stage the hostess rose and ran right out of the house—followed by her mother-in-law. They were both terrified. In due time both were delivered. They ran away because they were being probed. Spiritual disease was being uncovered; they realized the position but were afraid at first to face it. They ran away: and that was in a sense a good sign. It was a sign of life, of conviction. I am much more concerned when a person is really in great need and does not care, more or less adopting the attitude, 'Well, I'm like this and I'll die like this and you can bury me where I fall.' There is no spark of life. If they are running, at least you may catch them and persuade them to face up to things.

Now I may say to those of you who fear the dentist's chair: 'I know your dentist, he is a kind man and will treat you with great care, and when your extractions are all over, life will be wonderful. You'll have no more toothache at night and no more problems.' One can picture a person weighing it up. I personally used to have toothache every day in life. I had a fearful time as a boy. The dentist said I was too young to have certain of my teeth removed: it could have affected the shape of my jaw, and he did not want to do that to me. As a result, for years I had toothache almost every day. It used to come about four o'clock each day (I don't know why it came at that time), and it was awful. My memory is of this continuing year after year

after year. What a difference it would have made to life if I could have got rid of the pain! You will find that when a person has had serious pain ended by an operation he has no regrets that he went through with it. I would have loved to have had my teeth extracted.

Last night you were not only hearing a preacher, but the Holy Spirit was probing, and I sensed the incoming of God. Now when God comes in, the preacher does not need to indicate every separate sin and weakness. The Holy Spirit brings to our attention sins and issues that lie between ourselves and God. I am a great believer in leaving the Holy Spirit to do His own work. Were you to lay your life bare before me and ask what you should do, I might just not know. There are times when a sin is totally put away and God does not ask you to do another thing about it. There are times when the Holy Spirit will insist on restitution and a putting right of things that have been wrong. God knows in every life exactly what He wants that person to do. He comes over a gathering as He did last night and would reveal to you what He desires. We are forever wanting to have other humans outline courses of action for us. Get to a stage where you ask God to show you the way. If I tried to do this I might make things far rougher than God would make them. I might, on the other hand, make things far softer, and if I made a mistake in my diagnosis and prescription, that would not help you at all because you would still have God to face. My mistake would not change God's law. If I said, 'That's all right, friend, you can do that—there is nothing wrong with it,' and the Holy Spirit was forbidding you to do the thing, you might say, 'Mr Black said it; it must be all right.' Can I imagine God say, 'Who is Mr Black? and what has Mr Black's opinion or statement got to do with it? *I* am saying . . .' You see, no man may take God's place—so never put man in His place. While you may look to leaders for help, look to God ultimately for direction. At the end of the day it is His word that counts, not my word. It is the word of

the living God. If you find a bad teacher and a bad instructor who gives you bad advice, that will never cancel out the word of the living God in your deepest heart. There is no way of evading the divine, and it is the divine that you meet at the end of the day. It is to God that you are ultimately responsible.

Take Willie and Annukka, who just catch my eye as I am looking in their direction. I could say, 'Now, Willie, I don't really think you two should go to the mission field.' Does that make any difference to the will of God? If God calls these two to the mission field, who shall gainsay it? If Willie says, 'You're confusing me now. I'll go and speak to Mr X, who is particularly interested in mission work,' and if Mr X too says, 'No, I don't think you should go,' does that cancel the call of God? Many people said that to C.T. Studd—including the committee which had been formed for the express purpose of sending him out, but which wilted at a medical report. He got rid of them all: he said that he would have no more committees—he would take for his committee the Father, the Son and the Holy Spirit. He didn't want to have any more to do with doctors who forbade him to go to Africa or committees who accepted their views. Away he sailed blithely to evangelize a world because he heard the call of the living God. I am not saying that we should not defer to and take counsel of godly people. We should. We should all do that. We should listen carefully to the voice of others who are called of God, lest we be out on a foolish line of our own, but at the end of the day God is God and God is to be obeyed.

Now back to the dentist's or doctor's surgery. Realize that none of us is perfect, and some of us are less perfect than others—I don't mean in essential being but in having these matters dealt with by God. What has your response been? Are you quite happy to have God carry out a diagnosis—quite happy to say, 'Yes, Lord, I'd like to come into Your surgery. I'd like a complete spiritual examination of my condition. I want You to deal with all the

things that rankle from the past and all my present attitudes. I am willing to have everything laid out before You, and as you diagnose I will do exactly what You want me to do'?

I have found another interesting thing. Have you ever been annoyed with your doctor? You go in, and he may sort of casually say, 'Well, what's the trouble?' You proceed to give him a life story—and the discourteous man cuts you short. He is not prepared to listen to a review of the last ten years. You tell him ultimately where the pain is and how long you have had it, and he looks at you with mildly contemptuous eyes and you know that he's not fully believing you...and you just sort of stop talking when you realize it is not getting through. You then criticize him in your heart and say, 'Surely I should know what's wrong with me better than anyone else.' He doesn't believe that either. He doesn't think you really know very much about what's wrong with you, and he proceeds to examine you and make his own diagnosis of your condition and also provide you with a remedy. No doubt, with experience doctors know that lay people talk quite a lot of rubbish. You tell your dentist which tooth is causing you pain, and sometimes he tells you that it is not coming from that tooth at all, but from another tooth. You think, 'That's ridiculous,' but in fact he is right. He knows more about your teeth than you do. The doctor makes his diagnosis based on symptoms of which you may not be aware and he provides his remedy—you know, they're quite shrewd, are doctors.

In my school-days I took an infection on my cheek and went to our family doctor. 'Ah,' he said, 'ringworm.' And he prescribed medicine for me. Now I didn't believe it was ringworm. While I lived on a farm where ringworm was easily picked up, I had reasons for believing it was not ringworm. So I came out of that surgery and went a hundred yards further along the street to where I saw another doctor's plate. I went in and asked if he had any

idea what my trouble might be. I said, 'Do you think it might be ringworm?' 'Oh no, it's not ringworm,' he said. 'There's a simple test for ringworm. If I pull that hair (in the middle of the affected part) it will come out.' He pulled, and it didn't! 'No,' he said, 'I'm not sure what this is, but I'll look up the book'—a real honest doctor—and he literally looked up a book in front of me and said, 'It's impetigo.' He wrote out a prescription and, lo and behold, both prescriptions were the same. The first doctor, I think, realized before I was out of his surgery that it wasn't ringworm, but he wasn't telling that to a boy after committing himself at the beginning. He kept it to himself. (It is possible, of course, that the same ointment could have been prescribed for both conditions.)

You will find that doctors have very definite ideas, and you are not always sure whether they are right or not, but when it comes to the heavenly physician, He is *never* wrong. His diagnoses are always absolutely accurate. He knows about you altogether, and when He examines He knows exactly what is needed. He may see that living inside people there are a whole lot of interlopers, entities that ought not to be there. It reminds me of Paul and Susie's 'country mansion' up in the corner of the estate (really a very primitive shack!). There are others living in that house who are not supposed to be there—they are referred to as 'our furry friends': lots of lovely little mice. They were never invited in. They are there and they shouldn't be there. Now they are comparatively pleasant little creatures, but if the uninvited guests had been rats that would have been somewhat different, and had we been living in a foreign land and it had been snakes of a poisonous variety, that would have been much more serious. That house would have been a dangerous place—really a horrible place.

It is obvious as we read the New Testament and examine our own experiences that there are people whose bodies are holding not only the spirit and the soul of the

individual but entities that ought never to have been there, demons: just as simple as that. We read that from one individual a whole legion of demons was cast out by Christ; in another case a man was so fierce and violent that people attempted to chain him, but he burst the chains and dwelt in desolate places—a fearsome man, violent, awful—wicked, with powerful evil operating within him.

You find in Christ's ministry that He is continually meeting demon-possessed people. Now those of you who are observant and thoughtful may well be asking, 'How do these entities ever get into the body of a man or woman?' I have always found this a fascinating matter. I believe people have guardian angels; Scripture teaches it. In a more general sense, if you look back on your own life I think you too may find that there has been a guard which you instinctively know it is dangerous to breach. Perhaps at a fairly early stage you wilfully broke through that guard. You went through a barrier that you maybe only vaguely knew was there—a barrier of light. You did something that was wrong and you knew it to be wrong, and in a strange way things were never quite the same for you again. You destroyed something. The crisis does not come with a trumpet blaring. You are not warned in that way. In my own case I was in primary school and was being harshly treated by a very cruel teacher (who I now think was really quite unwell). We were all treated similarly. I was in no way singled out for personal victimization. I was belted daily. This was standard for poor spelling, and my spelling was very poor. It never seemed to occur to me to do my homework; I just endured my daily punishment. I began, however, to change inside. I became aggressive at home. I found that if I didn't just *pretend* to kick but *actually* kicked it was much more effective. I took the law into my own hands in many things. I was aware of a hardening inside. Real hardness came in—and I never got back to what I would call childlike innocency until I found Christ. Then the hardness went. I had gone through a

barrier that I ought never to have broken. When a person is treated brutally he can become brutal.

I am sure that many people break through barriers that are there for their protection—and barriers can be broken in many ways. Alcoholism can do it. A psychiatrist who himself had a very deep out-of-body experience has described how he saw the entrance of a spirit into a young man who got deliberately drunk in a pub. The man had opened himself. The guard was down and the demon got in.[1]

Where you break any of the moral rules you are in danger of being affected. Alcoholism is an obvious one, smoking is another, drug addiction, unbridled lust, inordinate anger, resentment and hatred are all highways to the entry of dark powers. People become bound in their condition. Obsession passes to possession and suddenly people realize they are not free. They cannot do what they want to do. They are controlled by their weakness and addiction. They are bound. At first they may feel lightly held, but then the chains tighten until in many cases they are in absolute bondage. There are many, many people whom we deal with who cannot break their bondages. It is not normal in some Christian circles today to speak very much about this—it is not popular teaching. Some things drop out of Christian vocabulary, the further away from revival we get: things like conviction of sin, eternal punishment. We don't like to speak too much about sin. We speak of deviation and lack of balance and use many other euphemisms. Talk of demons is not at all acceptable to many religious leaders. I remember once I was dealing with a university professor in my early days. He had no time for the doctrine of hell. He could not stand it, and he thought he had trouble enough in presenting his subject without bringing in the idea of a devil. What we teach is not popular. It is derived directly from the Bible and from experience. There are demons—literal entities with intelligence within the bodies of people, within the bodies of

non-Christians, within the bodies of Christians—yes—
and within the bodies of Pentecostal Christians—oh, yes.
What an awful conception! Many people want to shut this
out of the door, but it is in the door. Scripture confirms
that evil powers come into the bodies of men and women.

I love to think of God being present as the various cases
come for ministry. I love to stand, as it were, with God;
He views the bad cases as well as the not-so-bad cases. My
human reaction might be, 'Oh, no, I can't face this. There
is no hope here!' Think of God for a moment. I see Christ
with a lovely smile on His face and the light of victory in
His eyes and the glory of God in His countenance. A bad
case?—a bad case to the Lion of the Tribe of Judah? 'I
came into the world for such. I came into the world for the
bad cases.' There are no hopeless cases with Christ. We
look from our vantage point and say, 'Oh, dear, no,' and
Christ regards the situation so differently. He came into
the world to save sinners. He came into the world to
deliver from the power of darkness, from the power of
hell. He came into the world to destroy the works of the
devil.

So you go dancing into the fight. You do not go with the
attitude, 'O God—I'm in a terrible state, and how will we
ever get through this?' You go dancing in with a sword in
your hand. It is lovely to see Christ smite the enemy, and
we now see it regularly: almost every week, and sometimes
frequently in one week. Yes, Christ sets people free. He
came for that purpose. When we are called of God into this
side of ministry we know beyond doubt that this is what
Christ came for. Christ wants people to be totally delivered. He wants you to be totally delivered. You say, 'It's
not a bad case with me. I don't think there are demons
controlling me at deep levels at all. I just feel as though
I've got a skelf* in my finger.' Well, for preference I'd
rather have the skelf out of my finger than in it, because
you know what it's like at night—it's just that bit of your
finger that touches the blanket and upsets you very badly.

Why go to bed with a skelf in your finger? You are better to get it out. You sleep far better that way. Now we find that from comparatively small things, such as fear of mice, spiders, snakes, etc., people can be set free very readily. I am not confusing phobias with rational fears. The person, for example, who has a crocodile for a pet is a fool and if I was in his house I would be afraid. This would not be an irrational fear. It would be a perfectly normal fear, quite different from irrational phobias.

To come directly to you—what about these dreams that disturb you by night, these nightmares that recur? Sometimes you have pushed things that were too horrible to face, away deep down into your subconscious. Nature has a way of doing that—of burying disagreeable things. Sometimes people have covered over horrors of a lifetime, until they come to Christ and these horrors come to the surface: that is because God wants to take them away. He wants to clean out from the very bottom. Most of us will cover a thing over, in the sense that if it is not causing trouble we ignore it. But when it troubles us we have to deal with it. Now the Holy Spirit knows the things that trouble us at conscious levels, and if the roots are away down in the subconscious He does not cover that over, but goes right down there to take out the roots and also removes the trouble at the conscious level. It is a very wonderful thing that God does in this. I want you to treat this subject as a glorious subject, not painful or distasteful, but something wonderful: 'Whereas I was blind, now I see. Whereas I was demon-driven, now I am driven of God and the evil power has no more hold over me at all.'

I know very well that last night many of you would be deeply concerned about your condition, and my message to you is quite simple. I have told you facts. It is true that people have demons, and that while sometimes possession is very deep and exorcism very sensational, in many cases

---

* Scots word meaning 'splinter'.

this is not so and deliverance takes place easily. You heard last night that you can be set free just where you sit without individual ministry: that is very true. I remember reading of one case in particular. One group of Christians, not long saved, had demon trouble amongst them (as I may say is normal in Christian groups. You say, 'Do you mean that?' Yes, I actually do. In the majority of Christian groups there is a great deal of demon trouble that has to be dealt with, and in many cases it is never dealt with at any time). But there came into that company one or two men who had deliverance ministry, and even as one of them preached, suddenly there came from across the congregation just a series of coughs, and many people were set free. Entities came out quickly and easily. Sometimes it is no more than a sigh as the entity passes out. Sometimes there is no outward sign of it at all. Sometimes, on the other hand, if the possession is deep a person may crash to the floor and there can be quite a scene before he or she is set free.

Now Christ came to set you free, to deliver you into glory—and I want to pause at this point. In spiritual life there are gradations downward, hellward, and there are gradations upward, skyward, gloryward. When you experience deliverance you are left in a neutral position. God wants the space then to be filled with the Holy Spirit. As you aspire after righteousness you may find that there is more silt that comes to the surface. There are things which may not be touched until you go through into the bright light where no dark power has any sway over you at all, until the wicked one no longer has anything in you.

I want us to see ourselves as a company of people at various stages in the spiritual heavenly adventure, and to come up higher and to bring the things that cause us trouble—jealousy, role-seeking, position-seeking, ill feelings one toward another within or outwith the company, pride, our reaction to being caught in a fault—everything that is un-Christlike in our nature: our every selfishness,

our every self-centredness, our every laziness—just every-thing that we know instinctively is not like Jesus Christ. Open your life as a book. Say to the Doctor, 'Here I am. This is all I know about myself. Now you can test me as you like and please prescribe the cure.' When he lays you on the operating table, go gladly. You will come off it better than you go on. Don't be afraid, because the hand that holds the knife is the hand of the heavenly physician; just relax in God and ask Him to sort you. It is as simple as that.

Now that is not a comprehensive study of the subject of deliverance—but rather an introduction, and I want to leave space for contributions on the subject from Mrs Grace Gault, Mrs Diana Rutherford and Mrs Susan Sharkey, who are used in this ministry.

Note

1 George G. Ritchie with Elizabeth Sherrill, *Return from Tomorrow* (Fleming H. Revell Company; original publisher Chosen Books Publishing Co., Ltd., 1978), pp. 59–61.

15

Observations of Practitioners

Grace

Looking back over the years, I realize that there was an inner preparation for the ministry of deliverance. I did not analyse it at the time; it is in retrospect that I can see it. I grew up in the church, and sometimes in our very early days there would come someone into our midst who was very obviously in need of deliverance. The ministry was almost unknown, as far as I am aware, in Christian circles at that time. There was always a power in our midst to prevent such a person dominating: they were always contained, they were subject. But my impression is that deliverance ministry was not particularly in operation, and though I was very young, I was aware of a need in that area. I can remember when many years ago the ministry began to come into operation very powerfully through Mr Black and Miss Taylor. It was tremendous to know then that that was there—it brought a feeling of great security. But as the years went by, I became quite anxious. I thought, 'What will happen if they pass on before Christ comes? What will happen to that ministry? There will still be people in need.' I can remember often praying that God would give ministries of exorcism. I don't ever remember praying during that time for the ministry for myself, but I

was very aware of the church's need for it. At the same time the thought of actually being used in that ministry seemed a million miles away from most of us—at least from me; I don't know how other people felt. It seemed something really to be quite scared of. Sometimes in our earlier days there would be an eruption in the middle of a service and the deliverance would take place right in the midst of the gathering. I think the normal reaction was one of fear. We just held a very tight grip on God and concentrated our minds as much as we could on Him, until the incident was past and covered.

Then a change came. I can distinctly remember the night when I realized that it had happened for me. It was many years ago, and it was not until quite recently that I connected it with an occasion when Miss Taylor had prayed with me. She used words that were prophetic regarding that ministry, and it was some time afterwards that the incident happened. Somebody in the middle of a meeting was delivered, and I wasn't the least bit afraid; I was absolutely in exultation. I could feel Christ in action, the Christ whom we love so much, who is so gentle, who is so tender, who is the Lamb of God—but who, when moving against the powers of darkness in setting free His child, is the Lion of the tribe of Judah. And I knew, I could feel, that He went down into the realms of darkness against darkness, and against iniquity He is the Lion. But He is the Lion for us, not against us, if we are walking with Him. For us He is that beautiful, tender Lamb of God. And I can remember I just felt such a pride in Christ. There was a longing inside that I would see Him like that—that I would actually see that ministry in operation, I suppose, through myself, because I wanted to see Christ like that. I don't know if that was very selfish, but I longed to see Him like that. I had seen Him—He had revealed Himself to me in other ways, but I longed for that revelation in a more personal way.

Time passed, and I sometimes resigned myself, thinking, 'Well, I'll see Him like that in eternity, if I don't see Him now.' Then God really began to speak to me about it. Through *Daily Light* the verse came three times: *This is the confidence that we have in him, that if we ask anything according to his will, he heareth us* (1 Jn 5:14). I had not said anything about it to anyone, when my father Mr Black asked me one night if I wanted to be involved. From that time the ministry gradually began to come into operation, perhaps over the course of a year. And then one night when Diana and I were praying with somebody at an August camp, it came very much more fully and completely. That night I saw Him the way I had longed to see Him. I saw that Lamb of God. I couldn't sleep all night, because I was in the presence of the Lamb of God. There was an absolute thrill and joy and wonder: I just could not sleep; I was so alive in God, because I had seen a person in deep need, to whom the Lamb of God came. I have noticed again and again that this can happen at a critical point, maybe especially when the case is difficult for one reason or another. I remember one young life: it wasn't that she was deeply possessed, but her case was difficult and there was a sense of hopelessness, which was almost seeping into me, when suddenly Christ came. As soon as the words were said, 'Behold, the Lamb of God,' it was as though a light came on inside her, and a flicker of hope came into her being as she looked toward the Lamb of God. He took all the darkness away, and He took her in His arms. He is absolutely glorious. I am never completely satisfied with a life that has been prayed for unless they come, not just out of the darkness, but into the light of Christ. In such an hour a person's barriers are down. Their self-restraint and self-consciousness have to be broken in order for them to be delivered, and if they are desperate enough, they will let these barriers down. I sometimes feel that God has a golden opportunity then to bring them into the revelation of Christ, because in the

moment the barriers and the darkness go, they are less self-conscious than usual and are open to being pulled out into the spiritual world and into the revelation of Jesus Christ.

He is a wonderful Christ. I just love to see Him in power, in victory. I hate the darkness that tries to flaunt itself. I hate it most of all when it is connected with the occult; again and again occult spirits try to give the impression to the person concerned that they are too strong to be moved. Sometimes just as soon as you say to the person that that is what they are thinking, instantly the power of God is there. There comes in me an indignation that anybody can believe so poorly of Christ, and that demons can try and flaunt themselves before the face of Christ.

I have a deep heart-cry that the power of God will come more and more into our midst and that inner things will be revealed.

Sometimes, for example, people come into our midst who don't really want to be freed, but are there almost to make a mockery of the ministry. There is a deep desire that such will increasingly be exposed and terrified—the thing inside terrified—by the power of Christ. But for the life that really wants God, and just wants to be right with God, there is absolutely no doubt about it: Christ will come and set the life free into Himself. I have felt sometimes an immense compassion of Christ for the life that really wants Him. His love is so intense that it is as though He shields the person as much as He can from the painful side of deliverance—He quickly sorts the matter, and brings them into the love of His own presence and into the fold of His arms. Blessed be His Name.

Diana

I always find it extremely difficult to explain some aspects of deliverance. I never feel I put across the sheer joy and glory that deliverance can bring. I came into the ministry

through Miss Taylor. One night, it must be ten or twelve years ago now, as she prayed with me, the anger of God and the authority of Christ came over me like a mantle; I think I was out of the body on the occasion. Eventually I was found shaking my fist before Miss Taylor's face!— such was the anger of God and the holy hatred against Satan. I had no idea that I had come into the ministry at that point. All I knew was that something was born inside against the works of darkness, and there came a terrible inner drive to see lives free from every bondage, every barrier; and there also came a tremendous desire to see other lives coming under the same anointing that I myself had received, that others would learn to fight against the powers of darkness.

There was a witness very clearly with one or two, right back in the early days when I was still at Jordanhill College. I remember praying with Susie, and immediately there was a flame within her, the same flame that was in myself, against Satan, and there was the feeling of a kindred spirit with her.

Around that same time, possibly just before Miss Taylor prayed with me, I remember being in the Spirit as I was going about my household chores, and becoming aware of the terrible need that there was in the church of Christ for the ministry of deliverance to be in operation. At the same time there came a real burden over me for the ministry to flow, not through me in particular, but through me if God wanted it that way. I went down on my knees before Him immediately the burden came, and happened to open my Bible at these words, *Behold, they shall come*. There were two particular desires: one was to see souls set free from demon power, and the other was to bring lives into the revelation of the Lord Jesus Christ. And the word was given immediately: *Behold, they shall come*.

And one of these ministries—that of bringing others into the revelation of Christ—was born within me almost

at once. It really was wonderful. It happened during a meeting in Glasgow, when I was very new and young in things. There was somebody seeking the baptism in the Spirit, and Mr Black took them through next door into the vestry to pray with them and asked me to take the prayer time with the general company. I had no idea how to take a prayer time. Actually all you need to do is to be in the Spirit and go through to God yourself and you find that others come too. I remember that as I sat down I felt physically a mantle fall on me—I felt the weight of it fall on my head and on my shoulders. There was absolute knowledge to go and to pray with one member of the company there. As I did so I went out of the body. I totally lost consciousness of myself and everything around, I lost consciousness that I was praying with anyone. I went out into the heavenlies, and I knew that that person's spirit had come with me and that he was seeing Christ in a way he had never seen Christ before. This kind of ministry flowed from then on. I remember in the Jordanhill days it came again and again and again, the revelation of Christ the Deliverer, the One who was able to set free, not into nothingness, but into the beauty and the glory and the revelation of Himself.

About eight years after Miss Taylor had prayed with me, the ministry began to come more fully into operation. Looking back now, I think that I had been used in it many times without realizing it. I can remember Jordanhill meetings when I would be in prayer with somebody, and would see the barrier within the person; I would see Christ come and smite the barrier, enabling the person to go through into complete liberty and glory. Yet I had no idea of what was really happening—I didn't analyse it and conclude that the deliverance ministry was operating through me. The full realization came later that this was actually what I had been seeking for: the ministry of deliverance. I found again and again that Satan opposed that ministry more than he opposed anything related to my

own growth as a Christian. I felt that it was like going up a gravel slope—taking one step up and three back. Again and again I felt that I wasn't making any progress, and I became very, very burdened that I should get through. It happened at the July camp, just before the August camp of which Mrs Gault speaks, when something particularly significant happened for herself in this realm. It was the perfect timing of God. On two occasions when praying with two different individuals I saw Satan in the room, and I knew that he had to acknowledge that the power of God within me was greater than his own power. He was unable to say anything. He was unable to speak in that presence: he was totally powerless in the presence of the living Christ that was in that room. And I knew that I had crossed the line that I had been longing to cross for years.

At the August camp it was with tremendous joy that I entered a new phase. I don't know how to put this into words. I found that when I prayed along with Grace for another life, it was as though almost exactly the same ministry flowed through both of us. It sounds a strange thing to say—but it was almost like praying with another 'you', if I can put it that way. What was coming through Grace was exactly what was coming through myself. One part of the revelation might unfold through me, and then a part would come through Mrs Gault. It was lovely, the dovetailing and the oneness, and it has happened repeatedly. I often find that I am more reluctant to speak than Mrs Gault is; I let her take the lead, and again and again as the visual side is given I have heard her describe exactly, absolutely exactly, the revelation given to myself—over and over again. When that happens, a tremendous confidence arises to go in against the powers of darkness, to go into the living Christ and see Him glorified. It is wonderful when the purity of Christ comes into a life that has been tormented by uncleanness. The vileness, the horror and the filthiness go, and Christ comes in to replace them. The two situations are, gloriously, poles apart. It is so wonder-

ful that Christ comes right in in such cleansing, transforming power. Praise His Name.

Mr Black's comment

At a recent meeting, when perhaps over one hundred people came forward for ministry, Diana was asked to say a few words about the visual side of her ministry. This she did just prior to the appeal, with what I felt was tremendous effect. 'Yes,' she said, 'I see demons. I sometimes see them in individuals as I walk along the street. I see them here in this church now.' She then proceeded to name a number of them and indicate some of their reactions, and I was not surprised at the hush that fell or at the many who came for help. It is indeed a glorious ministry which God is now giving to an increasing number of His servants.

Sūsie

It is really very difficult to explain how certain gifts function. You can't always say how a thing happens or why it happens. Quite a number of years ago I found that there would come on me real burdens of prayer: it could be for a particular individual, or it might be for a company; but at specific times God would bring particular people and situations before me. I found that at the same time there came a real clarity about what Satan was doing in the situation. As I was praying I could have given a running commentary on what was actually happening and on how the forces of darkness were being pushed back. If demons were being cast out and there were maybe still more to come, it was almost like watching a film. By revelation I could tell what was happening and could say, 'That's it—Christ has come totally into that situation.'

This went on for quite a few years, and then about two years ago certain specific incidents occurred. At the time of Jean Darnall's visit there were many people being prayed with. They stretched from one wall of the main auditorium in the City Halls to the other. I sat there just

praying for the people who were being ministered to. When there remained about half-a-dozen, I thought I would go home and I got up from my seat. Then I really felt God saying to me, 'No, you have to stay there and you have to wait until every single person has been prayed with.' I could not hear what was being said at the front as people received ministry; I was too far back, and the hall was very big. Those ministering came to one woman in particular, and I could have told exactly the second she was totally free: I could have said, 'Yes, that is it. God has come fully into that situation: she is completely free.'

Time went on, and last year again a similar thing happened at the July camp. A whole row of people were receiving ministry, and there were certain cases where I knew either that the work had been completed or that there was something further to be done and they had not been set absolutely free: there were still things lying there that hadn't manifested themselves. I was talking to Mr Black between the camps and mentioned these things; and then there was opportunity to be with him at the August camp in ministering to people. I don't know how revelation comes; I don't altogether know how it operates; but I just know that there comes a real clarity about what is happening within people. Sometimes deliverance takes place and there may be a lot of noise. Eventually things may quieten down, but I find at that point that I can tell if there is still something else there, or if the person is completely clear.

Now I also know that if I am physically tired I have to be careful, for tiredness can hinder the clarity. I've got to keep myself in proper condition to be used. There are things I have to be really disciplined in at a practical level.

It is God who gives revelation. There is nothing that you can conjure or work up yourself. I could not tell what is going on in a person, of myself, but I can do so under the operation of the Holy Spirit. You know, He does reveal what is happening within a person, and He also

reveals what He wants accomplished. Sometimes a person can be saying, 'Such-and-such is the problem,' and when you turn to pray there can be completely different things that come to light. God gives revelation and deliverance can take place at quite unexpected levels. I don't profess to understand what actually happens, but I thank God that it does happen and that people don't have to go away only partially set free. There is a place of total liberty in Christ for all of us.

PRAYER: *Lord our God, we thank Thee for the ministries that Thou art putting into Thy church. We thank Thee that provision is being made that Thy whole church may be set free in the total liberty of the sons of God. We pray now that if there are those who are in need of deliverance they shall do business with Thee. We ask it in Christ's Name.... Lord our God, we pray that Thou shalt meet all who are in need and we would like it to happen early— today, Lord—that the joy and glory of God may flow throughout the camp. We ask it in His Name and for His sake. Amen.*

16

A Door Opens

[A very lovely instance of inner healing occurred for one of our number at the July camp of 1989. The account she gave a few days later at that same camp has been integrated with a written version she kindly supplied more recently for the purpose of this book. Something of the freshness and spontaneity of the original version is retained. This lady's healing has been deep and permanent. Now she speaks for herself.]

Her own account

The ringing phone was shrill and jarring to nerves already taut. The doctor's words, though laced with sympathy, were like sharp arrows and the wounding was deep. For my mother, life was over. For me, life without her seemed inconceivable.

She had always been supportive, always understanding, and I had enjoyed a very close, harmonious relationship with her. Although the bereavement unearthed precious 'treasures of darkness', much had happened in the four intervening years since her death, and the direction my life was taking seemed terribly unfamiliar. Fear and insecurity, which I had prided myself on keeping under control, rose to the surface and worsened significantly when I

started at Jordanhill College. A housewife for many years, I was afraid of leaving the house with its security and going into a world which was totally alien to me. That was a really difficult experience, yet one which I believed God was asking me to follow through.

Discouraged, I wondered how these deep-seated emotions could ever be different. In reading the book of Numbers, however, I was struck by the similarity and relevance of the fears the Israelites experienced as they contemplated the giants who occupied the promised land. Also, one of my daily readings emphasized that it was only as the Israelites advanced toward the new land that they met the giants. The writer went on to encourage readers not to be put off by the giants but to look for God. I identified my giants as being Fear and Insecurity. I had been acquainted with them as far back as memory went, and often they had felt close and menacing. I thought of the Israelites as their courage failed them on the brink of entering Canaan, and it seemed almost inevitable that I too would succumb under the challenge and mockery of my own giants.

Then one afternoon in June 1989, while sitting alone in my living room, I heard an inaudible yet unmistakable Voice. The words were penetratingly clear:

Are you not tired of all this fear? ...Are you not weary of it?

For a moment I turned round, because I thought somebody had come into the room—then I realized it was the Lord who was speaking to me, and He was putting into words exactly what the problem was: a tiredness of fear, a weariness of spirit because of fear. I felt that it had been there for such a long, long time. It was a general fear, rather than a fear of specific things like heights or enclosed spaces; and I was also afraid to trust God completely and really step out in faith. I asked Him, 'Where did this fear come from?' for it seemed to me that it had always been there.

Almost immediately a childhood experience which had intermittently troubled me flooded my thinking....

It was a sunny day for October. I obediently hurried downstairs for a neighbour as my mother had instructed. Suddenly my world seemed insecure and disordered. Not only was one neighbour bustling about, but others came in as well. My mother seemed to be in pain although she assured me that she was fine, and that I had to do what I was told. But I knew she was not fine, and it is hard not to get in the way, and to do what you are told, when you are four-and-a-half years old, very confused, and worried about the most important person in your world.

From this hive of activity I was deliberately excluded. At one point there arose a commotion in the room where my mother was. Suddenly the door opened, and I was in like a flash. What I then saw really terrified me. I was very quickly pushed back outside by a neighbour and the door shut in my face. It was a huge brown door with a little brass handle three-quarters of the way up—distinctly beyond my grasp, even on tiptoe. With my mother, who was my security, out of reach on the other side of the door, I began screaming with fear and was duly removed.

My twin brothers were born that day in that room and carried off in an ambulance with my mother. Oh, how I disliked them!

Given the circumstances of the birth, my mother became seriously ill and seemed to disappear out of my life. Children were not permitted to visit the hospital, nor were their emotional needs, I believe, as well considered then as they are today.

Approximately two months later the red-letter day came when I gathered with the rest of the neighbourhood to welcome my mother home. I was excited and felt important too as the big black taxi drew up with my parents in it—*but these two babies were still there: incredibly, she had brought them back home with her!*[1]

As the memory of the incident came back so vividly all

these years later, I began to cry. I cried a great deal that morning, because the pain was still very real. I realized that it was after that experience that I felt a fear of the dark and had to have a light left on. I could not suffer the curtains or the door being closed. For the following six years my nights were dominated by a recurring nightmare of a wall I could never get over; my parents always seemed to be on the other side of that wall. I would waken up in a state of fear; it was as though fear had entered into me. Life was irreversibly changed.

I believe God was now giving me insight into this childhood experience and showing me that through it a sense of insecurity had become an intrinsic part of my personality and had affected me in varying degrees ever since. I saw with spiritual sight a tree, old and gnarled, with strong roots, which had been like a sapling in my childhood development, and it seemed a picture of how fear can grow within a human heart.

A prophecy was given that night in a meeting in Greenock, and the first line of it lived for me: *The axe is laid to the root of the tree.* I became increasingly aware of the intention of the Lord Jesus to set me free and in doing so to change an integral part of my character. Already when God had spoken that Saturday morning a song had started in me (and it was not I who was singing):

*I have loved you with an everlasting love and have continued my faithfulness to you. Again I will build you and you shall be built, and I will be your God, says the Lord.**

It brought tremendous comfort, just listening to that song.

Camp time came round and I could hardly wait to get to the meetings. Since the prophecy a few days earlier there had been a growing anticipation that a spiritual experience

* See Jer 31:3–4.

of great significance was drawing near.

The first thing that happened was significant in a rather unexpected way. Early on in the camp, when asked to testify, I was really afraid and expressed the fear quite openly. Afterwards I felt very troubled. I knew that something had been exposed; fear had been made public in some way. Mr Black noticed my emphasis on fear and, feeling that the public expression of it could not be allowed to pass unchallenged, spoke openly about it. I should say that the troubling I felt was not in a bad sense: it was like the angel's troubling of the pool at Bethesda, when there was going to be healing. There was an anticipation that God was really going to do something. I did not sleep a wink that night; I thought about the matter all the time and I could not wait to get back to the meeting on the following night. I knew that was when God was going to act. I have never been in the habit of seeking ministry, for so often I find that the remedy lies in my own hands. But this time I knew I needed help, for the thing was too great for me. I asked again that there would be confirmation in the meeting that it was right to go forward and that God really would set me free. The meeting was very much along deliverance lines, and at the end two people testified to having been set free from fear.

After the meeting quite a number of us waited for ministry. As I was wondering who would come and pray with me, again the Voice said, 'No, this is not going to be any human action. This is going to be Me: just seek Me.' I turned my mind and began to think about Christ—and He came quickly with such reality and power. What struck me most of all was the sense of His rejoicing: He was moving forward in tremendous joy, and I couldn't help but be caught up in His rejoicing that He was coming to do something for me that He had waited a long, long time to do. I was ready for it to happen.

Just then Mr Black came over. His opening remarks staggered me: ' . . . tired and weary of this fear.' *Tired and*

weary of it—exactly the same words that I had heard three weeks earlier, and I had not spoken about it to anyone—because I somehow wanted to keep it to myself. When Mr Black spoke these words, something burst within me: this really was of God. It wasn't any human action; it was something that God was revealing to him, the tiredness and the weariness. I couldn't get over it—I nearly hugged him! I was so pleased that he knew exactly what it was.

As I began to move out in prayer and as Christ was coming nearer, the memory of my childhood trauma came back more and more strongly, and I felt the tears coming. There it was, the brown door with the little brass handle. A child stood outside it, screaming in fright and bewilderment. I watched with fascination as the scene continued to unfold and felt a start as I realized that the scream was coming from me and not from the child. But in the very same instant that the scream began—without a second's gap—there came an unutterable sense of ointment being poured in. I sensed laughter, rich, infectious, and full of joy. Suddenly He was there and I became conscious of the tremendous joy Christ has when He comes to set a child of His free. The giants shrivelled up without His even giving them a casual glance, such was the power streaming forth before Him.

Fear and insecurity could not breathe in such an atmosphere. I sensed He had come from a golden place and it was as though I had a sighting of it. The child's screaming turned to delight as this wonderful Being gathered her up. Forgotten was the human separation, the closed door, the confusion and the fear. Jesus had come into the situation and a locked door within me was opened; fear and insecurity, once inhabitants of that place, were banished. Rays of beautiful light flooded the darkness, and a sweet, healing love was poured on old scars. There came the absolute certainty that Christ had been on both sides of that door: it had not been a shut door to Him.

I knew that this experience was precious and I had the

feeling that the Lord Jesus had waited a long time until I was ready to receive it. I had actually said to someone previously, 'You know, I've heard people saying they've been delivered in an instant, and that doesn't happen to me.' But it did. In an instant the healing came, and there was no scarring whatsover. I knew that my fear was totally gone and my spirit totally healed.

As I returned home from camp that evening, I was acutely aware of a change within. It was as though something snarled and deeply engraved in my personality had been completely removed. I kept looking for something I seemed to have lost: my stomach felt hollow—as if a concrete thing had been removed and I was breathing at a much deeper level than I had ever done in my whole life. As Mr Black said, 'When the tide of God comes in, it fills every nook and cranny'—and it did. The song we were singing, *The Lord thy God in the midst of thee is mighty*, was very personal, because I felt that in the midst of me He was mighty; He was rejoicing over me and His happiness was so infectious that I felt as though I was watching something happening and at the same time was very much a part of it.

In place of the old insecurity there came a tremendous sense of well-being and a new level of confidence in the Lord. This change strengthened in the days which followed, and two and a half years later has not diminished. Although there have been occasions when the threat of the giants' return has seemed imminent, there has also been a continuing ability to recognize that they have no substance in the light of Christ's power. They have not regained their old ground. As Corrie Ten Boom once wrote: when a bell stops ringing, for a time the echo of it remains, but the bell itself has ceased. The giants of Fear and Insecurity have no more impact than that bell which has stopped ringing.

Mr Black's comment, given on the occasion:
I'd just like to enlighten you a little. I wanted to go out of

the hall for a moment before I ministered to you, and had allocated various helpers to go to particular individuals. I was about to let you know that I would be with you later, but you erupted before I got there and I found I had to stay. I had become aware, when you had been testifying earlier, of fear in you, and I told you I was tired, weary as it were, of this fear. I knew about it, and the time had come.

Note

[1] Needless to say, my feelings for my brothers were to undergo a change with the passing of time, and I can gratefully record that one by one over the last twenty years every single member of my family has come to Christ. But subsequent events did not undo the original trauma.

17

Sheila's Healing

[Mrs Sheila Robertson experienced a remarkable healing at the July camp. I reported this briefly in *Christ the Deliverer*.[1] Here is her own account, given at camp a year later.]

Sheila

It is with great joy that I give my testimony to healing. Sometimes you speak of what God has done for you and as you speak you relive the experience—praise His Name.

My healing took place a year ago yesterday. Let me briefly sketch the background. When my friend Alison* and I moved to Millport in 1986, the removal seemed to last for months, during which we must have shifted a mountain of furniture. That was the first time I realized I had really hurt my back. I remember being in terrible pain and crying with it in the New Year of 1987. I had gone to the doctor in Millport and he said, 'You have been shifting too much furniture—you need to rest.' I tried to rest and things improved, but the pain would come back with the slightest provocation. A little over a year ago, I don't know exactly what I did—it may have been shifting storage

* See chap. 18.

heaters—but I remember one night knowing that I had hurt my back again, really badly. It just didn't get better although I did all the right things. I went to the doctor, I took a week of bed rest and the household had to cope without me, I lay flat on my back and took very strong pain killers. Gradually my back grew worse and, what was even more alarming, my spiritual condition grew more and more shadowed.

There really was a horrible aspect to this ailment. It wasn't just like being ill. There had been a time before in my life when I had been quite ill after my husband had died, but God had used that time very fruitfully. I had been afraid of being on my own, and afraid to take to my bed, because I thought one had to fill one's life with business. And so I had gone back to work full time, was working too hard, and had made myself ill. I found myself flat on my back, and it was in that time that God really spoke to me and told me He wanted me for His service and wanted me to be with the children. I was not to go around chasing after this, that and the other, using up my energy in wrong directions. That time of illness had been very, very fruitful. But this sore back was something else. There was a binding in me spiritually: it was a horrible thing.

I can't say that anything particularly good came out of that week in bed, although I did come to the point where I said, 'Well, God, if I have to live the rest of my life in this pain (and it was intense), then that is all right.'

Alison was just saying, coming down in the car this week, that you can get to a stage where pain actually possesses you. I am sure that any of you who ever have been in real agony will agree that you come to a point where you can think of nothing but the pain: it takes you over—body, mind and spirit. The strong painkillers I was taking were so upsetting to my stomach that my body really began to waste away. I could not get above my situation physically, and I couldn't get above it spiritually: there was a real binding in it. Mr Black had been down at

Millport previously and I had asked him to pray with me, but not much had happened that night: it obviously wasn't God's time. But last year at the youth camp (July 1989), when I was in real need, someone had very kindly gone to Mr Black and said, 'Mr Black, you are really going to have to do something about Sheila.' But Mr Black couldn't move, because it was not God's time. I was hobbling about; I would sit down there at the front of the meeting and I would think, 'How will I get through this meeting?' That was all I could think about—not, 'What is God saying to me? Isn't the singing lovely?' but, 'How can I get through the meeting? How can I possibly sit for two hours!!!' The pain was consuming the front part of my mind.

It was at the point of my utter desperation that God met me. In many ways it was similar to one of the deliverances we have heard about. Though consumed by pain, I felt I couldn't ask any more for prayer. I had asked before and it seemed as if the prayer wasn't going to be answered. I would have to come to terms with my condition.

On the Tuesday morning of the adult camp a week later, as I sat at the front I became aware that Mr Black had shifted the person sitting next to me and sat down beside me himself.[2] I felt a bit like what someone described earlier: I was sinking in blackness and couldn't hear what anybody was saying; I couldn't concentrate on anything. But during the singing of 'Amazing Grace', one line in the song came through to me: *The Lord hath promised good to me*. There was enough in that to quicken something in my spirit: 'Yes, God has promised good to me!! He doesn't want me to live like this.' There is a kind of illness that God can be in and can be using to draw you closer to Him, but I knew that this was not that type of thing. I said, 'The Lord *has* promised good to me.' Then we went on to sing from another hymn, *My chains fell off, my heart was free*. Mr Black put his hand on my back. I had

not told him where it hurt, but he put it on exactly the right spot.

Three of our number who are physiotherapists[3] had all been working on my back and had told me that if it didn't get better I would have to go back and see the doctor. They really thought I would need an operation to remove a disc, which was so severely damaged that with the slightest movement pain would radiate from the spine right down to my foot. With manipulation this could be cleared, but as soon as I moved, it would radiate again, and the pain was excruciating.

Without knowing about this, without knowing which part of my back was sore, Mr Black put his hand on the precise spot and instantaneously I was healed. I am reminded of Kenneth's giving testimony to healing.[4] There are times when you know you have been healed gradually—when a couple of hours or a couple of days later you realize that the pain is no longer there. But this wasn't like that. It was literally as if I could hear the chains falling off and clanking to the ground. Instantly I was healed, and not only healed, but something happened inside: I was free! and the blackness lifted. Praise His Name!

There is a postscript that Mr Black doesn't know yet! Just before Christmas an old schoolfriend who now teaches English at a girls' school in London was organizing a mountain expedition to Wales with a party of schoolgirls. They were arranging it for this June—just about a fortnight ago. Now, before my children were born (more than twelve years ago), I did a lot of hillwalking and climbing. My husband and I used to spend every summer in the mountains. We would take our tent and our boots and go away climbing up in Torridon ... Skye ... you name it, we climbed there. I was really fit. But after the children were born we didn't have the chance to continue this kind of activity. When my friend Lorraine suggested that I join their party, it felt right. But I thought, 'Lord, my back—

you know, it's a long time since I've done any climbing anyway and, well, I know I'm healed, Lord, but what about my back?'

Yet it began to grow and grow and grow that this was the right thing to do. The woman who was organizing the trip didn't know me, but she said I could go along as a member of staff and I wouldn't need to pay. All I had to do was get myself to London.

'A week in Wales!' I thought. 'This is really odd—this woman doesn't know me, and I've to go along as a member of staff!' It seemed increasingly right, and I thought, 'Oh, Lord, a mountain centre!' When the prospectus came in, saying things like 'white water rafting, canoeing, rock climbing,' Alison said, 'Right, you can go walking, but none of that canoeing nonsense and none of that white water rafting!!'

So out of the bottom of my wardrobe came my dusty old climbing boots with twelve years of non-use on them, and down came the rucksack and climbing breeches—you know, all the gear that climbers have to wear because you've got to look the part! It's like golfers or foot-ballers—if you don't have all the right gear on, you just can't begin! Out came all the gear and I thought, 'Right, I'm away—Welsh mountains, here I come!'

The first day out on the hills I did really well. We walked a long way, but it wasn't going up very far, and all I prayed was, 'Lord, I've not had these boots on for so long, please don't let me get blisters!'—I was so unaware of my back. The next day it was really lashing and we were all wearing our big cagoules and our boots, and we really were beginning to climb. The weather was terrible—rather like Scottish weather when it rains all the time and the midges are out—oh, it was awful. But as I was climb-ing God began to speak to me again, and I thought, 'You know, I really am well!' There is a place that is different from merely being healed and going a bit tentatively in case the trouble comes back. What I was doing was not of

my timing. I began to climb and not only was I climbing, but I was keeping up with the leaders, who were trained, experienced mountaineers, and I wasn't even tired!

Over my spirit and over my body came this terrific feeling of wellness, of health—whatever it is, it is not just being healed; it is another level. I thought, 'For the first time in years, I think for the first time since Ian died seven years ago, I feel really well—and I feel so vibrantly well, in this rain!' I climbed and I climbed and I climbed. It was another step up from being healed—it was like bursting with life. I thought, 'Lord, are you speaking to me about something?' And I know that He was. I know that He has taken me on to yet another level.

A fortnight ago I got back from Wales. A year yesterday I was healed. But I want to emphasize that there is a further place than the healing itself. It is like what Pauline in her recent testimony was saying about the bird soaring.[5] My friend Lorraine, a keen bird watcher, was telling me about a little bird which lives in the high altitudes. It lives in the air and only comes down to lay its eggs. It eats and lives and goes round the whole world in the air without coming down. I thought, 'Lord, You are speaking to me. There is a place of living where you are above your circumstances, you are above your pain. Lord, that's where You want me to be. I'm not there yet. I've caught a glimpse of something'—you know how you catch a glimpse of something and it is contested. I have said, 'I don't care if this is going to be contested. I am standing up here tonight saying I am vibrantly alive and vibrantly well, and there is this place of living—and tomorrow if I'm flat on my face it doesn't mean that I haven't seen this place, and it doesn't mean that this place doesn't exist.' It does exist. It is a place of wholeness of being, a place of health, a place of vibrant aliveness. It is just wonderful, the place that I have glimpsed. I pray that many of us will be able to go into that place this week—whether it is by deliverance from demon entities, or deliverance from ill health or tiredness or

lethargy, there is a place up there where you can circle the whole world and you don't need to come down. Praise His Name!

Notes

1   Hugh B. Black, *Christ the Deliverer* (New Dawn Books, 1991), pp. 65–7.
2   The detail of how Sheila got from her bed to that meeting is heartrending. She had to manoeuvre from her bed by way of Alison's bent back to a standing position and move painfully from stage to stage until she eventually reached the hall.
3   One of whom had herself experienced healing, as recorded in *Christ the Deliverer*, pp. 74–6.
4   For Kenneth's instant healing from post-viral syndrome, see *ibid.*, p.65.
5   See Pauline's description of this experience in *Christian Fundamentals* (New Dawn Books, 1991), p. 73.

18

Sheila's Further Testimony

The Valley of Achor—A Door of Hope

[I have felt it appropriate to have a fuller testimony from Sheila included in this book, although much of the detail was not revealed until two years later. She continues in her own words.]

Sheila

> *Therefore, behold, I will allure her, and bring her into the wilderness, and speak comfortably unto her. And I will give her her vineyards from thence, and the valley of Achor (Troubling) for a door of hope: and she shall sing there, as in the days of her youth ...thou shalt call me Ishi (My husband), and shalt call me no more Baali (My master) (Hos 2:14–16).*

The song 'The Valley of Achor' really speaks to me, because at a point in my life in 1985 when I was about to take a wrong turning after my husband had died, the Lord spoke to me through the second chapter of Hosea: 'Don't run after the enticements into which you are being drawn. It was I the Lord your God who gave you your vineyards: I am the One who gives you your wealth and abundance—it is I.' Hosea's message to Israel when she is playing the harlot is: 'Don't run after your lovers.' In my heart (not at a physical level) I was desiring other things—especially

151

fulfilment in relationships. It was not to be given to me and the Lord said to me: 'I will be your husband. Don't run after other things,' and He made for me the valley of Achor a door of hope. I have now come to the other side of that door: I have come through the valley.

I have never known a time when I did not love Jesus. When I was about three years old He was as real to me as my parents were. That is why the song based on these verses from Hosea speaks to me: 'I will make you to sing again as in the days of your youth.'

In my teens other allurements came in—not of drink or drugs or smoking, but relationships: basically the male/female relationship and good friendship. In my late teens I said to the Lord, 'I've had enough of Your cold love: You are too far off, You're not real. Give me the best of ordinary human love.' Within a couple of months I met the man who became my husband. My mother's death during those years strengthened my resolve to marry Ian and hold on to this relationship when I had lost the other.

No sooner was I married than I looked for the Lord again—and in His mercy He took me back.

After a few years I began to teach in a school in Greenock, where I met Mary Black—and my life turned round again at the age of twenty-nine. I had a husband, a fine home, children; Ian was an assistant headmaster. We were really going places—yet I knew I was not fulfilled. I knew that Mary had something I didn't have. In my abundance, in all the relationships one could hope to have, I was empty. I thought, 'I'll have to find out what that woman has.'

One night she invited me to her home, and I knew that night my life was going to change. I knew nothing of the baptism in the Holy Spirit or of the things of Pentecost—but I knew that night was going to be a turning-point. I went running out of my house—running to meet God. I knew I was going to meet God again as I had known Him as a child, but even better; and I ran straight into the Lord

that night. He baptized me in the Holy Spirit instantly. Knowing nothing of the doctrine, I just felt the love of Christ and knew that my life would never be the same again. I had played the fool, but my time of restoration had come.

That was May 1982. Within a few months my husband was seriously ill with leukaemia. I had known that my baptism in the Holy Spirit was an empowering to live and an empowering for service. How does one know these things? Yet I did know—and within months Ian was desperately ill, and I really needed that power. I needed that sense of love.

I prayed to God then: 'Lord, don't let Ian turn his back on You now. It's too serious.' All the years Ian had resisted going to church with me, but now old habits began to fall away, and at Christmas time he began to open his heart to the Lord: just quietly to let Jesus in. It wasn't anything I said, for I said nothing. But softly Jesus began to penetrate his defences: so much so that when he was in remission and got home, he said, 'Sheila, I'm going to come to church with you.' Because it was so serious and my heart was bursting, I said by way of playing it down, 'Do you want the walls to collapse?—still, come anyway!'

We went to church (not Struthers) that Sunday morning, and it was a pretty ordinary service. Ian looked at me with hurt eyes that said, 'I've come looking for God, and what are you giving me?' He was dying, and the minister had stood there and preached about lack of money in the church and people not giving properly. My heart sank. That afternoon while we were out for a run in the car with the children, Ian said to me, 'I think I'll come with you to Struthers tonight.' I knew then he was really serious, because he had mocked my commitment to Struthers; he thought I had really lost the place! Yet that night he came, and it was not long afterwards that he gave his life to Christ. God had come in and had made us one. What had been one flesh now became one spirit, and I knew that

from then into eternity it did not matter whether it was life or death. I began to feel that Ian was going to die, and there was a preparation for that.

God stood by us through the last days and finally took Ian peacefully home.

In the days that followed there was a real desire in me to give everything to God—not to make the mistakes I had made before. But this desire in a strange way did not lead to service: it led to stripping. If God is going to trust you with anything, then He is going to strip you first. I found it hard to believe that God expected me to go on without a husband, because from the age of nineteen to thirty my life had been largely focused on Ian. I could not believe that God now expected me to stay single, when all my adult life I had been used to having a partner. I could not comprehend that one could be whole without a partner. I did not really understand the teaching of this church on the matter.[1] I had been brought up to believe that you were not whole if you were not married. God began to reveal to me that this was not what He wanted for me for the rest of my life. Although I understood at a head level, I had to go through it internally. I had to go through again the whole pain of potential relationships, of relationships that could have led to marriage but which God did not allow. There was nothing wrong with the relationships; they would have been perfectly legitimate. I was a widow, after all, and only thirty. But God was calling me to be single. I could not believe the pain of it: the pain of not being allowed to be what I thought was 'normal'. And when you are a widow, people urge you to remarry. They want you to be normal and to fit into a mould, and by not doing that you become a 'rub'—a source of pain and friction. The amount of invitations I had to dinner parties to make up numbers!—and I could not explain that it was very kind of them, but I wasn't going that way!

I really had to go through it; it wasn't a head decision— it was something being ripped out of my being. It wasn't

as if my assent at a mind level was enough—God had to do something inside me. I had to go through the pain of it all to let it go. I had to go through it in actuality, not just in theory. I had to feel the pain and I had to say 'no'. I had to feel the draw and the desire, and in the height of the desire, I had to choose Christ. Now, you have to go through that to understand what I am saying; but it is God's way. It is not enough in a cold moment to say, 'I choose Christ.' In the heat of passion, in the heat of desire, you must choose Christ.

I chose Christ, and He became as real to me as a husband, and He said to me from Isaiah 54: *I, your maker, will be your husband*. He has fulfilled that promise to me—but I had to go through the renouncing process, and that was part of the growing up for me. God was not going to allow me to be 'normal'. He was going to call me into a different way of living, a way that would go against the grain—because I am very average and very normal and have a desire to be like everybody else. I didn't want to be different.

It took nearly two years to that camp in 1985 when the Lord spoke to me from Hosea. He said, 'You touch that relationship which is not from Me, and you are spiritually dead. Go that way, and your spiritual life is ruined.' I knew that He meant it. More than that, He said, 'Your children will be the children of whoredom' (Hosea 2:4), and I thought, 'O Lord, not the children.' The words, I now feel, were directed towards possible future children of a forbidden marriage, but for a time I feared they might apply to the two I already had, and this I could not bear. He had promised to take care of my children. For myself I might have taken some risk—but not with my children. 'They belong', I said, 'to You, Lord. They are the inheritance of the Lord.' For the sake of the children and for the sake of my own love for Christ, I didn't touch the forbidden thing. In the moment of its going, I moved into another place spiritually.

So there wasn't to be another husband, and there wasn't to be a job—there was nothing into which I was allowed to put my energies. He brought me to a low place. One Saturday morning in the swimming baths in Greenock (I remember it quite clearly), I said to God: 'If I never *do* anything for You, if there is never any outward sign in my life of my love for You or Your love for me—can I accept that? If no one ever hears my name, nobody ever knows I have ever done anything for You—then that is OK!' He brought me to the point that if I just lived my life for Him, then it was perfectly acceptable.

I would like to go on from 1985. Usually I stop here and let Alison Speirs tell the rest, but it is the story of both our lives and our lives in conjunction.

I got to know Alison through our boys. Neil and Fraser were both dreadful boys—they were utterly awful. When I see parents at camp struggling with boys on their knees who won't sit still, I remember what it was like with Neil. He always seemed to be too big for me—he was a huge big boy and I couldn't even carry him. He would always get the better of me; he used to run rings round me—so much so, that he was running me into the ground.

I couldn't get him into a state nursery, because they decided we were too prosperous and he didn't merit a place! But it is strange how God leads you. One day when I was driving near a private nursery in Greenock I had a real feeling that if I went in, even though it wasn't the beginning of the term, Neil would get a place there.

Ian and I had great debates about it, because Ian was quite a socialist and he didn't approve of private education (although he had gone to a private school himself). His son wasn't going to a private nursery—so I said, 'Do you want me to have a nervous breakdown? I don't care, I'll find the money! But that boy's going to a nursery—because I can't stand it!!'

Poor Neil. By this time Kirsty had arrived and she was an angel. She sat up in her pram, all beautiful with blond

hair, with this boy climbing all over the pram, trying to haul her out!

And so Neil went to the nursery. It was here that he met an equally bad boy, Fraser Speirs. The pair of them struck up a friendship—they just took to one another. Fraser went home to his mum with a screwed-up bit of paper in his hand with our phone number on it. He said to his mum: 'Phone that number,' and she said: 'Go away! I'm not phoning that number.' Then she thought, 'Aha! It might be a friend for Fraser.'

So she phoned up and we arranged that the boys would play together, and it was from Neil and Fraser's choice of one another that our friendship grew. The leading of God is quite remarkable.

When I first saw Alison she was in her 'hippy' phase. She had long hair, jeans and anorak, and she was smoking outside the posh nursery. I was all dressed up in my Marks and Spencer's gear, because it was the West End, after all, and all of the mums would be at the nursery at nine in the morning with their make-up on and wearing their designer track-suits. I was playing up, trying to be a wee bit smart—but Alison just didn't care!

She came up to me and said, 'Are you Neil's mum?' I looked at her and thought, 'Oh, no! I can't let my son go to her house!' and she was thinking about me, 'What a pretty little stuck-up madam!' Our first impressions of one another were, 'No way!' But we were both so desperate that our boys should have a friend and we thought we might get a cup of coffee in peace—so we decided to meet up. Within that first afternoon of speaking to one another, we really did become friends. There was just something there, and we laughed a lot—it was really good fun.

Within a couple of months Ian had taken ill, and Alison more or less took over the children for me to allow me to go to hospital, although I hardly knew her. She felt strangely committed to me, which was odd, because she wasn't a Christian; and she felt committed to taking care of

my children. Even her family, quite understandably, questioned the extent to which she became involved, as she didn't know me. But she told them, 'This is something I have to do, and I have to see it through.'

Through her kindness and her help for me our friendship developed. I didn't ever try to convert her—never, not once. I was even frightened at first to ask her along to church, and when she began to ask what church I went to, I was really evasive. I just knew she wouldn't understand. She said, 'What kind of church is it?' and I said, 'Evangelical.'

'What kind of evangelical?' I didn't want to say the word 'Pentecostal'.

'And where is this church?'—'It's in the centre of town!'

'Whereabouts in the centre of town?'—'It's just along from Tesco's!'

'*Struthers!!!*'

We didn't talk very much about this at the time, but the subject came up again later. When Ian died, Alison, who was a convinced atheist, was afraid that I was temporarily buoyed up with a false religious emotion which would soon pass, with disastrous consequences. A true friend, she stayed close to me in order to pick up the pieces when I collapsed, as she was sure I would! Through the various hard times I had after Ian's death, I confided in her the problem of potential friendships and possible remarriage that was facing me. She told me I ought to get married again. For goodness' sake, if there was someone there who wanted to marry me, what was the problem! What was all the difficulty?

I began to explain to her that that wasn't what God was asking me to do—that I had to be obedient to Him. I thought she wouldn't understand, and I was frightened to tell her these things, thinking she would just laugh at me—but she didn't! She did listen. At times she would prepare the evening meal for us and make sure that I got to

church at night. She didn't mock me, beyond a gentle teasing.

When we went for a caravan holiday in Millport it was not a set-up thing. I had no intention of seeing Alison Speirs converted; nothing could have been further from my mind! Neil and Fraser had wanted to get together for their eighth birthday (around the same date), and Alison's husband was putting in a new fitted kitchen while we were away with the four children. But God had other plans.

Right from the word go, I found that our friendship was being torn in two and seemed to be slipping away from us. Various things happened. We sat in the Ritz café, drank hot chocolate and talked. It was mooted that we should go to the pictures, because it was really wet. Strangely, I'd had a particularly bad experience at the cinema just some weeks before when I had gone with the children to see *Ghostbusters*. It seemed just a laugh—I had taken them twice—and after that I'd had to go and seek prayer from Miss Black because I had felt such a power of evil in the cinema that I was scared. I knew God was saying to me, 'Sheila, you'll never go to see anything like that again!' There was something emanating from that film that wasn't funny. Other people were laughing, but I felt a cloud of darkness over me and the children. I said to the devil that night: 'You may be getting other people's children, but you are not getting mine! Because my two will never be in a cinema again—it will be over my dead body, and I don't care if I have to nail their feet to the floor!!'

I made that commitment to God, and I knew, because I'd had a terrible fright, that these things were real. The power of evil coming from that screen was real. As far as I was concerned, it was finished. The children knew me well enough to accept it: they don't argue if I really have a word from God. If it's just what I might think or not think, then that's up for grabs! But if I really stand my ground then they know better than to push.

Now here was Alison saying, 'I think we might go to the

pictures!' and I thought, 'What do I do here?' Again, I was afraid of her mocking, but I had to stand my ground. So we sat in the café and I explained to her why I wouldn't go to the pictures. She was really angry.

'This is ridiculous! You are going *too* far! I've seen this before! I've seen these extremist sects, and I know what they do to their children! You're going to turn them into narrow this and narrow that—you're going to ruin their lives! As your friend I have to counsel you that you are going too far!'

She went on and on—she was so angry. She saw our friendship being split in two, and I saw it, too. But I thought, 'I'm not going to the pictures—if I fall out with her and this is the end of our friendship, that's too bad! but I'm not going.'

I am more afraid of God than I am of other people. I don't care what other people think of me, but I am afraid, if I have had a word from God, to transgress that word. It is really serious.

That night we did not go to the pictures, but a way was opened up spiritually for speaking. We got the children to bed and began to talk about life: what was it all about? There was no thought in my mind of conversion—in fact, with Alison I would have found it really embarrassing if she had asked me; although we were good friends it would have been embarrassing at that stage to talk so intimately.

But God really turned the tables on us, that night. We were sitting up in our sleeping bags, Alison on one side of the van and I on the other, the children safely tucked up in bed. I was reading a magazine and she wanted to talk to me seriously. I was humming and hawing—then I realized she really did want to talk to me, and I began to speak to her about spiritual things.

At one point I said, 'What have you to lose? It is better to find out now if God is real than to spend the rest of eternity in hell!'

You can picture the scene. She was in one bunk and I in

the other, and we were trying to pray. We were so embarrassed! I wanted her to pray. She said, 'No, no—you pray! But don't pray out loud!' This was our approach to the great conversion experience—'Don't pray out loud! Don't do this ... don't do that!'

It was at that point that we realized that she could not say, 'I believe.' She said, 'Sheila, you'll have to come over here and help me!'

I went over and put my hand on her head. What happened next was like nothing I had ever known in my life. It was as if a force was trying to push my hand off. I had never come into contact with demon power till that point; I knew almost nothing about it. I knew that Mr Black and others in the church were used in combating it, but it was a totally alien realm to me. I think I had caught a glimpse of it through God's warning in the *Ghostbusters* episode. God was saying to me: 'Sheila, this dimension is real and you don't dabble in it.' He knew He was going to take me Himself into that dimension, which is why He showed me the seriousness of it.

It was as if another hand tried to push my hand off: it was physical and it was real. If I tried to press my hand down on her forehead, this force tried to push my hand off.

I thought, 'Oh, help!' I knew it was serious and I was out of my depth—at least I knew enough to know this.

I had to call on the living God. It was a question of 'being in the way', in the sense of the text *I being in the way, the Lord led me* (Gen 24:27): I was the one who was there. It wasn't because of anything I was doing right; I was just there—in the way of Christ's plan for Alison.

At that point we were both catapulted into another dimension. It wasn't like praying with someone for the baptism in the Spirit, or even with someone you don't know for deliverance, when normally you have a measure of control over the situation: you can stop the interview ('Off you go! Come back later when you're sorted out').

This time it wasn't like that. I had to see this thing through—there was no walking away from it. I couldn't say, 'Well, Alison, that's enough for tonight!' Once the process had started it had to be finished: I knew there was going to be no rest for us until the whole thing was completed.

We prayed that whole night—and yet, as with Maureen and Jimmy's encounter with the angels,[2] there was an altered concept of time. I don't know enough words to pray all night—but I prayed in tongues, not in English.

Alison saw and felt things that I knew nothing of. They were inside her head or in her spirit—wherever she was at that point. I was only aware of her body lying out in the caravan.

She did at one point try to get up to run away, and her legs just went from under her. I didn't touch her—but I witnessed it. Her feet literally went up into the air and she landed flat on her back.

Surprisingly, the children didn't waken up, and nobody heard us, in spite of the hullabaloo!

All night we prayed. I don't know even yet what all these things were in Alison, but after prayer came deliverance.[3] We would stop in the middle of the night for a cup of tea and then we'd summon up enough energy to start again. It went on until the dawn broke.

The strange thing was that after having had no sleep, only endless cups of tea, we got up in the morning when the children arose and went through the day as normal. Neither Alison nor myself ate all that week. Yet it wasn't a conscious decision to fast. We just couldn't eat. We were so aware of this other dimension that normal things were not real—and yet we were able to lead our normal lives. It was like being suspended between two worlds. I have never known anything like it before or since.

We were living almost a double life. We knew that when night-time came, we would have to commence praying again. Neither of us said it to the other; we just knew

that when the children went to bed it would start all over again. Sunday night: up again in the morning, still existing on cups of tea. Took the children to the beach, fed them— no hunger, no need for food. Saturday, Sunday, Monday, Tuesday: four whole nights praying.

It was during Tuesday night that Alison was baptized in the Holy Spirit. It really was remarkable. That night was a night of tremendous revelation for me too. I *did* fall asleep after she was baptized and then we had a cup of tea.

But there was a desire to get before God again. He revealed to us things that were going to happen in the future, things which at that time didn't make a lot of sense. He told us, for example, to 'pray for the peace of Jerusalem'. It meant nothing to us, because we weren't ones given to the cause of the Jews: I knew nothing about that. But that was one of the instructions given.

He told us there was a work that we would do together. Now Alison was in Bearsden, I was in Gourock—and the caravan was in Millport. It seemed at that point not sensible. Yet it has since come to pass.

There were other things that He asked of me that night. I had been afraid of preaching in the open air. I used to find it terribly embarrassing as a child if I saw people preaching at a street corner: it was mortal agony till I got safely past. I would think, 'How can adults humiliate themselves like that? How can they do it? Why don't they just grow up and act like sensible people?' My mum and dad would want to stop and listen, but I'd be dragging them away! Now the Lord began to put images before me: would I be willing to preach in the open air for Him? He presented me with the picture of a figure on a corner in Millport and asked me if I would preach there. When I consented, I realized the figure was not me—but Neil (who has since been involved in open-air work with our young singing group, Radical Alternative!).

He also asked me if I would look straight in the face of the devil and not be afraid. All the time the deliverance

had been going on, I hadn't been looking at him. It was like being a channel for God, but not looking at the wicked thing—which is quite correct, but God wanted to take the fear from me. God said, 'Look at him, look him straight in the face and he will flee.' *Resist the devil, and he will flee from you*! (Jas 4:7) I had to do that thing, and it seemed that all the darkness evaporated as I stared at it—there was nothing to be afraid of.

It was a night of tremendous revelation, so much so that I believed that the end had come. There was such a sense of God with us, such a sense of another world, that I would not have been surprised if Christ had come back again that very moment. Even the body wasn't the same: the need for food, for bodily comfort, didn't exist. Then we were catapulted back into normal life.

I will not go in detail now into the last part of my life. There were years of difficulty and of pain—but out of that grew a work, out of the pain, out of the suffering, out of the sacrifice (because there is a sense in which you get nothing for nothing in the spiritual world, just as you get nothing for nothing in this life). I don't regret a minute of it, because the joy of the place God brought us into is utterly glorious. In a place of new dying to one's own desire for service, for a normal life, a husband, a family, children, job—in the place of the death of all that, came Life!

In Radical Alternative we sing, 'How can death bring life to me? How can I gain through loss?' *But* you do! You gain through the loss of yourself: Christ gains in you. What you lose of you—the more you die to what you are and what you think you ought to have—the more Christ has control of you.

During those years Alison and I moved with my father and our children to Millport—she after a traumatic domestic experience. There the Valley of Achor became a door of hope. In the stripping and dying and vulnerability, Christ had His way in us. Out of that came life—for

ourselves and also in the outward work for God that was born there. We didn't look for it, we didn't go out to evangelize: people just came and the work grew. I praise God for what He has done. I give Him thanks that our dying can mean life for others. In our death, is life for Christ. Die to your own right to your life—it is the way to real life.

I was right to resist Alison's promptings to 'do something!' The world wants us to 'do something'—it wants us to be seen to be doing. But that isn't God's way, or the way of this fellowship to which we belong. The way to spiritual life is through death. It is through Christ's death and your death—it is not through our own zeal or activity.

It is through stillness in the place of appointment. The life that springs up round about you is almost incidental. It is the relationship with Christ that matters.

Notes

[1] For the teaching referred to, see chapter 9 above.
[2] See *Christ the Deliverer*, appendix 3.
[3] It is hoped to give more details of Alison's side of events in a later book. She came through a fearful experience as evil entities that had deeply gripped her life were exposed and driven out. She saw hell and its unspeakable horror.

PART 3

THE LAST TIMES

Introduction

The closing studies in our camp gatherings always have a particular flavour. Frequently there is a concentration on End Times and how our lives should be regulated in the light of these. This year was no exception, and it is hoped that something of the atmosphere will be transmitted in the writing.

19

Evidence from the Past

PRAYER: *Lord our God, we are conscious that this is the last gathering of this occasion, and it is very unlikely that this whole company of people will ever be together in the way we are tonight. It may be there are those who will be here a year from now: it may be there are those of us who will be in the glory, or in hell. Lord, we realize the seriousness of last things, and we pray that the solemnity of Thy presence shall be deeply upon us as we read and we look into these things tonight. We feel the touch of Thy Spirit, the sense of Thy power. Lord, there are those of us who are further along the road than others in age, and for whom the reality of eternity becomes a practical proposition. As we look forward and backward and look around, Lord, there is no levity but there is joy. Lord our God, we pray that the deep seriousness and the deep joy of the living God shall come upon Thy people tonight. We ask it in the Name Lord Jesus Christ, for His sake. Amen.*

As I contemplated the sermon tonight, I realized that it is Friday, the last of the series, and recollected other last nights of camp series. Occasionally at these times I have spoken of Christ's going from earth. After His death and resurrection, He ascended into Heaven; but prior to ascension He spoke very serious words to those He was leaving behind. From time to time I have pondered the situation should I personally be speaking for the last time, never again to address a company, but going home to God: and

from time to time I have indicated what I might say. My mind began to move along that line for tonight, but I had no real freedom to pursue this course.

But there occurred to me certain words from Acts 2. Speaking of the outpouring of the Holy Spirit predicted by Joel and experienced on the day of Pentecost, Peter said, *Your young men shall see visions and your old men shall dream dreams*. I thought, does that mean that I begin to go over the past and in a nostalgic kind of way like a venerable greybeard say, 'Oh, when I was a boy, it was like this and this and this'? Do I give the people a survey from the year dot to the year dash? Do you know, my spirit did not settle on that at all. I began to ponder that word: *Your old men shall dream dreams*. You are very wrong if you get the notion that that means dreaming of the past on an easy chair. It is not a case of dreaming life away. As I pondered with an open spirit and an open mind, I suddenly thought of the late David du Plessis as an old man. He was one of the liveliest people I ever met. With both feet almost in the grave, he had more go in him than nearly any young man I have known. He reminded me of Caleb, who with Joshua ultimately came into the land of promise. Caleb had said away back forty years earlier, 'We are well able to take the land.' The people did not believe him and ultimately all of his own generation died except himself and Joshua. The day came when the next generation of Israel came into the land and Caleb's own inheritance was to be possessed. I don't know if you have ever read around that story and looked at it deeply. It's an awful story—the old man: the poor old man! Do you know what they did to the old man? There was a mountain that was to be his inheritance, and do you know who lived up there? The Anakim—the giants. Caleb had said, 'We are well able to go in and take the land.' Now, Caleb, old man or not, if you want your inheritance you go up that mountain, and take it. He had to go up and kill the giants. *God* was with the old man.

You don't need to waste any sympathy on that old man. He was overflowing with life.

As for du Plessis, I heard him preach when he was very aged, and I'll never forget it. I saw the shining of the light of God through a skin that was parchment thin, almost transparent. The 'old man' was disintegrating, but the new man after Christ Jesus was alive in power—gloriously. It was being renewed day by day.

So as I pondered *Your young men shall see visions and your old men shall dream dreams*, the next scene that flitted across my vision was my own retirement. I retired from my head teacher's post a number of years ago, and it was very interesting watching the attitude of people generally and of my colleagues who were retiring round about the same time, and the attitude of the world. Suddenly—from a position where you are making very important decisions (or so they seem at the time), at the very hub of activity, influencing the careers of many people, and all is in your hand—one fine morning you retire and it is all gone. In a moment of time it is gone. Some people find this very painful and quite difficult to cope with. Life begins to run down. They begin to move slowly and they think slowly. They are really subconsciously preparing for the end. There is the feeling of life fading into a grey drabness and a nothingness, a going slowly or quickly down to the grave.

Do you know, I have not found it that way at all? Not for one moment have I found it that way. From time to time we all look back. I can recollect early days when as a boy I lived on a farm. I recall the people who were around me, the things that they thought and the things that they said: a whole way of life—and now it has gone, totally gone.

Primary school days came, and there were things which were terribly important at the time. It's all gone.

Secondary school—we were alive and active; life was opening before us. We were going to live forever, as it

were—and do you know, it's all gone. Some of their names I cannot even recollect.

Early teaching days came—and the world of that day has gone, all faded from memory.

Older people tend to go back into these things and think about them and live in them. It means they are going back into a dead past: scenes that change and change and change. The world of each successive scene seemed so permanent, and they have all changed and passed away. I think that God has never really allowed me to live in the past in any serious way. Occasionally I can look at it and review it, but I live forward most of the time. I don't look at the 'dear dead yesterdays', as the poet speaks of them. I look forward. I do not decide that I am going to look forward and then do it. I do it, and I find that I have done it. And you know, in the glory there are my mother and my father and my dead brothers and sisters. There in the glory are people I have known and loved. There in the glory is the Lord Jesus Christ. There are the angels, there are the saints of the Old Testament, there are the saints of the New Testament. The saints of the ages are over there, God is over there and glory is over there, and I'm probably much nearer Heaven than most of you folks—I'm far better off than you are! Many of you are going to be in this vale of tears, I reckon, for a considerable time longer than I am, unless the Lord comes. Why should I feel the shadows of death rather than the rays of glory and the power of the world to come? So much depends on where you are looking, and I am looking forward and upward tonight: I am not going to produce a sentimental sermon saying, 'Friends, I'll soon be dead. I hope—I hope you'll remember me.' One thing I have never understood all my life is the fuss that people have about burials. I have always reckoned that whether I died without a penny or not, I would be got rid of anyway. I have never worried all my life about burials; I have never understood the degree to which people worry about them. If you are looking for-

ward, you are not too worried about that. I never reckoned that anybody would stuff me and keep me—that's for sure!

So I find myself looking and reaching forward, and the message I want to leave with you tonight, the last message of this camp, is this: *The coming of the Lord draweth nigh* (Jas 5:8 AV).

Those of you who have read *The Incomparable Christ* will find in it a section that I can very, very highly recommend; and I can do this without blushing because I didn't write it. I culled it from another's writings and used it in its context. Let me sketch the background.

The Old Testament is full of prophecy, much of which relates to the coming of Christ. There was a fundamental problem about the coming of Christ, because there were two quite distinct lines of Messianic prophecy. One regarded Him as a coming king of whose kingdom there would be no end, and the other as a suffering, dying Saviour. I have often thought of what it must have been like for some of the ancient scholars to try to understand this. They seemed to have clear Scripture on both sides of the question, and I can imagine that sceptical people of earlier ages would probably just say, 'The predictions are rubbish. They cannot be true—they are totally contradictory, cancelling each other out. There is no coming Christ. How could He die and live forever? Die by crucifixion and live eternally? It just doesn't add up.'

Now we who live after the event can look backward over the prophecies. Some scholars have given particular attention to this, and one whom I highly recommend to you is Josh McDowell. I sometimes say that if as a young man I was to be banished to a desert island and could only take one book with me apart from the Bible, it would be the first volume of *Evidence that Demands a Verdict*.[1] Can I give a much higher recommendation than that?

Scholars have examined the subject carefully and have

found that there are a remarkable number of major prophecies regarding the coming of Christ. McDowell lists sixty-one and shows the mathematical probability of these predictions being fulfilled in any individual by chance. He shows that they came over centuries referring to one person and that when that person was born and lived and died all of these predictions were fulfilled in Him. The chances of that being by accident are billions to one against. With reference to eight of the predictions, one of McDowell's sources[2] presents the statistical probability in colourful terms. He has silver dollars, only one of them marked, covering the face of Texas to a depth of two feet; the likelihood of your happening to pick out the marked dollar is as great as was the likelihood of the Messianic predictions coming by chance on one individual. As you examine the subject, you find for instance that Christ was to be born in Bethlehem (Mic 5:2) and that God was to call His son from Egypt (Hos 11:1). He was born miraculously at Bethlehem, He was taken into Egypt because of Herod, and He was called out of Egypt. Not a bone of Him was to be broken, and as He hung on that cross and the soldiers came, they saw that He was dead already and they did not break His legs, but they broke the legs of the two beside Him. It had been predicted that they would look on Him whom they had pierced, and a soldier having a spear thrust it into His side, from which there immediately flowed blood and water—sure evidence that death had already taken place. They did not thrust a spear into the sides of the two who were dying with Him on the other crosses. Their bones were broken; His were not. They were not pierced; He was. *He keepeth all his bones*, the Scripture had said. *Not one of them is broken* (Ps 34:20), and again, *They shall look unto me whom they have pierced* (Zech 12:10).

He rode into Jerusalem on a donkey, as it had been predicted: *Rejoice greatly, O daughter of Zion; shout, O daughter of Jerusalem! behold, thy king cometh unto thee: he is*

just, and having salvation; lowly, and riding upon an ass, even upon a colt the foal of an ass (Zech 9:9).

He was to be betrayed by a friend (Ps 41:9), and He was by Judas. He was to be sold for thirty pieces of silver; the money was to be thrown to the potter in God's house (Zech 11:12–13): *And [Judas] cast down the pieces of silver into the sanctuary, and departed ...And they took counsel, and bought with them the potter's field, to bury strangers in* (Mat 27:5–7).

He was to be dumb before His oppressors (Is 53:7): *And when he was accused by the chief priests and elders, he answered nothing* (Mat 27:12).

I would like to draw attention to further remarkable prophecies. Christ was to be smitten and spat upon: *I gave my back to the smiters, and my cheeks to them that plucked off the hair: I hid not my face from shame and spitting* (Is 50:6). We read that the soldiers *spat upon him, and took the reed and smote him on the head* (Mat 26:27).

It was predicted: *They part my garments among them, and upon my vesture do they cast lots* (Ps 22:18). Note the accuracy of the fulfilment: *The soldiers therefore, when they had crucified Jesus, took His garments, and made four parts, to every soldier a part; and also the coat: now the coat was without seam, woven from the top throughout. They said ...Let us not rend it, but cast lots for it, whose it shall be* (Jn 19:23–4).

Again, *They also gave me gall for my food, and for my thirst they gave me vinegar to drink* (Ps 69:21). As Christ hung on the cross, *they gave Him wine to drink mingled with gall: and when he had tasted it, He would not drink* (Mat 27:34).

In a strangely paradoxical prophecy, Isaiah asserted that *they made his grave with the wicked, and with the rich in His death* (Is 53:9). The mystery was resolved in Christ. *Then are there crucified with Him two robbers* (Mat 27:38)— but after He died, *there came a rich man from Arimathea, named Joseph ...and asked for the body of Jesus.... And*

*Joseph took the body, and wrapped it in a clean linen cloth,
And laid it in his own new tomb* (Mat 27:57–60).[3]

I have dealt here with barely a quarter of the sixty-odd
major prophecies regarding Christ's first advent and their
fulfilment; I recommend that you study them all. Now I
want you to watch the logic of the next point. These
prophecies, referring to Christ's coming as the suffering
Messiah, were accurately fulfilled. Is not that a very good
reason for basing faith in the fulfilment of the other prophecies that refer to the second coming? If the one has been
so gloriously, wonderfully, miraculously fulfilled, may we
not confidently expect the same for the other—particularly when Christ Himself positively confirmed it? I
think that we could well borrow McDowell's phrase: *evidence that demands a verdict*.

Notes

[1] Josh McDowell, *Evidence that Demands a Verdict*, vol. 1 (1st
     British ed.: Scripture Press, 1990; published in U.S. by
     Here's Life Publishers, 1981).
[2] Peter Stoner, in McDowell, *Evidence*, p. 167.
[3] For these and many more Messianic prophecies and their
     fulfilments, see McDowell, *Evidence*, pp. 141–76.

20

Christ's Predictions

When Jesus came out of the temple for the last time, His disciples drew His attention to the amazing stones with which it was built, and He said: 'Do you see these stones? There will not be one of these stones left upon another which will not be thrown down.' They then asked Him three questions: 'When shall these things be? and what shall be the sign of Thy coming and of the end of the age?' Now in their minds they ran the three questions together. He answered two of their questions, and if you study Matthew 24 and the corresponding parts in the other gospels you will find quite clearly that the temple that was to be destroyed was that temple. This happened in A.D. 70, its destruction was bitter, and the Jews resisted with great courage and strength. About 1,100,000 of them were carried into captivity and 900,000 were hung on trees outside of Jerusalem until they could scarce find trees whereon to hang the bodies. They had said of Christ, *His blood be on us and on our children* (Mat 27:25). Christ Himself had predicted that all the righteous blood shed on the earth would *come upon this generation* (Mat 23:36), and upon that generation it came. His prediction of the fate of Jerusalem was subsequently reinforced by prophetic utterance in the local church, and all the Christians got out of

Jerusalem before it was finally encompassed by armies and destroyed.

Now let me come to the heart of the matter. He gave very clear predictions regarding His second coming. Many, he said, would be deceived:

> *Many shall come in my name, saying, I am the Christ; and shall lead many astray ... Then if any man shall say unto you, Lo, here is the Christ, or, Here; believe it not. For there shall arise false Christs, and false prophets, and shall shew great signs and wonders; so as to lead astray, if possible, even the elect. Behold, I have told you beforehand. If therefore they shall say unto you, Behold, he is in the wilderness; go not forth: Behold, he is in the inner chambers; believe it not* (Mat 24:4, 23–6).

Over the centuries there have been hundreds of false Christs; some of them have been very potent and have led many people astray. In my own early days, Father Devine in America claimed to be God and had about six million followers (more than the population of Scotland)—and Krishnamurti was another. This has been going on through the ages: people rising and claiming to be the Son of God. Christ said that His coming would not be private, but *as the lightning cometh forth from the east, and is seen even unto the west; so shall be the coming of the Son of man* (v.27). *For the Lord himself shall descend from heaven with a shout, with the voice of the archangel, and with the trump of God* (1 Thess 4:16), and *with ten thousands of His holy ones* (Jude 14). It will not be a secret, private matter. There is no such thing as a secret, silent rapture: that is a heresy perpetrated initially by Jesuits who greatly opposed Luther's interpretation of the book of Revelation and his identification of the Antichrist with the Papacy. The Jesuit view has been carried into evangelical circles largely through two unlikely bedfellows—Edward Irving, an early believer in the gift of tongues, and followers of the Brethren movement. A hallmark of the Futurist school of prophecy, it is still accepted in some quarters—and in my view it is

untenable. The truth, as it seems to me in plain Scripture, is that when He comes He will come with clouds and every eye shall see Him, and there are those who will mourn because of Him (Mat 24:30). One of the signs, He said, would be the appearance of many false Christs, and that sign is being and has been fulfilled throughout the years.

He predicted a time of coming danger, when the days would be shortened for the elect's (i.e. his followers') sake, because if these days were not shortened no flesh would be saved (v.22). He is speaking of 'flesh' here: He is not speaking of spirit. He is speaking of the danger of a holocaust upon earth that would obliterate humanity. The First World War was a bloodier war than the Second World War. And yet if both of these wars had gone on indefinitely there would have been no danger to world population, for it was greater at the end of each war than at its beginning. There was no danger of human obliteration. But, you know, from the moment man got his hand on a nuclear device, something new happened. Man now has in his hand the power to devastate the world a thousand times over, with the stockpiling of nuclear energy. I tell you a strange, an awful thing: man has never through the ages been able to keep himself from war, and the fact that we are not at war now is not a reflection of grace growing in the human heart. It is a reflection of fear, because the major powers all know that there can be no winners in that war. The devastation would be so fearful and the nuclear weapons, the atomic and hydrogen bombs, are in fact in one sense the keepers of the peace because of men's fear of such a holocaust breaking out.

Christ also said, *Ye shall hear of wars and rumours of wars* (v.6). They rejected the Prince of Peace, and the years from the destruction of Jerusalem up to our own day have been the bloodiest years recorded in human history. Two-thirds of the total time from the destruction of Jerusalem until now have been occupied with major wars somewhere or other on earth. He said of that age beginning with the

destruction of Jerusalem, *Then shall be great tribulation, such as hath not been from the beginning of the world until now, no, nor ever shall be* (v.21). The 'tribulation' is not a short three-and-a-half year period—the latter half of Daniel's seventieth week—but is quite clearly identified with the destruction of the temple of Christ's day. It is a lengthy period, running from then until Christ returns. In my view it will intensify towards the end. It is a strange paradox that those who are in the kingdom are under the rule of God while those outside the kingdom are in a time of tribulation.

There sound in my ear these words: *When they are saying, Peace and safety, then sudden destruction cometh upon them* (1 Thess 5:3). Just now the major nations are pursuing a policy of peace and reducing their nuclear stocks, or at least promising to do so. I would love to think it true that peace is coming upon the world, but the Bible does not tell me that; the Bible tells me that when they say, 'Peace, peace,' then cometh sudden destruction. This is the prediction of Christ: *Except those days had been shortened, no flesh would have been saved* (v.22). You say, are we at that point? and I say no, we are not at that point yet. You say, could Christ not come back tonight? No, I say categorically, Christ could not come back tonight. Oh, you reply, but I've heard lots of preachers say He could come at any time. The Bible makes it quite clear that He *cannot* come at any time. Get rid of the idea of planes crashing as pilots are taken to glory while passengers are destroyed in falling to earth, and of trains going off the lines, and all that kind of Futurist thinking. It doesn't work that way. 'What?' you say, 'What do you mean, He couldn't come back tonight?' He said that this gospel must first be preached in all the world, and He cannot come back until it happens—but thank God, it is happening; it is happening increasingly. More missionaries are on the field than there have ever been. Modern means of communication are so effective that the world is shrinking. Television and

radio are able to flash news almost worldwide, and one can see how a nation could be born in a day. It seems that more young people are training for the mission field than there have ever been. The great task committed to the church is about to be fulfilled, and I believe that from the moment the gospel has gone into all the world, the second coming will be very near. Then you may well go to bed wondering if you will ever waken up again on earth, or if you will be wakened by the trumpet call. But it cannot be, until the word of the Lord has been fulfilled.

You say, 'But they asked for signs of His coming: did He not give them any?' Yes, indeed He did. He said, *From the fig tree learn her parable* (v. 32)—and there would be only one fig tree in their minds. He had cursed a fig tree a few days earlier and they had wondered that immediately it had begun to shrivel and die. The story of the fig tree is a very interesting one. Foolish people may try to maintain that Christ was small-minded and that it was the act of a petulant person to curse the tree because it had no fruit when He came to it. Now the fig tree is an unusual type of tree. For only two months in the year has it no fruit. Its fruit is of two types: fruit that sets before the leaves appear and fruit that sets afterward. At the time when there are no leaves on the trees there is no expectation of fruit, and it happened to be in one of these two months that Christ sought fruit. He sought fruit because, unusually, the tree was showing leaves, and there ought to have been fruit if the leaves were there. When He looked for the fruit there was none. He said, *Let there be no fruit from thee hencefor- ward for ever* (Mat 21:19), and immediately the tree began to wither. The disciples could not understand. Later He expounded the parable:

When her branch is now become tender, and putteth forth its leaves, ye know that the summer is nigh; Even so ye also, when ye see all these things, know ye that he is nigh, even at the doors. Verily I say unto you, This generation shall not pass away, till all these things be accomplished (Mat 24:32–4).

The fig tree is usually taken as a symbol of the nation of Israel. When Christ came there was a profession of religion in Israel, but fruit was lacking. As surely as He cursed the tree, Christ was so soon to say, *Ichabod, your house is left unto you desolate*: the glory of God is departed, the tree is cursed—but when signs of life begin to appear on the cursed tree, know that the end is drawing near. The generation which sees it will not pass till all be accomplished. It will witness the second coming. We have seen the beginning of the outworking of this. There came a day when a people which was no people became a people, became a nation. Multitudes went back into the land and extended their borders.

The restoration of Israel is a sign of the coming of the Lord Jesus. I believe that there are some of you here tonight who will see that: you will be there. From an age point of view, I would guess that the majority of you who are here tonight will be there when Christ comes. Events move fast, and may move even faster towards the end. When men say, 'Peace, peace,' sudden destruction comes. Talk of peace will increase, but even now strife continues. Some of the nations emerging on the breakup of former power blocks are even now in turmoil. The human heart has not changed. The history of the ages bears witness to the wickedness of the human heart and man's readiness to kill.

God is on His throne and the whole wide world is in His hand. No sparrow falls to the ground that He does not know about, and no nuclear war will come of which He has no knowledge. For the elect's sake the age will be suddenly terminated. The voice of the archangel and the trump of God will sound, and He will come with ten thousands of his holy ones. This will be glorious. Blessed be the Name of the Lord.

21

The Glorious Coming

Of the second coming of Christ in relation to the believer, Paul said,

> *But we would not have you ignorant, brethren, concerning them that fall asleep; that ye sorrow not, even as the rest, which have no hope. For if we believe that Jesus died and rose again, even so them also that are fallen asleep in Jesus will God bring with him* (1 Thess 4:13–14).

In other words, said Paul, don't think for one moment that if you are alive and left, you are going to have the advantage and meet Him before those who have gone before. *For this we say unto you by the word of the Lord* (it is not a mere opinion of Paul's) *that we that are alive, that are left unto the coming of the Lord, shall in no wise precede them that are fallen asleep* (v.15). *For the Lord himself shall descend from heaven*—isn't this lovely? and so understandable, and so logical, so very logical? He was caught up in a cloud and His disciples saw Him, and the angels stood by them and said, *Ye men of Galilee, why stand ye looking into heaven? this Jesus, which was received up from you into heaven, shall so come in like manner as ye beheld him going into heaven* (Acts 1:11).

For the Lord himself: not just the angels now, the Lord

185

Himself. I think that this will be wonderful for Christ Himself, if I might put it that way. Coming back to His world in this wonderful hour of consummation and triumph, He will *descend from heaven, with a shout, and the voice of the archangel*—oh, it is not going to be a quiet meeting that day: I tell you that there will be a shout and the voice of the archangel and *the trump of God*—oh, the sounding of that trump! Ah, maybe in a sense those of you who are alive then will have one advantage over those of us who have gone on—I'd love to hear the trump! But, you see, I will be coming with Him... and no doubt I shall hear it too.

And the dead in Christ shall rise first (1 Thess 4:16). You say, 'Ah, you are going too far—I don't believe the dead in Christ shall rise!' Why don't you believe the dead will rise? Do you realize that almost every physical particle that was present in your body seven years ago is gone forever, and yet a photograph of seven years ago shows you remarkably like what you are now? When you get to my age, you will have had several bodies, totally different each from the other, each having died and, as it were, risen again. Throw a potato in the ground; in due time a new potato grows, and the old one dies: there is resurrection. Paul teaches resurrection from nature (*doth not nature itself teach you?*): you sow the seed, it goes in the ground and dies; new life springs year by year (1 Cor 15:35–44).

The God who gave me these various bodies through the years is well able to give me another one—well able. When we see Christ we shall be like Him, for we shall see Him even as He is, and we shall have bodies, we read, like unto His own glorious body: a body that could be touched and yet could pass through physical objects. He could eat, He could be handled, He was real—His body was real, and so will yours and mine be on that day. Scripture teaches that those who go down into the ground (whether buried or cremated makes not the slightest difference) will be raised and changed *in a moment, in the twinkling of an*

eye (1 Cor 15:52). *Then we that are alive, that are left, shall together with them be caught up in the clouds, to meet the Lord in the air: and so shall we ever be with the Lord* (1 Thess 4:17).

I love to think around this theme, because the rapture is here, the marriage of the Lamb is here, the judgment of saints is here—I am not speaking of the great white throne judgment before which the lost shall appear, but the judgment of the saints. Just think of it for a moment. When revival comes to an area the first thing that normally happens is that Christ draws near and there is a burning conviction of sin, repentance and salvation and restoration. In the resurrection there is one thing which cannot happen: sin-soiled souls joining Christ. As Christ comes and we rise to meet Him, I believe that in a moment of time there will be judgment. In the spiritual dimension you do not count time in our normal way. A moment can be like a day, a day can be like a moment. I believe (and since this is speculative, I want to be very careful: I don't want to give, as authoritative, teaching which has an element of speculation in it) that we will be judged as we rise to meet Him. I do not for a moment think that the awarding seat of Christ is like the old Sunday school occasions where each child went up for a prize. I believe that in a moment, in the twinkling of an eye, we shall be raised, changed, judged and joined to Christ.

Some will shine as the stars forever, perchance in close proximity to Christ, while some may be further away, having sent little treasure up from earth. Some will be impoverished yet saved as by the skin of their teeth. I believe that the marriage of the Lamb takes place at that moment. What is a marriage? Basically it is a joining. And prior to meeting Christ in the air we will first be joined to those who have died in Christ, then together we will be caught up to meet Him and be joined to Him. So shall we be forever with the Lord.

Now I am not going down sidelines tonight about the

detailed views of various schools of prophecy—Futurist, Historicist, Praeterist or A-millenial; nor am I speculating as to what will happen here, there and yonder, when Christ comes. One thing I will say, however. I am persuaded that planes will not go off course and trains will not crash in that momentous hour. I once was in an atmosphere on the isle of Lewis where Christ appeared and where the glory of God shone. As I looked at the heavens and saw what I saw, I found prophetic power coming upon me and I spontaneously prophesied in the open street in the middle of the night, having physical effects of the experience on my body for weeks afterwards. I knew in that hour something of the power of the world to come. Nothing would accidentally fall out of the sky—the control of Christ was absolute. When He comes again, everything will be under His hand. Blessed be the Name of the Lord.

Let us pray for His coming. Let us greatly desire it.

Every one that has this hope set in him purifieth himself, even as he is pure (1 Jn 3:3). Let us be purified.

NOTE TO READERS

If you would like to enquire further about issues raised in this book or if you feel that the author could be of help, you are invited to write to him at 27 Denholm Street, Greenock, PA16 8RH, Scotland, or telephone 0475 87432.

It may also be of interest to know that the author is normally involved in five conferences in Scotland each year—New Year, Easter, July, August and October. Friends gather from many parts of Britain. An open invitation is extended to all and particularly to those interested in the Baptism in the Holy Spirit and related themes. Details will be provided on enquiry.

By the same author

Reflections on the Baptism in the Holy Spirit £2.25 This book is already proving very popular and is being used in bringing people into the baptism in the Spirit. It has been described as one of the clearest, most incisive books on this subject.

Reflections on the Gifts of the Spirit £2.75 Deals in an original way with its subject. The chapters on miracles, healings and discernment (with exorcism) have roused great interest and led to positive action. Anecdotes and illustrations have been much appreciated.

Reflections on a Song of Love £1.25 A highly original commentary on 1 Cor 13. The drawing power of love pervades this fascinating study. The author shows very clearly how this chapter fully supports and in no way detracts from the doctrine of Pentecost.

A Trumpet Call to Women £2.50 Presents a strong case from Scripture for greater involvement of women in ministry. It throws much light on those portions which on the surface seem to put women in a subject role. It includes the testimony of Elizabeth H. Taylor, a lady much used of God. A stirring book, demanding a response—a call to action.

Consider Him £2.25 Considers a number of the qualities of Christ. He Himself seems to speak from the pages of the book, both in the main text and in the testimony of Jennifer Jack, whose selfless presentation truly leaves the reader to consider Christ.

Battle for the Body £2.95 It will take courage to face the

truths highlighted in this original approach to fundamental issues of sanctification. The second part presents the powerful testimony of John Hamilton—a preacher widely known and loved.

The Clash of Tongues: with Glimpses of Revival £2.75 Part One is a commentary on 1 Cor 14. It deals in detail with some of the more difficult questions. Part Two deals with the relationship between revival and Pentecost and refers to the 1939 and 1949 revivals in Lewis, introducing a number of people who were involved in the first of these— particularly Mary MacLean, whose remarkable testimony is related. This book may particularly appeal to people studiously inclined.

The Incomparable Christ £2.75 Part One deals with the gospel. It faces honestly the questions of Christ's resurrection and that of all men. It deals in a direct way with the doctrine of hell and eternal judgment, and gives practical instruction on the way of salvation. Part Two presents the remarkable testimonies of two young ladies.

Gospel Vignettes £2.95 Focuses attention on various facets of the gospel, with chapter titles like: Ye Must Be Born Again, The Life-Giving Water, Weighed in the Balances, Behold I Stand at the Door and Knock, The Hour of Decision. Includes testimonies of three people whose lives have been transformed by Christ, to one of whom Christ Himself appeared. Useful in the gospel, but introducing the Pentecostal dimension.

Reflections from Abraham £2.50 Outlines spiritual principles seen in the life of Abraham. It deals with his call and ours, the mountain as distinct from the valley life, intercession, Lot in Sodom, the sacrifice of Isaac and the way of faith. Part Two tells of the action of God in the life of

Dorothy Jennings, to whom Abraham has been of particular significance.

**Reflections from Moses: with the Testimony of Dan
McVicar** £2.99 Part One shows the outworking of spiritual principles such as the calling and training of a man of
God, the need to start from holy ground, deliverance from
bondage, and the consequences of Moses' failure in a
critical hour. Part Two presents the well-known evangelist
Dan McVicar's story in his own words. The conversion of
this militant communist and the intervention of God in the
lives of his parents make thrilling reading.

Christ the Deliverer £2.99 Deals with both physical and
spiritual deliverance. It includes a number of remarkable
testimonies to healing, e.g. from blindness, manic depres-
sion, ME, rheumatoid arthritis, spinal injury, phobias,
nightmares. It speaks of the appearance of angels, touches
on revival and analyses the theory of 'visualization'.

Christian Fundamentals £3.50 Part One deals with the
individual and his needs in the realms of Salvation, Baptism in the Spirit, and Deliverance. Part Two focuses on
the outflow of the life of God to meet the needs of others
through Vocal, Hidden and Open Power Ministries. The
End Times are the subject of Part Three.

BOOK ORDERS

The books advertised on the previous pages are being made available to Christian booksellers throughout the country, but if you have any difficulty in obtaining your supply, you may order directly from New Dawn Books, c/o 27 Denholm Street, Greenock, Scotland, PA16 8RH.

· · · · · · · · ORDER FORM · · · · · · · ·

Please send me the books indicated below:

Quantity	Title	Price
	Reflections on the Baptism in the Holy Spirit	£2.25
	Reflections on the Gifts of the Spirit	£2.75
	Reflections on a Song of Love (A commentary on 1 Cor 13)	£1.25
	A Trumpet Call to Women	£2.50
	Consider Him (Twelve Qualities of Christ)	£2.25
	Battle for the Body	£2.95
	The Clash of Tongues: with Glimpses of Revival	£2.75
	The Incomparable Christ	£2.75
	Gospel Vignettes	£2.95
	Reflections from Abraham	£2.50
	Reflections from Moses: with the testimony of Dan McVicar	£2.99
	Christ the Deliverer	£2.99
	Christian Fundamentals	£3.50
	Reflections from David	£3.50

Signature . . . .

Address . . . .

. . . .

. . . .

When ordering please send purchase price plus 40p per book to help cover the cost of postage and packaging.